Shelby Foote

THE CIVIL WAR

A NARRATIVE

Shelby Foote

THE CIVIL WAR

A NARRATIVE

10

★ ★ ★

RED RIVER TO
SPOTSYLVANIA

40th Anniversary Edition

BY SHELBY FOOTE
AND THE EDITORS OF TIME-LIFE BOOKS,
ALEXANDRIA, VIRGINIA

All these were honoured in their generations,
and were the glory of their times.

There be of them,
that have left a name behind them,
that their praises might be reported.

And some there be, which have no memorial;
who are perished, as though they had never been;
and are become as though they had never been born;
and their children after them.

But these were merciful men,
whose righteousness hath not been forgotten.

With their seed shall continually remain
a good inheritance,
and their children are within the covenant.

Their seed standeth fast,
and their children for their sakes.

Their seed shall remain for ever,
and their glory shall not be blotted out.

Their bodies are buried in peace;
but their name liveth for evermore.

~ ECCLESIASTICUS XLIV

Contents

★ ★ ★

★

Prologue

---

*I*n early **1864,** George Meade's newest initiative against the Confederates, foiled by bad weather and tardy execution, had merely allowed Robert E. Lee to maneuver into an unassailable position at Mine Run, and both armies broke off and went into winter quarters. Around the same time down in Charleston, the South had failed to lift the Union blockade with the experimental *H. L. Hunley,* a submarine that sank to the bottom of the ocean after a successful attack on the Union's *Housatonic.* William Tecumseh Sherman's attempt to hook up with William Sooy Smith for a triumphal march from Meridian, Mississippi, to Selma, Alabama, was frustrated by Nathan Bedford Forrest, whose defeat of Smith at Okolona had forced Sherman to content himself with burning Meridian and withdrawing to Vicksburg.

The apparent stalemate created problems for Abraham Lincoln. Facing a campaign for reëlection, he needed more than a "mud truce" to attract voters in the fall. Seeking instead a few real victories or at least the hope of peace, Lincoln launched two expeditions into rebel territory aimed at helping to secure political advantages over his opponents, North and South. The idea that any Confederate state should be welcomed back into the Union if ten percent of its population signed a loyalty oath struck angry radical Republicans as far too liberal and outraged Southerners as yet another tyranny. And the loyalty oath forms carried by those Union forces invading central Florida and launching a full-scale cavalry raid on Richmond hardly ensured success. Indeed, the abject failure of both expeditions only underscored the confusion of political and military goals behind them and raised further questions about Lincoln's wartime leadership.

Jefferson Davis, also, had his problems. In the wake of Braxton Bragg's failures around Chattanooga, Davis had replaced him with Joseph E. Johnston only to bring the widely despised Bragg to Richmond as his military adviser. Beset by a vituperative opposition that included his own Vice President, by a sagging morale amounting in some quarters to defeatism, and by severe attrition in the armed forces, Davis suspended habeas corpus and extended the draft age down to 17 and up to 50, which only fed opposition complaints that he was undermining the very cause for which the South was fighting, the individual rights of states against the power of central government. Increasingly Davis placed his hopes not in any outright southern military victory but in maintaining a resistance strong enough to bring about Abraham Lincoln's loss of the upcoming election in the North.

Whether or not such an event would have led to peace, it certainly seemed a possibility in the spring of 1864. Salmon Chase, Lincoln's Secretary of the Treasury, had yet again become the center of a radical cabal seeking to deny the President a second term. But then Lincoln, for a second time, politically outmaneuvered Chase into offering his resignation, which Lincoln once more refused. Politically canny as always, Lincoln took the temper of Congress and colluded with its members to revive the rank of lieutenant general — George Washington's old rank — which Lincoln offered to the hero of Vicksburg and Chattanooga, Ulysses S. Grant. In the long run, Grant's elevation would alter the course of the war and perhaps help to save Lincoln's presidency. In the short term, it would take some of the sting out of the recent collapse of Nathaniel Banks's Transmississippi campaign and the soon-to-come Confederate successes in Paducah, Kentucky, and Plymouth, North Carolina.

Lieutenant General Grant was the grim mathematician Lincoln had long been seeking. After Grant's appointment, when he met with his chief subordinate, General Sherman, to plot the course of the war henceforth, his plan had seemed deceptively simple. "He was to go for Lee," Sherman wrote later, "and I was to go for Joe Johnston. That was his plan." But, in fact, Grant's design called for a total reorganization of the northern forces and the way they fought, operating on the dual principles of the highest concentration of forces and continuous action against the enemy. It would be a costly way to fight, as quickly became clear during the Wilderness Campaign on such bloody battlefields as Spotsylvania, but it was the way this war would be won.

★   ★   ★

Shelby Foote

A female visitor sits with officers of the 1st Brigade Horse Artillery at Brandy Station, Virginia, where General George Meade established headquarters.

O N E

Grant in Washington — His Plan

1864 ★ ★ ★ ★ ★ ★ Late afternoon of a raw, gusty day in early spring — March 8, a Tuesday, 1864 — the desk clerk at Willard's Hotel, two blocks down Pennsylvania Avenue from the White House, glanced up to find an officer accompanied by a boy of thirteen facing him across the polished oak of the registration counter and inquiring whether he could get a room. "A short, round-shouldered man in a very tarnished major general's uniform," he seemed to a bystanding witness to have "no gait, no station, no manner," to present instead, with his ill-fitting jacket cut full in the skirt and his high-crowned hat set level on his head, a somewhat threadbare, if not quite down-at-heels, conglomerate impression of "rough, light-brown whiskers, a blue eye, and rather a scrubby look withal . . . as if he was out of office and on half pay, with nothing to do but hang round the entry of Willard's, cigar in mouth." Discerning so much of this as he considered worth his time, together perhaps with the bystander's added observation that the applicant had "rather the look of a man who did, or once did, take a little too much to drink," the clerk was no more awed by the stranger's rank than he was attracted by his aspect. This was, after all, the best known hostelry in Washington. There had been by now close to five hundred Union generals, and of these the great majority, particularly among those who possessed what was defined as "station," had checked in and out of

★

Willard's in the past three wartime years. In the course of its recent and rapid growth, under the management of a pair of Vermont brothers who gave it their name along with their concern, it had swallowed whole, together with much other adjacent real estate, a former Presbyterian church; the President-elect himself had stayed here through the ten days preceding his inauguration, making of its Parlor 6 a "little White House," and it was here, one dawn two years ago in one of its upper rooms, that Julia Ward Howe had written her "Battle Hymn of the Republic," the anthem for the crusade the new President had begun to design as soon as he took office. Still, bright or tarnished, stars were stars; a certain respect was owed, if not to the man who wore them, then in any case to the rank they signified; the clerk replied at last that he would give him what he had, a small top-floor room, if that would do. It would, the other said, and when the register was given its practiced half-circle twirl he signed without delay. The desk clerk turned it back again, still maintaining the accustomed, condescending air

---

Here before them, in the person of this undistinguished-looking officer . . . was the man who . . . had captured two rebel armies, entire, and chased a third clean out of sight beyond the roll of the southern horizon.

---

he was about to lose in shock when he read what the weathered applicant had written: "U.S. Grant & Son — Galena, Illinois."

Whereupon (for such was the aura that had gathered about the name "Unconditional Surrender" Grant, hero of Donelson, conqueror of Vicksburg, deliverer of Chattanooga) there was an abrupt transformation, not only in the attitude of the clerk, whose eyes seemed to start from his head at the sight of the signature and who struck the bell with a force that brought on the double all the bellboys within earshot, but also in that of the idlers, the loungers roundabout the lobby, who soon learned the cause of the commotion in the vicinity of the desk. It was as if the prayers of the curious had been answered after the flesh. Here before them, in the person of this undistinguished-looking officer — forty-one years of age, five feet eight inches tall, and weighing just under a hundred and forty pounds in his scuffed boots and shabby clothes — was the man who, in the course of the past twenty-five months of a war in which the news had mostly been unwelcome from the Federal point of view, had captured two rebel armies, entire, and chased a third clean out of sight beyond the roll of the southern horizon. Now that he made a second visual assessment, more

★

deliberate and above all more informed than the first, the bystander who formerly had seen only an "ordinary, scrubby-looking man, with a slightly seedy look," perceived that there was more to him than had been apparent before the authentication that came with the fixing of the name. The "blue eye" became "a clear blue eye," and the once stolid-seeming face took on "a look of resolution, as if he could not be trifled with."

Such, then, was the effect of the gathered aura. And yet there was a good deal more to it than fame, past or present. There was also anticipation, and of a particular national form. Just last week, on Leap Year Day, the President had signed a congressional act reviving the grade of lieutenant general, and Grant had been summoned east to receive in person his promotion, together with command of all the armies of the Union, which he was expected to lead at last to final victory over the forces that had threatened its destruction. Forgotten now was the small top-floor room his modesty had been willing to accept. Instead, the clerk obsequiously tendered the distinguished guest "the best in the house": meaning Parlor 6, where Abraham Lincoln himself had held court in the days preceding his inauguration, less than one week more than three years ago today.

Grant accepted this as he had the other, with neither eagerness nor protest, which caused a second witness to remark upon "his shy but manly bearing." Still another even saw virtue in the dead-level way he wore his hat. "He neither puts it on behind his ears, nor draws it over his eyes; much less does he cock it on one side, but sets it straight and very hard on his head." A fourth believed he detected something else beneath the general's "rough dignity" of surface. "He habitually wears an expression as if he had determined to drive his head through a brick wall, and was about to do it." Just now though, here in the close atmosphere of the lobby of Willard's — which a disgruntled Englishman complained was compounded, in about equal parts, of "heat, noise, dust, smoke, and expectoration" — what he mainly seemed to desire was an absence of fanfare.

But that was not to be. For a week now the town talk had been of his imminent arrival, and now that the talkers had him within actual reach they intended to make the most of him. Returning downstairs presently for dinner in the main dining room, and holding his son Fred by the hand as if for mutual reassurance, he managed to get as far as his table and even to order the meal before he was recognized by a gentleman from New Orleans who came over for a handshake. Then, as before, all hope of privacy ended. Word of his presence "spread from table to table," according to one who was there; "people got up and craned their necks in an anxious endeavor to see 'the coming man.'" This reached a climax when one of the watchers, unable to contain his enthusiasm, mounted a chair and called — prematurely, for the promotion had not yet been conferred — for "Three cheers for Lieutenant General Grant!" These were given "in the most tremendous manner" and were followed by a pounding that made the glasses and silverware dance on the tables, "in the midst of which General Grant, looking very much astonished and perhaps annoyed, rose to his feet, awkwardly rubbed his mustache with his napkin, bowed, and resumed his seat." For a time, good sense prevailed; "the general was allowed to eat in peace." But when he rose again and began to make his way out, once more with his son in tow, a Pennsylvania congressman took him in hand and began a round of introductions. "This was his first levee," the witness added; after which his retreat through the crowded lobby and up the staircase to his rooms was characterized by "most unsoldierly blushing."

Hard as this was on a man who valued his privacy and was discomfited by adulation, before the night was over he would find himself at storm center of an even worse ordeal. Word of his arrival having spread, he found on his return to

This painting by Francis B. Carpenter depicts Grant and Lincoln greeting guests at a White House reception the evening before Grant's formal promotion to lieutenant general.

Parlor 6 a special invitation to come by the White House, presumably for a conference with the Commander in Chief, whom he had never met although they both were from Illinois and were by now the two most famous men in the country.

If he had known that the President's weekly receptions were held on Tuesday evenings he would perhaps have postponed his call, but by the time he completed the short walk up the avenue to the gates of the executive mansion it was too late. He found himself being ushered up the steps, through the foyer, down a corridor, and finally into the brightly lighted East Room, where the reception was in full swing. The crowd, enlarged beyond the norm tonight by the news that he would be there, fell silent as he entered, then parted before him to disclose at the far end of the room the tall form of Abraham Lincoln, who watched him approach, then put out a long arm for a handshake. "I'm glad to see you, General," he said.

The crowd resumed its "stir and buzz"; there was a spattering of applause and even "a cheer or two," which struck Navy Secretary Gideon Welles as "rowdy and unseemly." Lincoln turned Grant over to Secretary of State William H. Seward for presentation to Mrs Lincoln, who took his arm for a turn round the room while her husband followed at a distance, apparently much amused by the general's reaction to being placed thus on display before a crowd that soon began to get somewhat out of hand, surging toward him, men and women alike, for a close-up look and a possible exchange of greetings. Grant "blushed like a schoolgirl," sweating heavily from embarrassment and the exertion of shaking the hands of those who managed to get nearest in the jam. "Stand up so we can all have a look at you!" someone cried from the rim of the crowd, and he obliged by stepping onto a red plush sofa, looking out over the mass of upturned faces whose eyes fairly shone with delight at being part of an authentic historical tableau. "It was the only real mob I ever saw in the White House," a journalist later wrote, describing how "people were caught up and whirled in the torrent which swept through the great East Room. Ladies suffered dire disaster in the crush and confusion; their laces were torn and crinolines mashed, and many got up on sofas, chairs, and tables to be out of harm's way or to get a better view of the spectacle. . . . For once at least the President of the United States was not the chief figure in the picture. The little, scared-looking man who stood on a crimson-covered sofa was the idol of the hour."

Rescued from this predicament — or, as the newsman put it, "smuggled out by friendly hands" — Grant presently found himself closeted in a smaller chamber, which in time he would learn to identify as the Blue Room, with the President and the Secretary of War, Edwin M. Stanton. Lincoln informed him that he would be given his lieutenant general's commission at a ceremony here next day and would be expected to reply to a short speech, "only four sentences in all, which I will read from my manuscript as an example which you may follow . . . as you are perhaps not so much accustomed to public speaking as I am." For guidance in preparing his reply, he gave him a copy of what he himself would say, together with two suggestions for remarks which he hoped the general would incorporate in his response: first, something that would "prevent or obviate any jealousy" on the part of the generals about to come under his command, and second, something that would put him "on as good terms as possible with the Army of the Potomac," to which he was a stranger. "If you see any objection to doing this," Lincoln added as a final sign of consideration for a man about to be cast in an unfamiliar role, "be under no restraint whatever in expressing that objection to the Secretary of War."

Grant expressed no objection, but as he returned to the hotel after midnight for his first sleep in Washington he was perhaps regretful that he had ever left the West, where life was at once less pushy and more informal, and convinced no doubt of the wisdom of his resolution to go back there at the first opportunity.

Returning next day to the White House for the ceremony that would correspond to a laying-on of hands, he brought with him his chief of staff and fellow townsman, Brigadier General John Rawlins, who had come east with him from Nashville in response to the presidential summons, and the thirteen-year-old Fred. Promptly at 1 o'clock, as scheduled, the Galena trio was shown into the presence of the President, the seven members of his Cabinet, his private secretary John Nicolay, and Major General Henry W. Halleck, the present general-in-chief, over whose head the man they had gathered to honor was about to be advanced. Facing Grant, Lincoln handed him the official document and read the speech of which he had given him a copy the night before. "General Grant: The nation's appreciation of what you have done and its reliance upon you for what remains to

After receiving this commission certifying his promotion to the rank of lieutenant general, Grant told the President, "It will be my earnest endeavor not to disappoint your expectations."

do in the existing great struggle are now presented with this commission, constituting you lieutenant general in the Army of the United States. With this high honor devolves upon you also a corresponding responsibility. As the country herein trusts you, so under God it will sustain you. I scarcely need to add that with what I here speak for the nation goes my own hearty personal concurrence." Brief as this was, Grant's response was briefer by seven words. He took from his coat pocket a half-sheet of notepaper covered with a hasty lead-pencil scrawl. Either the light was poor or else he had trouble reading his own writing. In any case he read it badly. "Mr President," he replied, groping and hesitant as he strained to decipher the words: "I accept this commission with gratitude for the high honor conferred. With the aid of the noble armies that have fought on so many fields, it will be my earnest endeavor not to disappoint your expectations. I feel the full weight of the responsibilities now devolving on me and know that if they are met it will be due to those armies, and above all to the favor of that Providence which leads both nations and men."

"With the aid of the noble armies that have fought on so many fields, it will be my earnest endeavor not to disappoint your expectations."

— Ulysses S. Grant

The surprise in this, to anyone aware of the Blue Room exchange the night before, was that the general had not incorporated either of the remarks the President recommended for inclusion in his acceptance speech. Nicolay, for one, thought that Grant, in an attempt to establish an independence none of his predecessors had enjoyed, had decided it would be wise to begin his career as general-in-chief by disregarding any suggestions from above. Lincoln himself, on the other hand, seemed not to notice the omission which his secretary considered, if not a downright act of insubordination, then in any case a snub.

Once the congratulations were over, the two leaders had a short talk that began with Grant asking what special service was required of him. The taking of Richmond, Lincoln said, adding wryly that the generals who had been told this in the past "had not been fortunate in their efforts in that direction." Did Grant think he could do it? Grant replied that he could if he had the troops, whereupon Lincoln assured him that he would have them. That ended their first strategy conference, such as it was, and Nicolay observed that nothing was said as to the route or method to be employed, the jump-off date, or the amount of time the opera-

★

tion would require. All Grant said was that he could take Richmond if he had the troops, and Lincoln had been willing to let it go at that; after which the general took his leave. He was going down to Virginia today, specifically to Brandy Station, headquarters of the Army of the Potomac, for a consultation with its commander as a prelude to the planning of his over-all campaign.

One thing remained to be done before he got aboard the train. No truly recognizable photograph had been made of him since the early days of the war, when his beard reached the middle buttons on his blouse, and he had agreed — perhaps without considering that he thus would lose the near-anonymity he had enjoyed among strangers up to now — to an appointment that would remedy the lack. Accompanied by Stanton, who proposed to go to the station to see him off, he rode from the White House, down Pennsylvania Avenue, to the intersection of Seventh Street, where the carriage stopped in front of Mathew Brady's Portrait Gallery. The photographer was waiting anxiously, and wasted no time in getting the general upstairs into what he called his "operating room," where he had four of his big cameras ready for action. It was past 4 o'clock by now and the light was failing; so while Grant took his place in a chair on which the cameras, their lenses two full feet in length and just under half a foot in diameter, were trained like a battery of siege guns, Brady sent an assistant up on the roof to draw back the shade from the skylight directly overhead. To his horror, the fellow stumbled, both feet crashing through the glass to let fall a shower of jagged shards around the general below. "It was a miracle that some of the pieces didn't strike him," the photographer later said. "And if one had, it would have been the end of Grant; for that glass was two inches thick." Still more surprising, in its way, was the general's reaction. He glanced up casually, with "a barely perceptible quiver of the nostril," then as casually back down, and that was all. This seemed to Brady "the most remarkable display of nerve I ever witnessed."

It was otherwise with Stanton, who appeared unstrung: not only for Grant's sake, as it turned out, but also for his own, though none of the splinters had landed anywhere near him. Grasping the photographer by the arm, he pulled him aside and sputtered excitedly, "Not a word about this, Brady, not a word! You must never breathe a word of what happened here today. . . . It would be impossible to convince the people that this was not an attempt at assassination!"

★ ★ ★ *T*he train made good time from Alexandria, chuffing through Manassas and Warrenton Junction, on to Brandy, a distance of just under sixty miles; Grant arrived in a driving rain, soon after nightfall, to find that the Army of the Potomac, whatever its shortcomings in other respects — there was scarcely a place-name on the landscape that did not mark the scene of one or more of its defeats — knew how to greet a visitor in style. A regiment of Zouaves, snappy in red fezzes and baggy trousers, was drawn up to give him a salute on his arrival, despite the rain, and a headquarters band, happily unaware that Grant was tone-deaf — he once remarked that he only knew two tunes in all: "One was Yankee Doodle. The other wasn't" — played vigorous music by way of welcome as the army commander, Major General George G. Meade, emerged from his tent for a salute and a handshake. He and Grant, six years his junior and eight years behind him at West Point, had not met since the Mexican War, sixteen years ago, when they were lieutenants.

Tall and dour, professorial in appearance, with a hook nose, a gray-shot beard, glinting spectacles, and heavy pouches under his eyes, Meade was one of the problems that would have to be dealt with before other, larger problems could be tackled. Specifically, the question was whether to keep him where he was, a prima donna commander of a prima donna army, or remove him. His trouble, aside from a hair-trigger temper that kept his staff on edge and caused associates to refer to him, behind his back, as "a damned old goggle-eyed snapping turtle," was that he lacked the quality which Grant not only personified himself but also prized highest in a subordinate: the killer instinct. At Gettysburg eight months ago, after less than a week in command, Meade had defeated and driven the rebel invaders from his native Pennsylvania, but then, with his foe at bay on the near bank of a flooded, bridgeless river, had flinched from delivering the coup de grâce which Lincoln, for one, was convinced would have ended the war. Instead, the Confederates, low on ammunition and bled down to not much more than half their strength, had withdrawn unmolested across the rain-swollen Potomac to take up a new defensive position behind the Rapidan, where they still were. Meade had crossed in late November, with the intention of coming to grips with them in the wintry south-bank thickets, but then at the last minute had held his hand; had returned, in fact, ingloriously to the north bank, and ever since had seemed content to settle for the stalemate that resulted, despite practically unremitting prodding from the press and the politicians in his rear. Just last week he had been grilled by Congress's radical-dominated Joint Committee on the Conduct of the War, whose members for the most part, in admiration of his politics and his bluster, favored recalling Major General Joseph Hooker to the post he had lost to Meade on the eve of Gettysburg. Much bitterness had ensued between the Pennsylvanian and his critics; "My enemies," he called them in a letter this week to a kinsman, maintaining that they consisted "of certain politicians who wish me removed to restore Hooker; then of certain subordinates, whose military reputations are involved in the destruction of mine; finally, [of] a class of vultures who in Hooker's day preyed upon the army, and who sigh for a return of those glorious days."

This was accurate enough, as far as it went, but it seemed to Grant — as, indeed, it must have done to even a casual observer — that the trouble lay deeper, in the ranks of the army itself. Partly the reason was boredom, a lack of employment in the craft for which its members had been trained. "A winter in tents is monotonous," one officer complained. "Card playing, horse racing, and kindred amusements become stale when made a steady occupation." Moreover, Grant would have agreed with an assessment later made by a young West Pointer, a newcomer like himself to the eastern theater, that the trouble with the Army of the Potomac, predating both Meade and Hooker, was its "lack of springy formation and audacious, self-reliant initiative. This organic weakness was entirely due to not having had in its youth skillfully aggressive leadership. Its early commanders had dissipated war's best elixir by training it into a life of caution, and the evil of that schooling it had shown on more than one occasion."

Federal staff officers relax near Brandy Station.
After retreating from Gettysburg, the Federal
army was stationed north of the Rapidan River.

★

Before coming down to Brandy, Grant had rather inclined to the belief that the removal of Meade was a prerequisite to correction of this state of mind in the army he commanded. But once the round of greetings and introductions had ended and the corps and division commanders had retired for the night, leaving the two men alone for a private conference, Meade showed Grant a side of himself that proved not only attractive but disarming. He began by saying that he supposed Grant would want to replace him with some general who had served with him before and was therefore familiar with his way of doing things: Major General William T. Sherman, for example, who had been Grant's mainstay in practically all of his campaigns to date. If so, Meade declared, he hoped there would be no hesitation on his account, since (as Grant paraphrased it afterwards) "the work before us was of such vast importance to the whole nation that the feeling or wishes of no one person should stand in the way of selecting the right men for all positions. For himself, he would serve to the best of his

"I was much pleased with Grant, and most agreeably disappointed in his evidence of mind and character. You may rest assured he is not an ordinary man."

— George Meade

ability wherever placed." Grant was impressed. The offer, he said, gave him "even a more favorable opinion of Meade than did his great victory at Gettysburg," and he assured him, then and there, that he had "no thought of substituting anyone for him," least of all Sherman, who "could not be spared from the West." Now it was Meade who was impressed, and he said as much the following day in a letter to his wife. "I was much pleased with Grant," he wrote, "and most agreeably disappointed in his evidence of mind and character. You may rest assured he is not an ordinary man."

Mutual admiration on the part of the two leaders might be a good and healthy thing for all concerned, but the troops themselves, having paid in blood for the blasting of a number of overblown reputations in the drawn-out course of the war, were unconvinced and noncommittal. While this latest addition to the doleful list of their commanders was on his way eastward, they had engaged in some rather idle speculation as to his professional ability, and it did not seem to them that the mere addition of a third star to each of his shoulders would necessarily increase his military worth.

"Who's this Grant that's made a lieutenant general?"

"He's the hero of Vicksburg."

"Well, Vicksburg wasn't much of a fight. The rebs were out of rations and they had to surrender or starve. They had nothing but dead mules and dogs to eat, as I understand."

About the best thing they could say for him was that he was unlikely to be any worse than John Pope, who had also brought a western reputation east, only to lose it at Bull Run. "He cannot be weaker or more inefficient," a jaundiced New York veteran declared, "than the generals who have wasted the lives of our comrades during the past three years." For one thing, Grant was likely to find a good deal less room between bullets here in Virginia than he had found in the region of his fame. "If he's a fighter," another hard-case infantry-man put it, "he can find all the fighting he wants." Then he arrived and some of them got a look at him. What they saw was scarcely reassuring.

"Well, what do you think?" one asked a friend, who replied thought-fully, having studied the firm-set mouth and the level glance of the clear blue eyes:

"He looks as if he meant it."

Nodding agreement, the first allowed that they would find out for themselves before too long. Meanwhile he was willing to defer judgment, except as to looks. "He's a little 'un," he said.

Talk of Vicksburg brought on the inevitable comparison of western and eastern Confederates, with particular reference to the presence here in the Old Dominion of General Robert E. Lee, the South's first soldier. Grant could never have penned up Lee, as he had done John Pemberton, thereby forcing his surrender by starvation; Lee, they said, "would have broken out some way and foraged around for supplies." Thus the men. And Rawlins, as he moved among the officers on Meade's staff, found a similar respect for the southern commander, as if they took almost as great a pride in having opposed "Mars Robert" as the Virginian's tattered veterans took in serving under him. "Well, you never met Bobby Lee and his boys," they replied when Grant's chief of staff presumed to speak of victories in the West. "It would be quite different if you had." As for the campaign about to open here in the East, they seemed to expect nothing more than another version of the old story: advance and retreat, Grant or no Grant. They listened rather impatiently while Rawlins spoke of past successes, off on the far margin of the map. "That may be," they said. "But, mind you, Bobby Lee is just over the Rapidan."

In any case, whatever opinions had been formed or deferred, the new chieftain and his major eastern army had at least had a look at each other, and next morning, after a second conference at which both past and future campaigns in Virginia were discussed, Grant returned to the station and got aboard the train for Washington. Last night he had received a presidential telegram extending an invitation from Mrs Lincoln for him and Meade "to dine with us Saturday evening," and he had replied by wire that they were pleased to accept.

★

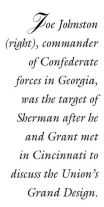

Joe Johnston (right), commander of Confederate forces in Georgia, was the target of Sherman after he and Grant met in Cincinnati to discuss the Union's Grand Design.

Overnight, however, he changed his mind. Today was Friday, March 11, and he would be leaving at once for the West — but only for a visit of a week or ten days, in order to confer with Sherman and other commanders there; after which, despite his previous resolution to avoid the political snares so thickly strewn about the eastern theater, he would be returning here to stay. Paradoxically, now that he had seen them at first hand, it was just those snares that determined his decision. "When I got to Washington and saw the situation," he later explained, "it was plain that here was the point for the commanding general to be. No one else could, probably, resist the pressure that would be brought to bear upon him to desist from his own plans and pursue others."

Not that the adulation and the invasions of his privacy did not continue to go against his grain. They did indeed. Closeted that afternoon with the President at the White House, he complained that the past three days, in Washington and at Brandy, had been "rather the warmest campaign I have witnessed during the war." Lincoln could sympathize with this, but he was disappointed that the general would not stay on through tomorrow night for the banquet planned in his honor. "We can't excuse you," he protested. "Mrs Lincoln's dinner without you would be *Hamlet* with Hamlet left out." But Grant was firm. "I appreciate the honor Mrs Lincoln would do me," he said, "but time is very important now. And really, Mr Lincoln," he added frankly, "I have had enough of this show business."

He left that evening on a westbound train, with stops for inspection at several points along the way, and reached Nashville in time to keep a St Patrick's Day appointment with Sherman, whose troops were advanced beyond Chattanooga, into northwest Georgia, to confront the main western Confederate army under General Joseph E. Johnston, around Dalton. They traveled together by rail to Cincinnati, the voluble red-head, "tall, angular, and spare, as if his superabundant energy had consumed his flesh" — so an acquaintance saw him at the time — and the new lieutenant general, who had once been described as "a man who could be silent in several languages" and who now seemed doubly reticent by contrast with his talkative companion. In the Ohio city they left the cars and checked into a hotel for privacy and room to spread their maps. There they worked on a preliminary draft of the over-all campaign which Sherman defined long afterwards: "He was to go for Lee and I was to go for Joe Johnston. That was his plan."

★ ★ ★ **T**hat was what it basically was. That was what it came to, in the end. At the outset, however, the plan — which might better have been defined, at this stage, as a plan for a plan — was a good deal more complicated, involving a great many other forces that were thrown, or were intended to be thrown, into action against the South. Grant had under him more than half a million combat soldiers, "present for duty, equipped," about half of them in the ranks of six field armies, three in the East and three in the West, while the other half were scattered about the country in nineteen various departments, from New England to New Mexico and beyond. His notion was to pry as many as possible of the latter out of their garrisons, transfer them to the mobile forces in the field, and bring the resultant mass to bear in "a simultaneous movement all along the line." Long ago in Mexico, during a lull in the war, he had written home to the girl he later married: "If we have to fight, I would like to do it all at once and then make friends." Apparently he felt even more this way about it now that the enemy were his fellow countrymen. In any case, the plan as he evolved it seemed to indicate as much.

"From an early period of the rebellion," he said afterward, looking back, "I had been impressed with the idea that active and continuous operations of all the troops that could be brought into the field, regardless of season and weather, were necessary to a speedy termination of the war." The trouble from the outset, east and west, was that the Federal armies had "acted independently and without concert, like a balky team, no two ever pulling together, enabling the enemy to use to great advantage his interior lines of communication." It was this that had made possible several of the greatest Confederate triumphs, from First Bull Run to Chickamauga, where reinforcements from other rebel departments and even other theaters had tipped the tactical scale against the Union. "I determined to stop this," Grant declared. Moreover, convinced as he was "that no peace could be had that would be stable and conducive to the happiness of the people, both North and South, until the military power of the rebellion was entirely broken," he held fast to his old guideline; he would work toward Unconditional Surrender. He had it very much in mind to destroy not only the means of resistance by his adversaries, but also the will. The Confederacy was not only to be defeated, it was to be defeated utterly, and not only in the field, where the battles were fought, but also on the home front, where the goods of war were produced. "War is cruelty," Sherman had said four months ago, in response to a southern matron's complaint that his men appeared hard-handed on occasion. "There is no use trying to reform it. The crueler it is, the sooner it will be over." Grant felt much the same way about the matter, and here at the start, in formulating his plan for achieving what he called "a speedy termination," he was determined to be guided by two principles of action: 1) "to use the greatest number of troops practicable," and 2) "to hammer continuously against the armed force of the enemy and his resources, until by mere attrition, if in no other way, there should be nothing left to him but an equal submission with the loyal section of our common country to the Constitution and the laws of the land."

To achieve the first of these, the concentration of fighting men on the actual firing line, he proposed that most of the troops now scattered along the Atlantic coast, in Florida, Georgia, and the Carolinas, be brought to Virginia for a convergent attack on Richmond and the army posted northward in its defense. All down the littoral, various forces of various sizes were attempting to make their way toward various objectives, few if any of them vital to Grant's main purpose. Accordingly, he prepared orders for abandoning all such efforts south of the James, along with as much of the region so far occupied as was not clearly needed to maintain or strengthen the naval blockade. The same would apply in the West, along the Mississippi River from New Orleans to Cairo, where the men thus gained were to be employed in a similar convergence upon Atlanta and the forces likewise posted in its defense. As for the troops held deep in the national rear, serving mainly by their numbers to justify the lofty rank of political or discredited generals assigned to duty there, Grant proposed to abolish some of these commands by merging superfluous departments, thus freeing the men for duty at the front. As for the generals themselves, useless as most of them were for combat purposes, he favored their outright dismissal, which would open the way for just that many promotions in the field. Though this last was rather a ticklish business,

*"War is cruelty. There is no use trying to reform it.
The crueler it is, the sooner it will be over."*

— William Tecumseh Sherman

verging as it did on the political, he thought it altogether worth a try because of the added opportunities it would afford him to reward the ablest and bravest of his subordinate commanders, even before the fighting got under way, and thus incite the rest to follow their example. By such methods (though little came of the last; out of more than a hundred generals Grant recommended for removal, Lincoln let no more than a handful go, mindful as he had to be of the danger of making influential enemies with the presidential election less than nine months off) he would reduce the ratio of garrison to combat troops from one-to-one to one-to-two, which in itself was a considerable accomplishment, one that no previous general-in-chief, from Winfield Scott through George McClellan to Henry Halleck, had conceived to be possible even as a goal.

As for his method of employing that continuous hammering which he believed was the surest if not the only way to bring the South to her knees, the key would be found in orders presently issued to the commanders involved: "So far as practicable all the armies are to move together, and toward one common center." This was to be applied in two stages. West and East, there would be separate but simultaneous convergences upon respective goals, Atlanta and Richmond, by all the mobile forces within each theater; after which, the first to be successful in accomplishing that preliminary task — the reduction of the assigned objective, along with the defeat of the rebel army charged with its defense — would turn east or west, as the case might be, to join the other and thus be in on the kill, the "speedy termination" for which Grant had conceived his grand design. It was for this, the western half of it at least, that he had come to Tennessee to confer with Sherman, his successor in command of the largest of the three main armies in this and the enormous adjoining theater beyond the Mississippi.

There the commanders of the Departments of the Gulf and Arkansas, Major Generals Nathaniel P. Banks and Frederick Steele, were engaged in the opening phase of a campaign of which Grant disapproved and which they themselves had undertaken reluctantly on orders from Lincoln, issued through Halleck before Grant was given over-all command. Advancing on Shreveport by way of Red River, which would afford them gunboat support, they were charged with the invasion and conquest of East Texas, not because there was much of strategic importance there, but because of certain machinations by the French in Mexico, which Lincoln thought it best to block by the occupation of Texas, thus to prevent a possible link-up between the forces of Napoleon III and those of the Confederacy, with which that monarch was believed to be sympathetic. Grant opposed the plan, not because of its international implications, of which he knew little and understood less, but because of its interference with, or in any case its nonfurtherance of, his design for ending the rebellion by concentrating "the greatest number of troops practicable" against its military and manufacturing centers. None of these was in the Lone Star State, so far at least

Nathaniel Banks, commander of the Department of the Gulf, would undertake the conquest of East Texas.

as he could see, or for that matter anywhere else in the Transmississippi, which he preferred to leave to the incidental attention of Steele alone, while Banks moved eastward, across the Mississippi, to play a truly vital role in the drama now being cast. Yet here he was, not only moving in the opposite direction, but taking with him no less than 10,000 of Sherman's best soldiers, temporarily assigned by Halleck to assist him in seizing the Texas barrens. Grant found this close to intolerable, and though he could not directly countermand an order issued by authority of the Commander in Chief, he could at least set a limit to the extent of the penetration and, above all, to the amount of time allowed for the execution of the order, and thus ensure that Sherman would get his veterans back in time for the opening of the offensive in northwest Georgia. Accordingly, two days before Sherman joined him in Nashville on March 17, he wrote to Banks informing him that, while he regarded "the success of your present move as of great importance in reducing the number of troops necessary for protecting the navigation of the Mississippi River," he wanted him to "commence no move for the further acquisition of territory" beyond Shreveport, which, he emphasized, "should be taken as soon as possible," so that, leaving Steele to hold what had been won, he himself could return with his command to New Orleans in time for the eastward movement Grant had in mind for him to undertake in conjunction with Sherman's advance on Atlanta. Above all, Banks was told, if it appeared that Shreveport could not be taken before the end of April, he was to return Sherman's 10,000 veterans by the middle of that month, "even if it leads to the abandonment of the main object of your expedition."

Sherman's own instructions, as stated afterward by Grant in his final report, were quite simple and to the point. He was "to move against Johnston's army, to break it up, and go into the interior of the enemy's country as far as he could, inflicting all the damage he could upon their war resources." For the launching of this drive on the Confederate heartland — admittedly a large order — the Ohioan would have the largest army in the country, even without the troops regrettably detached to Banks across the way. It included, in fact, three separate armies combined into one, each of them under a major general. First, and largest, there was George Thomas's Army of the Cumberland, badly whipped six months ago at Chickamauga, under Major General William S. Rosecrans, but reinforced since by three divisions from Meade for the Chattanooga breakout under Thomas, which had thrown General Braxton Bragg back on Dalton and caused his replacement by Joe Johnston. Next there was the Army of the Tennessee, veterans of Donelson and Shiloh under Grant, of Vicksburg and Missionary Ridge under Sherman, now under James B. McPherson, who had been promoted to fill the vacancy created by Sherman's advancement to head the whole. Finally there was the Army of the Ohio, youngest and smallest of the three, takers of Knoxville and survivors of the siege that followed under Major

General Ambrose Burnside, who was succeeded now by John M. Schofield, lately transferred from guerilla-torn Missouri. Made up in all of twenty infantry and four cavalry divisions, these three armies comprised the Military Division of the Mississippi under Sherman — redoubtable "Uncle Billy" to the 120,000 often rowdy western veterans on its rolls. This was considerably better than twice the number reported to be with Johnston around Dalton, but the defenders had a reserve force of perhaps as many as 20,000 under Lieutenant General Leonidas Polk at Demopolis, Alabama, and Meridian, Mississippi, in position to be hastened by rail either to Mobile or Atlanta, whichever came under pressure in the offensive the North was expected to open before long.

That was where Banks came in; that was why Grant had been so insistent that the Massachusetts general finish up the Red River operation without delay, in order to get his army back to New Orleans for an eastward march with 35,000 soldiers against Mobile, which would also be attacked from the water side by Rear Admiral David G. Farragut, whose Gulf squadron would be strengthened

★

At Fort Sherman on the eastern edge of Chattanooga, the men of Battery C, 1st Wisconsin Heavy Artillery, form up at the foot of their company street.

by the addition of several of the ironclads now on station outside Charleston, where the naval attack had stalled and which, in any case, was no longer on the agenda of targets to be hit. This double danger to Mobile would draw Polk's reserve force southward from Meridian and Demopolis, away from Atlanta and any assistance it might otherwise have rendered Johnston in resisting Sherman's steamroller drive on Dalton and points south. Later, when Banks and Sherman had achieved their primary goals, the reduction of Mobile and Atlanta, they would combine at the latter place for a farther penetration, eastward to the Atlantic and Lee's rear, if Lee was still a factor in the struggle by that time. "All I would now add," Grant told Banks in a follow-up letter sent two weeks after the first, "is that you commence the concentration of your forces at once. Preserve a profound secrecy of what you intend doing, and start at the earliest possible moment."

Such, then, was the nature of the offensive Grant intended to launch in the West, with Sherman bearing the main tactical burden. Similarly in the East, in accordance with his general plan "to concentrate all the force possible

★

against the Confederate armies in the field," he planned for Meade to move in a similar manner, similarly assisted by a diversionary attack on the enemy rear. But he wanted it made clear from the start that this was to be something more than just another "On to Richmond" drive, at least so far as Meade himself was concerned. "Lee's army will be your objective point," his instructions read. "Wherever Lee goes, there you will go also."

If past experience showed anything, it clearly showed that in Virginia almost anything could happen. Moreover, with Lee in opposition, that *anything* was likely to be disastrous from the Federal point of view. Four of the five offensives so far launched against him — those by McClellan, by Pope, by Burnside, by Hooker — had broken in blood and ended in headlong blue retreat, while the fifth — Meade's own, the previous fall — had managed nothing better than a stalemate; which last, in the light of Grant's views on the need for unrelenting pressure, was barely preferable to defeat. Numerical odds had favored the Union to small avail in those encounters, including Hooker's three-to-one advantage, yet that was a poor argument against continuing to make them as long as possible. Just now, as a result of the westward detachments in September, the Army of the Potomac was down to fewer than one hundred thousand men. By way of lengthening the odds, Grant proposed to bring unemployed Ambrose Burnside back east to head a corps of four newly raised divisions which would rendezvous at Annapolis, thus puzzling the enemy as to their eventual use, down the coast or in Virginia proper, until the time came for the Rapidan crossing, when they would move in support of the Army of the Potomac, raising its strength to beyond 120,000 effectives, distributed among fifteen infantry and three cavalry divisions.

Such assurance as this gave was by no means certain. Lee was foxy. No mere numerical advantage had served to fix him in position for slaughter in the past. But Grant had other provisions in mind for securing that result, involving the use of the other two eastern armies. In the West, the three mobile forces had three separate primary assignments: going for Johnston, taking Mobile, riding herd on Transmississippi rebels. In the East, all three were to have the same objective from the start.

Posted in defense of West Virginia and the Maryland-Pennsylvania frontier, the smallest of these three armies was commanded by Major General Franz Sigel; "I fights mit Sigel" was the proud boast of thousands of soldiers, German-born like himself, who had been drawn to the colors by his example. This force was not available for use elsewhere, since its left lay squarely athwart the northern entrance to the Shenandoah Valley, that classic avenue of Confederate invasion exploited so brilliantly two years ago by Stonewall Jackson, who had used it to play on Lincoln's fears, thereby contributing largely to the frustration of McClellan's drive on Richmond at a time when the van of his army could hear the hours struck by the city's public clocks. To Grant, however, the

★

"I fights mit Sigel," the proud boast of German-born soldiers in Major General Franz Sigel's command, gave rise to a comic wartime ballad.

fact that Sigel's 26,000 troops were not considered withdrawable, lest another rebel general use the Valley approach to serve him as Stonewall had served Little Mac, did not mean that this force was not usable as part of the drive on the Virginia capital and the gray army charged with its defense. It seemed to him, rather, that a movement up the Valley by a major portion of Sigel's command would serve even better than an immobile guard, posted across its northern entrance — or exit — to deny it to the enemy as a channel of invasion. Elaborating on this, he directed that the advance was to be in two columns, one under Brigadier General George Crook, who would march west of the Alleghenies for a rapid descent on the Virginia & Tennessee Railroad, along which vital supply line he would move eastward, tearing up track as he went, then north for a meeting near Staunton with Sigel himself, who would have led the other column directly up the Valley. There they would combine for a strike at Lee's flank while Meade engaged his front; or if by then Lee had fallen back on Richmond, as expected, they would join in the pursuit, by way of the Virginia Central — another vital supply line — to the gates of the city and beyond.

So much for the task assigned the second of the three Union armies in Virginia. The third, being larger, had a correspondingly larger assignment, with graver dangers and quite the highest prize of all awaiting the prompt fulfillment of its task.

One reason Grant expected Lee to fall back on Richmond in short order, before Sigel had time to get in position on his flank, was that he intended to oblige him to do so by launching a back-door attack on the capital, from across the James, at the same time Meade was effecting a crossing of the Rapidan, sixty-odd miles to the north. The commander of this third force would be Major

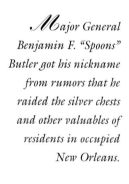

Major General Benjamin F. "Spoons" Butler got his nickname from rumors that he raided the silver chests and other valuables of residents in occupied New Orleans.

General Benjamin F. Butler, who had won a reputation for deftness, along with the nickname "Spoons," in the course of his highly profitable occupation of New Orleans, all of last year and most of the year before. Much as Sigel had been commissioned to attract German-born patriots to the colors, Butler had been made a general to prove to Democrats — at whose Charleston convention in 1860 he had voted fifty-seven consecutive times to nominate Jefferson Davis for President of the United States — that the war was not exclusively a Republican affair; Grant did not select, he inherited him, political abilities and all. For the work at hand, the former Bay State senator would have some 35,000 effectives of all arms, about half of them to be brought up from Florida and South Carolina by the commander of the Department of the South, Major General Quincy A. Gillmore, while the other half would be drawn from Butler's own Department of Virginia and North Carolina. He was to have naval support in moving up the James from his initial base at Fortress Monroe, as well as for the landing at City Point. That would put him within easy reach of Petersburg, the southside railroad center only twenty miles from his true objective, Richmond, which he was then to seize by means of a sudden lunge across the river. Or if Lee had managed a quick fall-back in such strength as to prevent a crossing at that point, Butler, having severed the city's rail connections with the granaries to the south, would combine with Meade and Sigel, upstream or down, for the resultant siege of the capital and its eventual surrender.

If all went as intended in the three-way squeeze he had designed to achieve Lee's encompassment, Grant himself would be there to receive the gray commander's sword at the surrender ceremony. For by now he had decided not only that he would return to the East for the duration of the war, so as to be able to interpose between the Washington politicians and the strategy they might attempt to subvert, but also that the most effective position from which to do this would be in close proximity to the headquarters of the Army of the Potomac. There were, indeed — in addition to the most obvious one, that being in the field would remove him from the constricting atmosphere of the District of Columbia and the disconcerting stares of over-curious civilians, in and out of government — several reasons for the decision: not the least of which was that Meade, in command of much the largest of the three armies in Virginia and charged with much the heaviest burden in the fighting, was outranked not only by Butler and Sigel, whose armies were assigned less arduous tasks, but also by Burnside, whose corps would move in his support and had to be more or less subject to his orders if he was to avoid delays that might prove disastrous. Although the problem could be ignored in the easier-going West — there Thomas, for instance, outranked Sherman, and McPherson was junior to several other major generals in all three armies — Easterners were notoriously touchy about such matters, and if a command crisis arose from the striking of personality sparks on the question of rank, Grant wanted to be there to settle it in person, as only he could do. If this resulted in some discomfort for Meade, whose style might be cramped and whose glory would no doubt be dimmed by the presence of a superior constantly peering over his shoulder and nudging his elbow, this was regrettable, but not nearly as much so, certainly, as various other unfortunate things that might happen without Grant there.

Besides, there was still another reason, perhaps of more importance than all the rest combined. For all its bleeding and dying these past three years, on a scale no other single army could approach, the paper-collar Army of the Potomac had precious few real victories to its credit. It had, in fact, in its confrontations with the adversary now awaiting its advance into the thickets on the south bank of the river it was about to cross, a well-founded and long-nurtured tradition of defeat. The correction for this, Grant believed,

"General Grant is all the rage. He is subjected to the disgusting but dangerous process of being lionized. He is followed by crowds, and is cheered everywhere."

— John Sherman

was the development of self-confidence, which seemed to him an outgrowth of aggressiveness, an eagerness to come to grips with the enemy and a habit of thinking of wounds it would inflict rather than of wounds it was likely to suffer. So far, this outlook had been characteristic not of eastern but of western armies; Grant hoped to effect, in person, a transference of this spirit which he had done so much to create in the past. Twenty months ago, it was true, John Pope had come east "to infuse a little western energy" into the flaccid ranks of the accident-prone divisions that came under his command in the short-lived Army of Virginia. Unfortunately, he had only contrived to lengthen by one (or two or three, if Cedar Mountain and Chantilly were included) the list of spectacular defeats; his troops had wound up cowering in the Washington defenses — what was left of them after the thrashing Lee had administered, flank and rear. But Grant, despite this lamentable example, had much the same victory formula in mind. The difference was that he backed it up, as Pope had been unable to do, with an over-all plan, on a national scale, that embodied the spirit of the offensive.

Sherman, for one, believed he would succeed, although the severely compressed and beleaguered Confederacy still amounted, as Grant said, to "an

★

empire in extent." He expected victory, not only because of the plan they had developed in part between them in the Cincinnati hotel room, but also because he believed that the struggle had entered a new phase, one that for the first time favored the forces of the Union, which at last had come of age, in a military sense, while those of the South were sliding past their prime. Or so at any rate it seemed to Sherman. "It was not until after both Gettysburg and Vicksburg that the war professionally began," he later declared. "Then our men had learned in the dearest school on earth the simple lesson of war . . . and it was then that we as professional soldiers could rightly be held to a just responsibility." Heartened by the prospect, he expressed his confidence to Grant before they parted: he to return to Nashville, the headquarters of his new command, and his friend and superior to Washington for a time, riding eastward past crowds that turned out to cheer him at every station along the way.

Nor was there any slackening of the adulation at the end of the line. "General Grant is all the rage," Sherman heard from his senator brother John the following week. "He is subjected to the disgusting but dangerous process of being lionized. He is followed by crowds, and is cheered everywhere." The senator was worried about the effect all this might have on the man at whom it was directed. "While he must despise the fickle fools who run after him, he, like most others, may be spoiled by this excess of flattery. He may be so elated as to forget the uncertain tenure upon which he holds and stakes his really well-earned laurels." Sherman, though he was pleased to note that his brother added: "He is plain and modest, and so far bears himself well," was quick to jump to his friend's defense, wherein he coupled praise with an admonition. "Grant is as good a leader as we can find," he replied. "He has honesty, simplicity of character, singleness of purpose, and no hope or claim to usurp civil power. His character, more than his genius, will reconcile armies and attach the people. Let him alone. Don't disgust him by flattery or importunity. Let him alone."

Let him alone, either then or later, was the one thing almost no one in Washington seemed willing to do; except Lincoln, who assured Grant that he intended to do just that, at least in a military sense. "The particulars of your plan I neither know nor seek to know," he was to tell him presently, on the eve of commitment, and even at their first interview, before the general left for Tennessee, he had told him (according to Grant's recollection of the exchange, years later) "that he had never professed to be a military man or to know how campaigns should be conducted . . . but that procrastination on the part of commanders and the pressure from the people at the North and Congress, which was always with him, forced him to issue his series of 'Military Orders' — one, two, three, etc. He did not know but they were all wrong, and did know that some of them were. All he wanted or had ever wanted was someone who would take the responsibility and act, and call on him for all the assistance needed."

Welcome though this was to hear, Grant was no doubt aware that the President had said similar things to previous commanders (John C. Frémont, for example, whom he told: "I have given you carte blanche. You must use your own judgment, and do the best you can." Or McClellan, who quoted his assurances after Antietam: "General, you have saved the country. You must remain in command and carry us through to the end. I pledge myself to stand between you and harm") only to jerk the rug from under their feet a short time later, when their backs were turned; Lincoln had never been one to keep a promise any longer than he believed the good of the country was involved. However, in this case he supplemented his private with public remarks to the same effect. "Grant is the first *general* I have had," he was reported to be saying. "I am glad to find a man who can go ahead without me." To a friend who doubted that Grant should be given so free a rein, he replied: "Do you hire a man to do your work and then do it yourself?" To another, who remarked that he was looking

well these days, he responded with an analogy. "Oh, yes, I feel better," he laughed, "for now I'm like the man who was blown up on a steamboat and said, on coming down, 'It makes no difference to me; I'm only a passenger.'"

Partly Lincoln's ebullience was the result of having learned, if not the particulars, then at any rate certain features of Grant's plan. Of its details, an intimate said later that they "were communicated only to Grant's most important or most trusted subordinates" — Meade, Butler, and Sigel, of course, along with Sherman and Banks. "To no others, except to members of his personal staff, did Grant impart a knowledge of his plans; and, even among these, there were some with whom he was reticent." The President and the Secretary of War were both excluded, though he was willing to discuss with them the principle to be applied in bringing "the greatest number of troops practicable" to bear against the forces in rebellion; for example, that the units charged with the occupation of captured territory and the prevention of rebel incursions into the North "could perform this service just as well by advancing as by remaining still, and by advancing they would compel the enemy to keep detachments to hold them back, or else lay his own territory open to invasion." Lincoln saw the point at once, having urged it often in the past, although with small success. "Those not skinning can hold a leg," he said. Grant, as the son of a tanner, knew that this had reference to hog-killing time in the West, where all hands were given a share in the work even though there were not enough skinning-knives to go round. He liked the expression so well, in fact, that he passed it along to Sherman the following week in a letter explaining Sigel's share in the Virginia campaign: "If Sigel can't skin himself he can hold a leg while someone else skins."

Men of the 1st Connecticut Heavy Artillery and the rest of the Army of the Potomac were taken in hand by their new commander, Ulysses S. Grant, in March 1864.

By that time he was in the field, where he enjoyed greater privacy in working on his plan for the distribution of knives to be used in flaying the South alive. Having returned to Washington on March 23, he established headquarters three days later at Culpeper, six miles beyond Brandy Station on the Orange & Alexandria Railroad, about midway between the Rappahannock and the Rapidan. This was the week of the vernal equinox; tomorrow was Easter Sunday. Yet a fifteen-inch snow had fallen that Tuesday and the land was still locked in the grip of winter, as if to mock the hope expressed to Sherman that the armies could launch their separate but concentric attacks by April 25. To the west, in plain view, the Blue Ridge Mountains bore on their peaks and slopes deep drifts of snow, which Grant had been told by old-timers hereabouts would have to have melted away before he could be sure that bad weather had gone for good and the roads would support his moving trains and guns. Down here on the flat at least its whiteness served to hide the scars inflicted by commanders North and South,

The worst of the scars no snow could hide, for they existed in men's minds and signified afflictions of the spirit, afflictions Grant would have to overcome . . .

who, as one observer remarked, "had led their armies up and down these fields and made the landscape desolate." Roundabout Culpeper, he added, "not a house nor a fence, not a tree was to be seen for miles, where once all had been cultivated farmland or richly wooded country. Here and there, a stack of chimneys or a broken cistern marked the site of a former homestead, but every other landmark had been destroyed. The very hills were stripped of their forest panoply, and a man could hardly recognize the haunts familiar to him in his childhood."

Although at present much of this was mercifully blanketed from sight, the worst of the scars no snow could hide, for they existed in men's minds and signified afflictions of the spirit, afflictions Grant would have to overcome before he could instill into the Army of the Potomac the self-confidence and aggressiveness which he considered prerequisite to the successful prosecution of its offensive against an adversary famed throughout the world as the embodiment of the qualities said to be lacking on the near side of the river that ran between the armies. Discouraging to his hopes for the inculcation of the spirit of the offensive, the very landmarks scattered about this fought-over section of Virginia served as doleful reminders of what such plans had come to in the past. Westward beyond the snow-clad Blue Ridge lay the Shenandoah Valley, where

Banks and Frémont had been sorely drubbed and utterly confused, and north-eastward, leading down this way, ran the course of the Buckland Races, in which the cavalry had been chased and taunted. Cedar Mountain loomed dead ahead; there Sigel, thrown forward by bristly Pope, had come a cropper, as Pope himself had done only three weeks later, emulating the woeful example of Irvin McDowell on the plains of Manassas, where the rebels feasted on his stores, forty miles back up the railroad. Downriver about half that distance, Burnside had suffered the throbbing pain and numbing indignity of the Fredericksburg blood-bath and the Mud March; while close at hand, just over the Rapidan, brooded the Wilderness, where Hooker had come to grief in a May riot of smoke-choked greenery and Meade had nearly done the same, inching forward through the ice-cramped woods a scant four months ago, except that he pulled back in time to avoid destruction. All these were painful memories to the veterans who had survived them and passed them on to recruits as a tradition of defeat — a tradition which Grant was seeking now, if not to erase (for it could never be erased; it was too much a part of history, kept alive in the pride of the butternut scarecrows over the river) then at any rate to overcome by locking it firmly in the past and replacing it with one of victory.

In working thus at his plans for bringing that tradition into existence, here and elsewhere, he was assisted greatly by a command arrangement allowed for in the War Department order appointing him general-in-chief in place of Halleck, who was relieved "at his own request" and made chief of staff, an office created to provide a channel of communication between Grant and his nineteen department heads, particularly in administrative matters. The work would be heavy for Old Brains, the glory slight; Hooker, who had feuded with him throughout his eastern tenure, sneered that his situation was like that of a man who married with the understanding that he would not sleep with his wife. But Halleck thereby freed Grant from the need for attending to a great many routine distractions. Instead of being snowed under by paperwork, the lieutenant general could give his full attention to strategic planning, and this he did. From time to time he would return to Washington for an overnight stay — primarily, it would seem, to visit Mrs Grant, who had joined him in Cincinnati for the ride back east — but mainly he kept to his desk in the field, poring over maps and blueing the air of his Culpeper headquarters with cigar smoke, much as he had done a year ago in the former ladies' cabin of the *Magnolia*, where he planned the campaign that took Vicksburg.

★   ★   ★

Shelby Foote

The Lexington races through a break in the dam constructed by Federal workers at the upper rapids of the Red River near Alexandria, Louisiana.

T W O

Red River, Camden: Reëvaluation

1864 ★ ★ ★ ★ ★ ★

Of all these several component segments, each designed to contribute to Grant's over-all pattern for victory on a national scale, the first to go awry was the preliminary one — preliminary, that is, in the sense that it would have to be wound up before the more valid thrust at Mobile could begin — involving Banks and Steele in the far-off Transmississippi, hundreds of miles from the two vital centers around which would swirl the fighting that would determine the outcome of the war. It was the first because it had already begun to falter before Grant was in a position to exercise control. Moreover, once he was in such a position, as general-in-chief, his attempts along that line only served to increase the frustration which both subordinates, proceeding as it were against their hearts, had been feeling all along. Not that it mattered all that much, whatever he did or did not do, for the seeds of defeat had been planted in the conception. By then the only cure would have been to abandon the crop entirely; which would not do, since Lincoln himself, with a fretful sidelong glance at France's latter-day Napoleon, had had a hand in the sowing.

Promptly after the midsummer fall of Port Hudson opened the Mississippi to Union trade throughout its length, Halleck had taken the conquest of Texas as his prime concern in the western theater. It seemed to him the logical

★

next step. Besides, he had always liked to keep things tidy in his rear, and every success achieved under his direction had been followed by a pause for just that purpose. After Donelson, after Corinth, after Vicksburg, he had dismembered the victorious blue force, dispersing its parts on various lateral or rearward assignments, with much attendant loss of momentum. Consequently, although it was here that the North had scored all but a handful of its triumphs in the field, the war in the West had consisted largely of starts and stops, with the result that a considerable portion of the Federal effort had been expended in overcoming prime inertia at the start of each campaign. And so it was to be in the present case, if Old Brains had his way. With the President's unquestioning approval — which, as usual, tended to make him rather imperious in manner and altogether intolerant of objections — Halleck had been urging the conquest of Texas on Banks, who had been opposed in the main to such a venture, so far at least as it involved his own participation. A former Massachusetts governor and Speaker of

---

The war in the West had consisted largely of starts and stops, with the result that a considerable portion of the Federal effort had been expended in overcoming prime inertia at the start of each campaign.

---

the national House of Representatives, he was, like most political appointees, concerned with building a military reputation on which to base his postwar bid for further political advancement. He had in fact his eye on the White House, and he preferred a more spectacular assignment, one nearer the center of the stage and attended with less risk, or in any case no more risk than seemed commensurate with the prize, which in his opinion this did not; Texas was undeniably vast, but it was also comparatively empty. He favored Mobile as a fitting objective by these standards, and had been saying so ever since the surrender of Port Hudson first gave him the feel of laurels on his brow. Halleck had stuck to Texas, however, and Halleck as general-in-chief had had his way.

Texas it was, although there still was considerable disagreement as to the best approach to the goal, aside from a general conviction that it could not be due west across the Sabine and the barrens, where, as one of Banks's staff remarked, there was "no water in the summer and fall, and plenty of water but no road in the winter and spring." Halleck favored an ascent of Red River, to Shreveport and beyond, which would allow for gunboat support and rapid transportation of supplies; but this had some of the same disadvantages as the

★

direct cross-country route, the Red being low on water all through fall and winter. While waiting for the spring rise, without which the river was unnavigable above Alexandria, barely one third of the distance up to Shreveport, Banks tried his hand at a third approach, the mounting of amphibious assaults against various points along the Lone Star coast. The first of these, at Sabine Pass in September, was bloodily repulsed; the navy lost two gunboats and their crews before admitting it could put no troops ashore at that point. So Banks revised his plan by reversing it, end for end. He managed an unsuspected landing near the mouth of the Rio Grande, occupied Brownsville unopposed, and began to work his way back east by way of Aransas Pass and Matagorda Bay. There he stopped. So far he had encountered no resistance, but just ahead lay Galveston, with Sabine Pass beyond, both of them scenes of past defeats which he would not risk repeating. All he had got for his pains was a couple of dusty border towns and several bedraggled miles of beach, amounting to little more in fact than a few pinpricks along one leathery flank of the Texas elephant. By now it was nearly spring, however, and time for him to get back onto what Halleck, in rather testy dispatches, had kept assuring him was the true path of conquest: up the Red, which soon was due for the annual rise that would convert it into an artery of invasion.

By now, too, as a result of closer inspection of the prize, Banks had somewhat revised his opinion as to the worth of the proposed campaign. Mobile was still what he ached for, but Mobile would have to wait. Meantime, a successful ascent of the Red, as a means of achieving the subjugation of East Texas, would not only add a feather to his military cap; it would also, by affording him and his army valuable training in the conduct of combined operations, serve as excellent preparation for better and more difficult things to come. Besides, study disclosed immediate advantages he had overlooked before. In addition to providing a bulwark against the machinations of the French in Mexico, the occupation of Shreveport would yield political as well as strategic fruits. First there was Lincoln's so-called Ten Percent plan, whereby a state would be permitted to return to the national fold as soon as ten percent of its voters affirmed their loyalty to the Union and its laws. With Shreveport firmly in Federal hands, Confederate threats would no longer deter the citizens of West Louisiana and South Arkansas from taking the oath required; Louisiana and Arkansas, grateful to the Administration which had granted them readmission, would cast their votes in the November election, thereby winning for the general who had made such action possible the gratitude of the man who, four years later, would exert a powerful influence in the choice of his successor. There, indeed, was a prize worth grasping. Moreover, the aforementioned strategic fruits of such a campaign had been greatly enlarged in the course of the fall and winter, occasioned by Steele's advance on Little Rock in September, which extended the Federal occupation down to the Arkansas River, bisecting the state along a line from Fort Smith to

Napoleon, and posed a threat to Confederate installations farther south. Ordnance works at Camden and Arkadelphia had been shifted to Tyler and Marshall, Texas, where they now were back in production, as were others newly established at Houston and San Antonio. Cut off from the industrial East by the fall of Vicksburg, still-insurgent Transmississippians had striven in earnest to develop their own resources. Factories at Tyler, Houston, and Austin, together with one at Washington, Arkansas, were delivering 10,000 pairs of shoes a month to rebel quartermasters, and inmates of the Texas penitentiary at Huntsville were turning out more than a million yards of cotton and woolen cloth every month, to be made into gray or butternut uniforms for distribution to die-hard fighters in all three states of the region. Shreveport itself had become an industrial complex quite beyond anyone's dream a year ago, with foundries, shops, and laboratories for the production of guns and ammunition, without which not even the doughtiest grayback would constitute the semblance of a threat. If Banks could lay hands on Shreveport, then move on into the Lone Star vastness just beyond, the harvest would be heavy, both in matériel and glory. By late January, having considered all this, and more, he was so far in agreement with Halleck that he wired him: "The occupation of Shreveport will be to the country west of the Mississippi what that of Chattanooga is to the east. And as soon as this can be accomplished," he added, his enthusiasm waxing as he wrote, "the country west of Shreveport will be in condition for a movement into Texas."

Another persuasive factor there was, which in time would be reckoned the most influential of them all, though less perhaps on Banks himself than on various others, in and out of the army and navy, about to be involved in the campaign. This was cotton. Banks was intrigued by the notion that the proposed invasion not only could be carried out on a self-supporting basis, financially speaking, but could result in profits that would cover other, less lucrative efforts, such as the ones about to be launched through the ravaged counties of northern Virginia and across the red-clay hills and gullies of North Georgia. What was more, he backed his calculations with experience. On his march up Bayou Teche to Alexandria, in April of the year before, he had seized an estimated $5,000,000 in contraband goods, including lumber, sugar and salt, cattle and livestock, and cotton to the amount of 5000 bales. This last represented nearly half the value of the spoils — and would represent even more today, with the price in Boston soaring rapidly toward two dollars a pound in greenbacks. Yet those 5000 bales collected along the Teche were scarcely more than a dab compared to the number awaiting seizure in plantation sheds along the Red and in the Texas hinterland; Banks predicted that the campaign would produce between 200,000 and 300,000 bales. Even the lower of these two figures, at a conservative estimate of $500 a bale, would bulge the Treasury with no less than a hundred million dollars, which by itself would be enough to run the whole war for two months.

★

This .58-caliber rifle is one of only four that remain from the approximately 3000 made at the Confederate's Tyler Ordnance Works in Tyler, Texas.

Nor was that all. In addition to this direct financial gain, he would also put back into operation the spindles lying idle in the mills of his native state, where he had got his start as a bobbin boy and where the voters would someday turn out in hordes to express their thanks for all he had done for them and the nation in their time of trial. It was no wonder his enthusiasm rose with every closer look at the political, strategic, and financial possibilities of a campaign he formerly had thought not worth his time.

Perhaps the most persuasive factor of all, so far at least as Banks was concerned, was that he secured Halleck's approval of a plan, worked out between them, that assured the coöperation not only of Steele, who would move south from Little Rock to the vicinity of Shreveport with 15,000 troops, but also of Sherman, who was to send 10,000 of his veterans to Alexandria for a combination with the 20,000 Banks himself would bring to that point by repeating last year's profitable march up the Teche. Including a Marine Brigade and the crews of twenty-odd warships under Rear Admiral David D. Porter, which were to serve as escort for the transports bringing Sherman's men from Vicksburg and thenceforth as an integral part of the command in its ascent of the Red, this would

★

Confederate General Edmund Kirby Smith (right), commander of the Transmississippi region, angered Richard Taylor by not providing reinforcements quickly.

give Banks a total strength of just under 50,000; which he believed was sufficient, in itself, to guarantee success in the campaign. His opponent, General Edmund Kirby Smith, commanding that vast, five-state Transmississippi region already beginning to be known as "Kirby-Smithdom," had not much more than half that many soldiers in all of Arkansas, Louisiana, Texas, and the Indian Territory combined. Such opposition as Smith might be able to offer the veteran 45,000-man blue army and its hard-hitting 210-gun fleet, Banks was not unjustified in believing, would only serve to swell the glory involved in the inevitable outcome.

Sherman himself was inclined to agree with this assessment, though he was aware (as Banks perhaps was not, having had little time for theoretic study) of Napoleon's dictum that the most difficult of all maneuvers was the combination of widely divided columns, regardless of their over-all numerical superiority, on a field of battle already occupied by an enemy who thus would be free, throughout the interim preceding their convergence, to strike at one or another of the approaching columns. His only regret, the red-haired general said when he came down to New Orleans in early March to confer with Banks about his share in the campaign, was that Grant had forbidden him to go along. He stayed two days, working out the arrangements for his troops to be at Alexandria in time for a meeting with Banks's column on the 17th — the same day, as it turned out, that he would meet with Grant in Nashville, though he did not know that yet — then steamed back upriver to Vicksburg, declining his host's invitation to stay over for the inauguration on March 5 of the recently elected Union-loyal governor of Louisiana, one Michael Hahn, a Bavaria-born lawyer and sugar planter who had opposed secession from the start. Despite the delay it would entail, Banks apparently felt obliged to remain for the ceremony

— which was quite elaborate, one item on the program being a rendition of the "Anvil Chorus" in Lafayette Square by no less than a thousand singers, accompanied by all the bands of the army, while church bells pealed and cannon were fired in unison by electrical devices — then at last, after managing to get through another two weeks of attending to additional political and administrative matters, got aboard a steamboat for a fast ride up the Mississippi and the Red for the meeting at Alexandria with Sherman's men and his own, whose ascent of the Teche had been delayed by heavy going on roads made nearly bottomless by rain. Before leaving he had written to Halleck of the public reaction to the inaugural celebration, thousand-tongued chorus, electrically fired cannon, and all. "It is impossible to describe it with truth," he wrote. In the future, much the same thing would be said of the campaign he was about to give the benefit of his personal supervision.

It was March 24 by the time he reached Alexandria, one week late. Even so, he got there ahead of the men in his five divisions, who did not complete their slog up the Teche until next day. Plastered with mud and eight days behind schedule, they did not let the hard and tardy march depress their spirits, which were high. "The *soldier* is a queer fellow," a reporter who accompanied them wrote; "he is not at all like other white men. Tired, dusty, cold or hungry — no matter, he is always jolly. I find him, under the most adverse circumstances, shouting, singing, skylarking. There is no care or tire in him." Banks, for all the dignity he was careful to preserve, shared this skylark attitude when he arrived, and with good cause. The time spent waiting for him to show had been put to splendid use by Sherman's veterans, who had arrived on time, with one considerable victory already to their credit and another scored before the Massachusetts general joined them.

Three divisions under Brigadier General A. J. Smith, a Pennsylvania-born West Pointer, they had left Vicksburg on March 10 and gone ashore two days later at Simsport, just up the Atchafalaya from its confluence with the Red. While Porter's twenty-two heavily gunned warships — thirteen of them ironclads, accompanied by some forty transports and quartermaster boats — returned to the Red for a frontal attack on Fort De Russy, a once-abandoned but now reoccupied Confederate strongpoint about halfway up to Alexandria, the infantry crossed a lush, bayou-mazed prairie called Avoyelles to come upon the fortification from the rear. Such few rebels as they saw en route were quick to scamper out of reach, having no apparent stomach for a fight. By late afternoon of March 14 the bluecoats were in position for a mass assault, not only hearing the roar of Porter's guns, which showed that he too was in place on schedule, but also receiving a few of his heavy shells that overshot the fort. Just before sundown, at a cost of only 38 killed and wounded, they stormed and took it, along with its ten guns and its garrison of 300 bitter, shell-dazed men, who, according to a newsman with the attackers, "screamed in demoniac tones, even after our banners flaunted from their bastions and ramparts." This done, the victors got back aboard their transports for the thirty-mile ride to Alexandria: all, that is, but the men of one division, who stayed behind to raze the fort by tearing out and burning its wooden beams and leveling the earthworks, after which they gave it the finishing touch by blowing up the powder magazine.

They had received excellent schooling in such work under Sherman, especially on the recent expedition to Meridian, where, in Sherman's words, they had cut "a swath of desolation fifty miles broad across the State of Mississippi which the present generation will not forget." In such work they used sledges and crowbars more than rifles, and though it involved much vigorous exercise, it was not only a fine way of relaxing from the rigors of the Vicksburg siege, it was also a good deal safer, since their efforts were mainly directed against civilians. Moreover, this particular division had a commander, Brigadier General T. Kilby Smith, whose views along these lines coincided more or less with their own. "The inhabitants hereabouts are pretty tolerably frightened," the thirty-three-year-old former lawyer was presently to write home to his mother in Ohio. "Our western troops are tired of shilly shally, and this year they will deal their blows very heavily. Past kindnesses and forbearance has not been appreciated or understood; frequently ridiculed. The people now will be terribly scourged." Presumably such words had been passed down as well as out, for private residences had begun to burn in Simsport almost as soon as the transports ran out their gangplanks for the troops to go ashore, and their progress across the lovely Avoyelles Prairie was marked by the ruins of burnt-out houses, some with nothing to show they had been there except an unsupported chimney; "Sherman Monuments," these were called. Arcadians of the region, a gentle people with a heritage of freedom, many of whom had been pro-Union up to now, were indeed "terribly scourged." The pattern was set for the campaign, so far at least as the western troops — "Sherman's gorillas," they dubbed themselves — were concerned. Next would come the turn of the inhabitants of the piny uplands beyond Alexandria, although a correspondent of the St Louis *Republican* was already predicting that unless such practices were discouraged there was a danger of "our whole noble army degenerating into a band of cutthroats and robbers."

By way of proving their skill as fighters as well as burners, six regiments of gorilla-guerillas, accompanied by a brigade of Banks's cavalry that rode in ahead of his infantry, pressed on above Alexandria to Henderson's Hill, twenty miles up Bayou Rapides, on a forced reconnaissance which reached a climax on the night of March 21 with a surprise attack, through rain and hail and darkness, that captured a whole regiment of rebel cavalry, some 250 men and mounts, together with all four guns of a battery also caught off guard by the assault. Returning to base three days later, they paraded their captives before Banks, who had just arrived and was delighted to find that they had not wasted the time spent waiting

★

*U*nion forces under General Andrew J. Smith,
supported by a bombardment by Porter's fleet, storm the
Confederate garrison at Fort De Russy on March 14.

for him and the rest of the five divisions they were supposed to reinforce. When
these wound up their march next day, March 25, he had concentrated under his
immediate command by far the most impressive display of military strength ever
seen in the Transmississippi, on land or water. With ninety pieces of field artillery
and considerably better than twice that number of heavier guns afloat, he had
30,000 effectives on hand, practically all of them seasoned campaigners, and was
about to move up the Red for a conjunction near Shreveport with half that
many more under Steele, who he now learned had left Little Rock two days ago,
marching south-southwest toward the same objective. The outlook was auspicious,
especially in light of the fact that his troops had already proved their superiority,
first at Fort De Russy and again at Henderson's Hill, over such forces of the
enemy as they had managed to trick or cower into remaining within their reach.
But then next day, as he was about to order a resumption of the march, a
high-ranking courier arrived with Grant's eleven-day-old letter of instructions
from Nashville, written while waiting for Sherman to join him there.

This could not but give Banks pause, stipulating as it did that if he
did not feel certain of taking Shreveport by the end of April he was to return A. J.
Smith's command to Sherman by the middle of that month "for movements

east of the Mississippi." Discouraging as this was in part — for it not only fixed him with a tighter schedule than he had felt obliged to follow when he set out, it also threatened him with the imminent loss of the three best divisions in his army — Banks took heart at something else the letter said. If the expedition was successful, he was to leave the holding of Shreveport and the line of the Red to Steele, while he himself returned to New Orleans for an advance on Mobile as part of the new general-in-chief's design for a spring offensive in the central theater. This was the assignment he had coveted all along, and though he was aware of the danger of being over-hasty in military matters, this went far toward reconciling him to the step-up in the tempo of his march. With Mobile to follow, more or less as a reward for past successes, he wanted this Red River business over and done with as soon as possible. Accordingly, he put his cavalry in motion that same day and followed it two days later with his infantry, while A. J. Smith's men got back aboard their transports to accompany the fleet. The immediate

---

With Mobile to follow, more or less as a reward for past successes, he wanted this Red River business over and done with as soon as possible.

---

objective was Grand Ecore, sixty miles upstream or roughly half the total distance. His plan was to move rapidly to that point and to Natchitoches, four miles south of Grand Ecore and the river, after which would come the leap at Shreveport that would wind up the campaign.

Banks himself did not leave Alexandria until after April 1, having remained behind to supervise an election on that date, by such voters as had taken the loyalty oath, of delegates to a state convention whose task it would be to draw up a new constitution tying Louisiana more firmly to the Union. Meanwhile the troops had been making excellent progress, encountering nothing more than scattered resistance that was easily brushed aside. By the time of the April Fool election, both Natchitoches and Grand Ecore had been occupied by leading elements of the respective columns, one advancing by land, the other by water. This meant that the campaign was back on schedule, despite the delay at the start. So far all was well, except perhaps that the lack of opposition had resulted in a dwindling of public concern outside the immediate area of operations. "It is a remarkable fact," the New Orleans correspondent of the New York *Tribune* declared on April 2, "that this Red River expedition is not followed by that anxious interest and solicitude which has heretofore attended similar army movements. The success of our troops is looked upon as a matter of course, and the cotton speculators are the only people I can find who are nicely weighing probabilities and chances in connection with the expedition."

If anxious interest and solicitude were what he was seeking, he could have found them not only in the New Orleans cotton exchange but also up Red River, aboard the flagship of the fleet. Porter had already lost one of his prized vessels, the veteran *Conestoga*, sunk March 8 in a collision on the Mississippi while returning from Vicksburg with a heavy load of ammunition that took her to the bottom in four minutes. She was the eighth major warship the admiral had lost in the past sixteen months, and two of these had been captured and turned against him, at least for a time. What was worse, it had begun to seem to him that if he continued to go along with Banks he would be in danger of losing a great many more, not so much through enemy action — he had never been one to flinch from combat — as through an act of nature; or, rather, a non-act. The annual rise of the Red, which usually began around New Year's, had not thus far materialized. Perhaps it was merely late this year; but

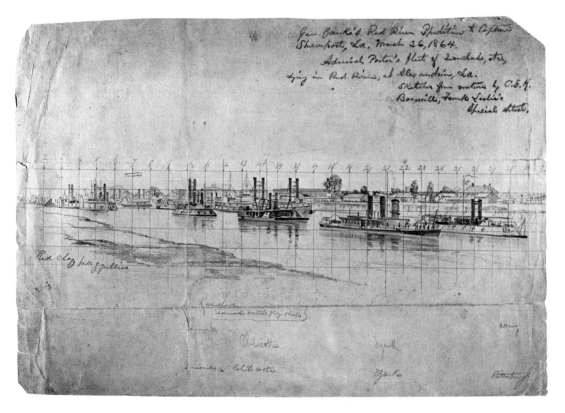

In this annotated sketch, Porter's flotilla lies at anchor in Alexandria on March 26 after bombarding the Confederate stronghold at Fort De Russy.

twice before, in 1846 and 1855, it had not occurred at all. That was a nine-year interval, and now that another nine years had elapsed, there were indications that if Porter got his boats above the mile-long falls and rapids at Alexandria, he might not be able to get them down again. If the river, instead of rising, took a drop, he would be left with the agonizing choice of blowing them up or having them fall into rebel hands, which would mean nothing less than the undoing of all the navy had accomplished in these past two years of war on the western waters. That was unthinkable, but he had boasted so often that he could take his fleet "wherever the sand was damp," the admiral now found it impossible to renege on his promise to stay with the army to the end of its up-stream trek. After three days of tugging and bumping — during which time the river, to his alarm, began to dwindle, then rose slightly — he got his largest ironclad, *Eastport,* over the falls; after which he followed with a dozen lighter-draft gunboats and twenty transports laden with troops. "The water is quite a muddy red and looks anything but inviting," a sailor wrote in his diary as the column began its winding crawl to Grand Ecore. "The transports from the head belch out three bellowing whistles which is caught up by the next, and sometimes two or three vie in a euphonious concert much resembling the bellowing of cattle at the smell of blood."

So far, except for the considerable slaughter of pigs and chickens encountered on the march, the smell of blood had been little more than a figurative expression. Moreover, if Banks could judge by indications, the Confederates were either content to have it remain so, or else they were incapable of having it otherwise, knowing only too well that most of the blood that would be spilled would be their own. In any case, the one thing they had not done was fight, and as he boarded his headquarters boat at Alexandria for an upstream ride on the evening of April 2 — a nattily dressed man in his vigorous prime, two years short of fifty, wearing highly polished boots and chinking spurs, a light-blue overcoat, buckskin gauntlets elbow-high, a bell-crowned hat, and a neatly groomed mustache and brief imperial — he got off a dispatch to Halleck expressing his confidence in "an immediate and successful issue" of the campaign, the end of which he believed was in plain view.

"Our troops now occupy Natchitoches," he informed Old Brains, "and we hope to be in Shreveport by the 10th of April. I do not fear concentration of the enemy at that point. My fear is that they may not be willing to meet us."

In the course of the past three years Lincoln had read other such dispatches, and all too often they had turned out to be prologues to disaster. Reading this one, when in time it reached Washington, he frowned and shook his head in disapproval.

"I am sorry to see this tone of confidence," he said. "The next news we shall hear from there will be of a defeat."

★

A defeat was what the Confederates had very much in
mind for the invaders: especially Major General Richard
Taylor, Kirby Smith's West Louisiana commander, who
had crossed swords with Banks before, first in the Shenandoah Valley, two years
ago, and then along the Teche the previous year. Tactically, the second of these
confrontations had not been as brilliant as the first, in which Taylor, serving as
one of Stonewall Jackson's ablest lieutenants, had helped to strip the former Bay
State politician of so many well-stocked wagons that he had been nicknamed
"Commissary" Banks; but the aptness of this nom-de-guerre had been redemon-
strated last summer, west of New Orleans, when Taylor's surprise descent on
Banks's forward supply base at Brashear City, yielding an estimated $2,000,000
in ordnance and other stores, helped immeasurably to equip the army he had
been raising for the defense of his home state ever since his transfer from Virginia.
A son of Zachary Taylor and brother of Jefferson Davis's first wife, now just past
his thirty-eighth birthday, he was described by one of his soldiers as "a quiet,
unassuming little fellow, but noisy on retreats, with a tendency to cuss mules
and wagons which stall on the road."

This tendency had been given a free rein for the past three weeks, in
the course of which he had been obliged to fall back nearly two hundred miles
before an adversary he was convinced he could whip, if he could only manage to
meet him on anything approaching equal terms. But there was the rub. With
fewer than 7000 troops in the path of better than four times that number backed
by the guns of the Union fleet, he had no choice except to continue his retreat,
hard though it was to suffer without retaliation the vandalism of A. J. Smith's
gorillas, not to mention such professional indignities as Fort De Russy and the
loss of most of his cavalry at Henderson's Hill. His consolation was that he was
falling back toward reinforcements, which Kirby Smith kept assuring him were on
the way from Arkansas and Texas. However — as might have been expected of a
young man who had served his war apprenticeship under the bloody-minded and
highly time-conscious Stonewall — he chafed at the delay. On the last day of
March, with his troops in motion for a concentration forty miles northwest of
Natchitoches and less than half that distance from the Texas border, he sent an
irate dispatch informing the department commander that his patience was near
the snapping point. "Had I conceived for an instant that such astonishing delay
would ensue before reinforcements reached me," he told Smith, "I would have
fought a battle even against the heavy odds. It would have been better to lose the
state after a defeat than to surrender it without a fight. The fairest and richest
portion of the Confederacy is now a waste. Louisiana may well know her destiny.
Her children are exiles; her labor system is destroyed. Expecting every hour to
receive the promised reinforcements, I did not feel justified in hazarding a general
engagement with my little army. I shall never cease to regret my error."

"Hydrocephalus at Shreveport produced atrophy elsewhere," he afterwards protested, complaining acidly that while his superior "displayed much ardor in the establishment of bureaus, and on a scale proportioned rather to the extent of his territory than to the smallness of his force," Smith neglected the more vital task of resisting blue aggression in the field. In thus indulging his fondness for classical allusion, while at the same time venting his spleen, Yale man Taylor was not altogether fair to a West-Point-trained commander who by now had spent a hectic year being responsible for a region the size of western Europe, much of it trackless and practically none of it self-sustaining, at any rate in a military sense, at the time he assumed his manifold duties. Not the least of these was the establishment of those bureaus of supply and communication scorned by Taylor but made altogether necessary by the loss, within four months of Smith's arrival, of all practical connection with the more prosperous half of his country lying east of the Mississippi. In short, he had been involved in a year-long strategic and logistic nightmare. If at times he seemed to vacillate in the face of danger, that was to a large extent because of the scantiness of his resources, both in manpower and equipment, in contrast to those of an adversary whose own were apparently limitless and who could move against him, more or less at will, by land and water. Missouri had been lost before he got there. Then had come the subtraction of the northern half of Arkansas, suffered while pinprick lodgments were being made along the lower coast of Texas. Now it turned out that all this had been by way of preparation for a simultaneous advance by two blue columns under Steele and Banks, converging respectively from the north and east upon his headquarters at Shreveport and containing between them more veteran troops than he had in his entire five-state department, including guerillas and recruits. If he was jumpy it was small wonder, no matter how resentful Richard Taylor might feel at being obliged to backtrack, across the width of his beloved home state, before the menace of a force four times his own.

Warned early of the double-pronged threat to his headquarters and supply base — the fall of which would mean the loss, not only of Louisiana and what remained of Arkansas, but also of much that lay beyond — Smith decided to meet the nearer and larger danger first: meaning Banks. He would hit him with all the strength he could muster, then turn and do the same to Steele when he came up. Accordingly, he alerted his Texas commander, Major General John B. Magruder, to prepare his entire force, garrisons excluded, for a march to support Taylor. In Arkansas, Lieutenant General Theophilus Holmes was given similar instructions, except that he was to retain his cavalry for use against Steele's column, slowing it down as best he could until such time as Taylor had disposed of Banks and was free to come in turn to his assistance. These alerting orders were issued in late February, before either enemy force had been assembled. In early March, though neither Federal column had yet set out, Magruder

★

Commander of the Confederate forces in Texas, John B. Magruder (left), known as "Prince John," sent men under Thomas Green to support Richard Taylor.

was told to put his men in motion. They amounted in all to some 2500 horsemen, combined in a division under Brigadier General Thomas Green, and left Magruder with only about the same number for the defense of all of Texas: a situation the Virginian considered not unlike the one he had faced two years ago, on the York-James peninsula, when he found himself standing with one brigade in the path of McClellan's huge blue juggernaut. Meanwhile Holmes, whose deafness was only one of the symptoms of his superannuation, had been relieved at his own request and succeeded by Major General Sterling Price, his second in command; Price was told to put his alerted troops — two small divisions of infantry under Brigadier General T. J. Churchill, with a combined strength of 4500 effectives — on the march for Shreveport. These were the reinforcements Taylor had been expecting all the time he was fading back across the width of Louisiana, protesting hotly at their nonarrival.

Green's progress was necessarily slow across the barrens and the Sabine, but Churchill's was impeded by Smith himself. By now the Transmississippi chieftain had begun to suspect that he had hoisted himself onto the horns of a dilemma: as indeed he had, since he thought he had. Having attended boldly to the threat posed by Banks, he feared that he had erred in leaving Price too little strength to hinder Steele, who might be able to descend on Shreveport before Taylor could dispose of Banks and come to its defense. Taking counsel of his fears, which were enlarged by information that Steele had set out from Little Rock on March 23, Smith held Churchill for a time at headquarters, so as to be able to use him in either direction, north or south, depending on whether the need was greater in Arkansas or Louisiana, then finally, in response to Taylor's increasingly strident dispatches, ordered Churchill to move south to Keatchie, a hamlet roughly midway between Shreveport and Taylor's latest point of concentration, just southeast of Mansfield. He had known what to do, but he had been so hesitant to do it that he had wound up not knowing what to do after all.

Dick Taylor had not helped with his hard-breathing threats to gamble everything on a single long-odds strike, provoked by desperation and congenital impatience. "When Green joins me, I repeat," he notified headquarters, "I shall fight a battle for Louisiana, be the forces of the enemy what they may." Horrified, Smith urged caution. "A general engagement should not be risked without hopes of success," he warned, reminding his impetuous lieutenant that rashness "would be fatal to the whole cause and to the department. Our role must be a defensive policy." Moreover, such resolution as he had managed so far to maintain, regarding his plan for meeting the two-pronged Federal menace, was grievously shaken by Taylor's expressed opinion that Steele, a "bold, ardent, vigorous" professional, might constitute a graver danger, despite his reported disparity in numbers, than the amateur Banks, who was "cold, timid, [and] easily foiled." Smith continued to waver under the suspicion that he had chosen the wrong man to tackle first. Finally on April 5, alarmed by news that Steele was making rapid progress, and in fact had completed nearly half his southward march by crossing the Little Missouri River the day before, he decided to ride down to Mansfield for a conference with Taylor. His intention was to revise his plan by reversing it. He would concentrate everything first against Steele, rather than in front of Banks, even if this meant standing a siege at Shreveport or retreating into Texas, where — it now occurred to him, as a further persuasive argument for postponing the showdown — a defeat would be more disastrous for the invaders.

Taylor was dismayed by his chief's vacillation. Asked for his advice three days ago he had been quick to give it. "Action, prompt, vigorous action, is required," he replied. "While we are deliberating the enemy is marching. King James lost three kingdoms for a mass. We may lose three states without a battle." He still felt that way about it, and he said so, face to face with Smith at Mansfield on the morning of April 6. Smith heard him out, a mild-mannered Floridian just under forty, outwardly unperturbed by the short-tempered Taylor, but left that afternoon to return to his headquarters, still gripped inwardly by indecision. Taylor, though he had been reinforced that day by Green, whose arrival raised his strength to 9000 effectives, still had been given no definite instructions. Churchill's 4500 were at Keatchie, twenty miles away, but when or whether they would be released to him he did not know. All Smith had said was that he would inform him as soon as he made up his mind — the one thing he seemed incapable of doing. Taylor apparently decided, then and there, that if anything was going to be done in this direction he would have to accomplish it on his own.

★

And that was what he did, beginning the following day, except that he had considerable help from his opponent, who presented him with a tactical opportunity he did not feel he could neglect, with or without the approval of his superior, forty miles away in Shreveport.

★ ★ ★   **B**anks came on boldly, still exuding confidence as he prepared at Natchitoches and Grand Ecore for the final stage of his ascent of the Red. Alexandria lay sixty miles behind him, Shreveport only sixty miles ahead. The first half of this 120-mile stretch had been covered in five days of easy marching, and he planned to cover the second half in less.

Such frets as he had encountered up to now came not from the rebels, who he was convinced wanted no part of a hand-to-hand encounter, but from internal complications. For one thing, smallpox had broken out in the Marine Brigade, with the result that it was returned to Vicksburg and Kilby Smith's division took over the pleasant duty of "escorting" — that is, riding with — the fleet. The loss of these 3000 Marines, who had not been included in his original calculations anyhow, was largely offset by the arrival of the 1500-man Corps d'Afrique, composed of Negro volunteers who had proved their combat worth to doubters at Port Hudson the year before.

Another complication was not so easily dismissed, however, for it had to do with money: meaning cotton. Banks had been getting very little of this because of Porter, who had been getting a great deal of it indeed — all, in fact, that came within his 210-gun reach. Unlike the army, which seized and turned over rebel cotton to the government as contraband of war, the navy defined cotton as subject to seizure more or less as if it was an authentic high-seas prize, the proceeds of which were to be divided among the officers and crew of the vessel that confiscated it, the only stipulation being that the bales had to have been the property of the Confederate government. Very little of it was, of course, but that did not cramp Porter or his sailors. They simply stenciled "C.S.A." on each captured bale, then drew a line through the still-wet letters and stenciled "U.S.N." below. When an army colonel remarked that the result signified "Cotton Stealing Association of the United States Navy," the admiral laughed as loud as anyone, if not louder, in proportion to his lion's share of the proceeds as commander of the fleet. This would not have been so bad, in itself; Banks, though punctiliously honest, had grown more or less accustomed to such practices by others, in the service as in politics. The trouble was that the upriver planters, hearing of Porter's activities below, began to burn their cotton rather than have it fall into his hands. By the time the civilian speculators, who had accompanied the army from New Orleans and were prepared to pay the going backwoods price for the hoarded staple, arrived in the wake of the gunboats, bearing trade permits signed by Chase and even Lincoln, there was nothing left for them to buy, either cheap or dear, for resale to the hungry mills of New England. Moreover, they directed their resentment less at Porter, who after all was doing nothing they would not have done in his place, than at Banks, who they believed had lured them up this winding rust-colored river only to dash their hopes by failing to deliver even a fraction of what he had encouraged them to expect. By the time they reached Alexandria it was evident there was nothing to be gained by going farther; Banks made it official by ordering their return. They had no choice except to obey, but they were bitter as only men could be who had been wounded in their wallets. "When General Banks sent them all back to Alexandria, without their sheaves," a staff officer later wrote, "they returned to New Orleans furious against him and mouthing calumnies."

It was of course no good thing, militarily or politically, for a man to have such enemies in his rear, but at least he was rid of a frock-coated clan who, he complained, had "harassed the soul out of me." And though they would be quick to fix the blame on him in case of a mishap, let alone an outright failure,

At Grand Ecore, a depot on the Red River, Union steamers land their cargoes of rations. Here, General Banks divided his land forces from Porter's fleet.

Red River, Camden: Reëvaluation

Banks was more confident than ever that nothing of the kind was going to happen. It was not going to happen because there would be no tactical occasion for it to happen; Taylor simply would not risk a probable defeat. After reviewing his troops at Natchitoches on April 4 — a frequent practice which always brought him pleasure and tended to enlarge his self-respect — the former Bay State governor said as much in a letter to his wife. "The enemy retreats before us," he informed her, "and will not fight a battle this side of Shreveport if then."

When two days later — April 6: the second anniversary of Shiloh — he set out on the final leg of his advance, his route and order of march demonstrated, even more forcefully than his letters to Halleck and Mrs Banks had done, the extent of his conviction that the rebels would not dare to stand and fight before he reached his goal. At Grand Ecore the land and water columns diverged for the first time in the campaign, the former taking an inland road that curved west, then northwest, through the villages of Pleasant Hill and Mansfield, and finally northeast, back toward the Red, for a meeting with the fleet abreast of Springfield Landing, roughly two thirds of the way to Shreveport,

which they then would capture by a joint attack. Banks chose this route either because he did not know there was a road along the river (there was, and a good one) or else because he thought the inland road, leading as it did through piny highlands, would make for better progress. If this last was what he had in mind, he was mistaken in that too. According to one of the marchers, a heavy rain soon made the single narrow road "more like a broad, deep, red-colored ditch than anything else." Heavy-footed, sometimes ankle-deep in mire, they cursed him as they slogged: particularly A. J. Smith's Westerners, who by now had acquired a scathing contempt for the former Massachusetts politician and the men of his five divisions, mainly Easterners from New York and New England. Paper-collar dudes, they called them, and referred with grins to the general himself, whose lack of military training and acumen was common gossip around their campfires, as "Napoleon P. Banks" or, even more scornfully, "Mr Banks."

Heavy-footed, sometimes ankle-deep in mire, they cursed him as they slogged: particularly A. J. Smith's Westerners, who by now had acquired a scathing contempt for the former Massachusetts politician . . .

Nor was the poor condition of the road itself the worst of the disadvantages an inland march involved. Beyond Natchitoches, in addition to being deprived of the support of Porter's heavy guns, the westering column would encounter few streams or wells, which would make for thirsty going, and little or nothing in the way of food or feed. One look at the sparsely settled region back from the river convinced a newsman that "such a thing as subsisting an army in a country like this could only be achieved when men and horses can be induced to live on pine trees and resin." Fortunately — at least from the subsistence point of view — Banks had brought along a great many wagons, no fewer in fact than a thousand, which assured that his soldiers would suffer no shortage of bacon or hardtack or coffee while crossing the barrens, although Smith's gorillas, whom Sherman had accustomed to traveling light, were so unappreciative as to sneer that they were loaded with iron bedsteads, feather bolsters, and other such creature comforts for the city-bred dandies under his command. That was of course false, or in any case a gross exaggeration, but it was altogether true that those thousand wagons and their teams did at once decrease the speed and greatly increase the length of the column: the more so because of the way they were distributed along it, with an eye for accessibility rather than for delivering or receiving an attack. Up front was a division of cavalry, followed by its train of 300 wagons. Next came the three remaining infantry divisions (the fourth had been left on guard at Alexandria, charged with unloading and reloading supply boats in order to get them over the low-water falls and rapids) of the two corps that had slogged up the Teche under Major General William B. Franklin, top man in the West Point class of 1843, in which he had finished twenty places above his classmate U. S. Grant, and a veteran of hard fighting in Virginia. Close behind them came their train of 700 wagons, with the Corps d'Afrique as escort. A. J. Smith's two remaining divisions (the third, Kilby Smith's, was taking it easy aboard transports, ascending Red River with the fleet) brought up the rear. However, so slow was the progress, so wretched the road, and so strung-out the column by the accordion action of all those interspersed mules and wagons, it was not until the following morning that Smith's jeering veterans lurched into motion out of Grand Ecore. By then the column measured no less than twenty miles from head to tail: a hard day's march under better conditions, by far, than here prevailed.

That was April 7, and before it was over Banks had cause to suspect that he had erred in his estimate of the enemy's intention. Three miles beyond Pleasant Hill by midafternoon of this second day out, the cavalry encountered mounted graybacks who, for once, did not scamper at the threat of contact. Instead, to the dismay of the Federal horsemen, they set spur to their mounts, some half a dozen regiments or more, and charged with a wild Texas yell. The bluecoats broke, then rallied on their reserves; whereupon the rebels fell back, as before. That was about all there was to it; but the cavalry commander, Brigadier General Albert Lee, a thirty-year-old former Kansas lawyer, began to reflect intently on the disadvantages of his situation, particularly with regard to those 300 wagons directly in his rear, between him and the nearest infantry support. Several times already he had asked Franklin to let him shift his train back down the column, combining it with the infantry's, but Franklin had declined; let the cavalry look after its own train, he said. Now that the rebs were showing signs of fight, Lee made the same request again, with a further plea for infantry reinforcements, and received the same reply to both requests. In fact, when the young cavalryman tried to make camp near sunset, six miles beyond Pleasant Hill, Franklin sent word for him to push on four miles farther, train and all, so that the infantry would have plenty of room to clear the town next morning. Lee obeyed, though with increased misgivings, and was brought to a halt at nightfall, just short of his objective, Carroll's Mill, where he found gray riders once more drawn up in a strong position directly across his front, midway between Pleasant Hill and Mansfield.

Depressed by the notion of what was likely to result if he was struck by superior numbers on the march next day, he repeated his plea for reinforcements

*Confederate cavalrymen charge from the woods to surprise
a wagon train and its cavalry escort, under
Brigadier General Albert Lee, near Mansfield, Louisiana.*

to Colonel John S. Clark, one of Banks's aides, who came forward that night to see how things were going. The colonel, agreeing that things were not going well, or in any case that the danger Lee foresaw was possible, rode back to present the cavalryman's request to Franklin in person, only to have him refuse it as flatly as before. So Clark returned to Pleasant Hill, where headquarters had been established that afternoon, for a conference with the army commander. Banks agreed that caution was in order, overruled Franklin, and directed him to send a brigade of infantry to reinforce the cavalry by daybreak. Franklin did so, though it went against his grain, and when Lee started forward next morning at sunrise he was pleased to find the rebel horsemen once more fading back from contact after each long-range exchange of shots, apparently intimidated by the steely glint of bayonets down the column, which signified that the front-riding cavalry now had close-up infantry support.

This continued for half a dozen miles: quick spatters of small-arms fire, followed by sudden gray withdrawals. It was hard for Lee to tell whether the Johnnies were really afraid of him or only pretending to be, in order to lure him on. Then the head of the column emerged from the dense pine woods to find itself on the rim of a large clearing, half a mile deep and half again as wide, with a broad, low hill in the center, on whose crest he saw a line of butternut skirmishers. He halted, brought his infantry to the front, and sent them forward, textbook style. The gray pickets gave ground before the massed advance, but when Lee rode up to the crest of the hill down whose opposite slope the rebs had scrambled for safety, he found his worst fears realized. There below him, in the woods along the far edge of the clearing, stretched a Confederate line of battle: not merely cavalry now, he saw, but infantry too, in heavy files, with artillery mixed in.

It was Taylor, and it was here, within twenty miles of the Texas border — only that bit short of having retreated across the entire width of his home state, leaving its people to the by no means tender mercy of the self-styled "gorillas" in his wake — that he was determined to make his stand. Last night, on his own initiative, he had sent Churchill word to march at dawn from Keatchie, twenty miles away; after which (but no sooner than the sun was four hours high, lest there be time for his order to be countermanded) he got off a note to Kirby Smith at Shreveport, saying laconically of Banks: "I consider this as favorable a point to engage him at as any other."

Sabine Crossroads, the place was called, three miles short of Mansfield, where four roads forked. One led east, allowing the Federals a chance to effect an early junction with their fleet; another branched northwest to Keatchie, which would place them in the path of the reinforcements moving toward him; while the other two ran generally north along parallel routes, giving the invaders a straight shot at Shreveport. Once they were where those four roads came together, free to choose whichever fit their fancy, Taylor's hope of blocking them would be gone, along with his chance to catch them out from under the umbrella protection of their heavy naval guns, strung out on a narrow, ditchlike road in a single, wagon-choked column. Moreover, in considering the tactical opportunity Banks was thus affording him, he had more in mind than a mere defensive stand, whatever numerical odds he might encounter. Like his old mentor in the Shenandoah Valley, he hoped to inflict what Stonewall had sometimes called "a speedy blow" or, more often, "a terrible wound."

Accordingly, while Tom Green and his Texans continued the harassment they had begun in earnest three miles this side of Pleasant Hill, Taylor chose his field of fight and began to make his preparations, including the summoning of the two infantry divisions then at Keatchie. The two already with him, under Major General J. G. Walker and Brigadier General Alfred Mouton, were ordered to return at first light, from Mansfield back to Sabine Crossroads, where they would take position along the near edge of the clearing, respectively on the right and left of the road that crossed the low hill just ahead. Cavalry under Brigadier Generals Hamilton Bee and James Major would guard the flanks, and a four-gun battery, posted astride the road, would stiffen the center. In Mansfield itself, by way of further preparation, private houses were selected and put in order for use as hospitals, and surplus wagons were sent rearward to clear the streets. Taylor was leaving as little as possible to chance, though he was also prepared to seize upon anything chance offered in the way of tactical opportunities; Green's

Taylor was leaving as little as possible to chance, though he was also prepared to seize upon anything chance offered in the way of tactical opportunities . . .

troopers, for example, the most experienced and dependable body of men in his command, were to be employed wherever they seemed likely to prove most useful in that regard when they arrived. This force of 9000 infantry, cavalry, and artillery would be increased to 13,500 when Churchill got there, and though Taylor would not enjoy a numerical superiority even then — there were 20,000 blue effectives in the twenty-mile-long column toiling toward him — he intended to make up for that with the sheer fury of his attack, which he would design to make the most of his intimate knowledge of the ground, having chosen it with just that aim in mind. Nor was terrain the only advantage on which he based his belief that he would win when it came to shooting. "My confidence of success in the impending engagement was inspired by accurate knowledge of the Federal movements," he later wrote, adding that he was encouraged as well by previous acquaintance with "the character of their commander, General Banks, whose measure had been taken in the Virginia campaigns of 1862 and since."

By midmorning, April 8, he had established the line of battle the blue cavalry commander found confronting him when he topped the hill at midday. Young Lee sent back at once for additional reinforcements, meantime getting his batteries into positions from which to probe the gray defenses. A long-range artillery duel ensued, in the course of which Banks arrived in person for a look

★

at the situation. He was undismayed. In fact, this was precisely what he had said he wanted on the day he set out from Grand Ecore: "The main force of the enemy was at last accounts in the vicinity of Mansfield, on the stage road between Natchitoches and Shreveport, and the major general commanding desires to force him to give battle, if possible, before he can concentrate behind the fortifications of Shreveport or effect a retreat westerly into Texas." Warned now by Lee that, in his opinion, "we must fall back immediately, or we must be heavily reinforced," Banks told him to hold what he had; he himself would "hurry up the infantry." That took time, partly because the cavalry train had two or three miles of the road blocked, but about 3.30 the other brigade of Franklin's lead division arrived to join the first. Hard on its heels came a courier with instructions for Lee to advance immediately on Mansfield. Shocked — for the town was three miles beyond the enemy line of battle, and he estimated that the rebels "must have some 15,000 or 20,000 men there; four or five times as many as I had" — the young cavalryman rode in search of Banks, who confirmed the validity of the order. Paraphrasing his protest, Lee said later: "I told him we could not advance ten minutes without a general engagement, in which we would be most gloriously flogged, and I did not want to do it." Given pause by this, although he was unwilling to abandon the attack, the army commander at any rate agreed to postpone it until another division of Franklin's infantry arrived, and he sent a staffer back to see that it was hurried forward with a minimum of delay.

Dick Taylor had bided his time up to now, but only by the hardest. Though he affected the unbuttoned, rather languid combat style of his father, Old Rough-and-Ready, sitting his horse with one leg thrown across the pommel of his saddle while casually smoking a cigar, he was anxious to force the issue. At one point, around 2 o'clock, when he believed he saw bluecoats massing for an attack on his left, he shifted one of Walker's brigades to Mouton and one of Bee's regiments to Major, but aside from this he did little except watch for an opening that would justify going over to the offensive before Churchill arrived from Keatchie. Meantime the Union buildup continued, although toward no apparent climax; Banks seemed unwilling to throw the punch that would invite the counterblow Taylor was eager to deliver. Finally, just after 4 o'clock, with a scant three hours of daylight still remaining, he decided to wait no longer. Mouton, on the strengthened left, was told to go forward.

He did so, promptly: "like a cyclone," one blue defender later said, while another described the charging graybacks as "infuriated demons." Mouton was among the first to fall, thirty-five years old, a West-Point-trained Shiloh veteran, son of the Creole governor who had helped to vote Louisiana out of the Union. His senior brigadier, Camille Armand Jules Marie, Prince de Polignac — "Polecat" to his Louisianians and Texans, who were unable to pronounce the royal name

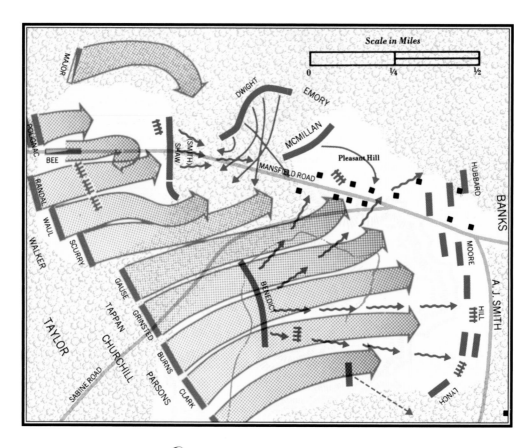

*On April 8, the Confederates routed Banks's army at
Sabine Crossroads. Banks retreated to Pleasant Hill where he
was attacked by Churchill, Walker, and Bee.*

of the young Crimea veteran with the dapper beard and spike mustache — took
over and pressed the uphill charge. His unleashed soldiers struck and broke the
Federal right, routing two of the regiments there, and turned three captured
guns on the fugitives as they fled. Taylor, observing the success of this while it
was still in midcareer, sent word for Walker and Bee to go in, too: which they
did, with similar results on the right, while Green threw his Texans into the
melee on the left, exploiting on horseback the confusion Mouton and Polignac
had begun on foot. All down the line, as the gray chargers emerged from the
pine woods into the clearing to strike at both ends of the confused blue line, the
high-throated rebel yell rang out.

Some on the opposite side did what they could to stay the rout. "Try
to think you're dead and buried," a Massachusetts colonel told his men, "and
you will have no fear." Either they did not try it at all, or else they tried and

found it did not work; in any case, they ran and kept on running. Apparently it was the abruptness of the assault that made it so demoralizing, and this applied as much to those in the rear as to those up front. "Suddenly," a journalist on Banks's staff would recall, "there was a rush, a shout, the crashing of trees, the breaking down of rails, the rush and scamper of men. It was as sudden as though a thunderbolt had fallen among us, and set the pines on fire. I turned to my companion to inquire the reason of this extraordinary proceeding, but before he had the chance to reply, we found ourselves swallowed up, as it were, in a hissing, seething, bubbling whirlpool of agitated men." Franklin was among them by then, having brought his second division up the hill in time for it to join the rout and add to the lengthening casualty list, which would include some 1500 captives and about half that many killed and wounded. One of these last was Franklin himself, who was struck by a bullet in the shin and lost his horse, then took off rearward on a borrowed mount to brace his third division for the shock about to come. Banks too was intimately involved in the confusion, and like Franklin he did what he could, which was not much. Removing his hat for easy recognition, he shouted to the skulkers running past him on the road: "Form a line here! I know you will not desert me." He knew wrong. "Hoo!" they cried, and kept running. So he drew his sword and waved it about; but that worked no better. By then the fleeing troops had become what one of them afterwards called "a disorganized mob of screaming, sobbing, hysterical, pale, terror-stricken men."

Taylor was intent on completing his triumph by pressing the pursuit. Near sundown there was an interruption by a courier who arrived from Shreveport with a letter Kirby Smith had written that morning, urging caution. "A general engagement now could not be given with our full force," he advised. "Reinforcements are moving up — not very large, it is true. . . . Let me know as soon as you are convinced that a general advance is being made and I will come to the front." Taylor scanned it hastily, then looked up smiling. "Too late, sir," he said. "The battle is won." However, he took time to get off a dispatch announcing the victory to his chief, so far as it had been accomplished up to now. "Will report again at the close of the action," he ended the message. "Churchill's troops were not up in time to take part [but] will be fresh in the morning. I shall push the enemy to the utmost."

He did not wait for morning; Jackson-style, he made full use of the hour of daylight still remaining, though the going was as rough for him as it was for the retreating Federals. Panicky teamsters, unable to turn around on the narrow road, had unhitched their mules for a mounted getaway and left the wagons behind as a barricade against pursuit, their bare tongues extended at all angles to trip the unwary. One result of this was the denial of the road to such guns as had avoided capture up to then; Taylor took no less than twenty of them in all, along with ten times as many wagons, some with and some without their teams, but all loaded. Meantime Franklin was putting his third division, which was as large as the other two combined, into a stout defensive position along a ridge just back from a creek in a ravine about four miles from Sabine Crossroads. The pursuers came up raggedly, attacked piecemeal in the dusk, and were repulsed. Taylor knew it was time to call a halt, but not quite yet if his men were to have water for the night; so he contented himself with driving the blue pickets back to their ridge and taking possession of the creek in the ravine. There he stopped, intending to renew the pressure in the morning, and the firing died away in the darkness, giving place to a silence broken only by the wounded crying for water and by the scavengers, back up the road, reveling on the good things found in the captured Yankee train.

As one of his own generals had predicted at the outset, to his face, Banks had been "most gloriously flogged." Out of 12,000 Federals engaged, 2235 had been killed, wounded, or captured, while Taylor, with 9000, had lost less than half as many. Nor was that the worst of it, by any means. In addition to twenty guns and two hundred wagons, Banks had also lost time — the one thing he could least afford to lose if he was to occupy Shreveport and get Sherman's soldiers back to him on schedule. And to make matters worse, caught as he was without water for his parched troops on the ridge, he must lose still more time by retreating still farther to reach another stream and another stout position in which to defend himself from the blood-thirsty graybacks, whom he could hear feasting on their spoils, back up the road, and who obviously intended to have another go at him tomorrow, probably at daylight. Even if he could stay here all night without water, it was doubtful whether A. J. Smith's two divisions, camped a dozen miles away at Pleasant Hill, could arrive in time for a share in the defense. A council of war advised the obvious, and the withdrawal got under way at 10 o'clock. By midnight all the survivors were on the march in a bedraggled column made up largely of stragglers blown loose from their commands, "men without hats or coats, men without guns or accoutrements, cavalrymen without horses and artillerymen without cannon, wounded men bleeding and crying at every step, men begrimed with smoke and powder, all in a state of fear and frenzy."

One among them saw them so, yet supposed in his extreme distress that Banks was the most dejected man of all. He had left Grand Ecore expecting to be in Shreveport within four days, yet here he was, marching in the opposite direction into the dawn of that fourth day. As he rode among his trudging men it must have begun to occur to him that a great deal more than the van of his army had been wrecked at Sabine Crossroads. Any general who could not capture Shreveport with the odds as much in his favor as these had been was not likely to be given the chance to take Mobile. And without that feather in his cap, his chances of occupying the White House were considerably diminished, if not abolished, especially when he recalled the scapegoat hunt that invariably followed every failure such as the one in which he was now involved. Who that scapegoat was likely to be, he knew only too well; perhaps he even had time to regret the cotton speculators he had sent back to New Orleans "without their sheaves," and who were there now, "mouthing calumnies." He was indeed dejected by the time he drew near Pleasant Hill, having failed to spot a good defensive position anywhere along the road, though it may well have improved his outlook to find A. J. Smith's hard fighters already disposed for battle and looking determined. "If it comes to the worst," an Iowa colonel had told his troops when he called them out at 2 o'clock that morning to give them news of the defeat a dozen miles away, "I ask of you to show yourselves to be men."

They showed that, and more, when Taylor came up eleven hours later, hard on the trail of the dejected bluecoats he had whipped the day before, and after a two-hour rest halt, required by Churchill's road-worn Arkansas and

---

The firing died away in the darkness, giving place to a silence broken only by the wounded crying for water and by the scavengers, back up the road, reveling on the good things found in the captured Yankee train.

Missourians, flung his reinforced victors forward with orders for them to "rely on the bayonet, as we had neither time nor ammunition to waste."

This was bravely said, but it was far from easily done. Taking heart from the stalwart look of Sherman's veterans, Banks had spent the morning hours preparing to defend the low, open, house-dotted plateau known felicitously as Pleasant Hill. During this time, according to a newsman, the area "had the appearance of a parade ground on a holiday, regiments marching to the right, regiments marching to the left, batteries being moved and shifted." Near the center of all this activity, in the yard of a house affording a panoramic view of the line thus being drawn, the journalist observed "a small cluster of gentlemen to whom all this phantasmagoria had the meaning of life and death, and power, and fame." It was Banks, surrounded by his chief lieutenants. He wore his light blue overcoat buttoned high against the April chill, and he passed the time "strolling up and down, occasionally conversing with a member of his staff or returning the salute of a passing subaltern." Franklin was there, limping on his wounded leg, his manner calm except for an occasional nervous tug at his whiskers, and so were A. J. Smith, sunlight glinting on his spectacles, and Brigadier General Charles P. Stone, who, after six months of confinement in army prisons and nine of unemployment, had been militarily resurrected by Banks as his chief of staff, thus giving the West Pointer a chance to dispel the cloud of suspicion that had gathered about his head and caused his arrest following Ball's Bluff, where he was accused of having treasonably exposed his men to slaughter. Not yet forty, "a quiet, retiring man who is regarded, by the few that know him, as one of the finest soldiers of our time," Stone sat on a rail fence, smoking cigarettes — a modern touch; cigarettes would continue to be rare and exotic until well into the following decade — and seemed to the reporter "more interested in the puffs of smoke that curled around him than in the noise and bustle that filled the air."

Gradually the noise and bustle died away as the various outfits settled down in their assigned positions and the day wore on and grew warmer. The genial cluster of uniformed gentlemen began to seem to the newsman "a rather tedious party," and apparently they themselves were of much the same opinion. Having done all they could in the way of preparation, the gold braid wearers had nothing to do now but wait, and while they did so they milled about rather aimlessly; "group after group formed and melted away," the reporter noted, "and re-formed and discussed the battle of the evening before, and the latest news and gossip of New Orleans, and wondered when another mail would come."

Whatever tedium his lieutenants might be experiencing, Banks had felt his confidence rise steadily with the sun. By noon, when the generals broke for lunch, he had convinced himself there would be no serious fighting today, and afterward, digesting the excellent meal while the sun swung past the overhead and began its long decline, he took such heart that he began to think of recovering the initiative and thereby repairing the damage his reputation had suffered yesterday. Surely Grant and Lincoln would forgive him for being a little behind schedule if he emerged from these piny highlands with a substantial victory in his grasp. He would go back over to the offensive; he would redeem his failure; he would salvage his career. Though his train was already well on its way to Grand Ecore — what was left of it, at any rate — he made up his mind to resume the advance on Shreveport, and he got off a message saying as much to Porter. "I intend to return this evening on the same road with General Franklin's and General A. J. Smith's commands," he informed the admiral. Today was Saturday, and he added that he expected "to be in communication with the transports of General Kilby Smith and the gunboats at Springfield Landing on Sunday evening or Monday forenoon."

Once more he was wrong in a prediction, but this time it was not for lack of a tactical success. Aware that the Federals were braced for an attack from straight ahead, Taylor took his time about deploying for an end-on strike by Churchill, designed to crumple and roll up the Union left while Walker held in front; Green meantime would probe and feint at the enemy right, working his way around it in order to cut off the expected blue retreat to Grand Ecore, and Polignac would be in reserve, since his division had suffered two thirds of the casualties yesterday, though he would of course be committed when the time was ripe. It was close to 5 o'clock before Churchill, having roused his men from their two-hour rest, had marched them into position in the woods due west of the unsuspecting Federal left.

He then went forward with much of the fury Mouton had shown the day before, provoking similar consternation in the Union ranks. To one defender, "the air seemed all alive with the sounds of various projectiles." These ranged, he said, "from the spiteful, cat-like spit of the buckshot, the *pouf* of the old-fashioned musket ball and the *pee-ee-zing* of the minie bullet, to the roar of the ordinary shell and the *whoot-er whoot-er* of the Whitworth 'mortar-pestle'; while the shrieks of wounded men and horses and the yells of the apparently victorious rebels added to the uproar." Back up the Mansfield road, Green and Walker chimed in with their guns, contributing new tones to the concert, and now that

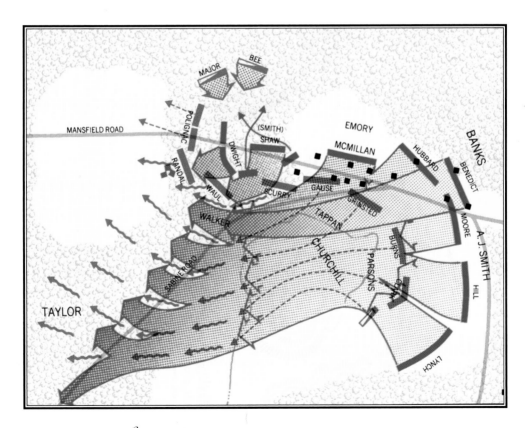

A. J. Smith's troops led the Federal counterattack at Pleasant Hill and forced the Confederates to withdraw. Banks told Smith that he had "saved the army."

the assailed enemy flank had begun to crumble, they put their troops in motion, mounted and dismounted, against the right and center. Churchill kept up the pressure, gathering prisoners by the score as Franklin's unstrung men fled eastward across the open ground of the plateau. Determined to make up for having missed it, the Arkansans and Missourians were intent on restaging yesterday's blue rout, about which they had heard so much since their arrival from Keatchie the night before, in time to share in the pursuit but not the glory.

A. J. Smith's two divisions had not been at Sabine Crossroads either, but they too were very much in the thick of things at Pleasant Hill: as Churchill's elated attackers soon found out. Smith had seen the flank give way, the graybacks whooping in pursuit of Franklin's rattled soldiers, who by now were in flight through the village behind their line, and had sent a reserve brigade in that direction on the double, soon following it with other units which he pulled out of his portion of the line to meet the graver threat. Attempting a

The cheering rebels at the extremity of the pivot were caught end-on by the advancing blue brigade, freezing the cheers in their throats and bringing them to a huddled, stumbling halt.

wide left wheel, which would enable them to assault the Federal center from the rear and in mass, the cheering rebels at the extremity of the pivot were caught end-on by the advancing blue brigade, freezing the cheers in their throats and bringing them to a huddled, stumbling halt. They wavered, lashed by sheets of fire, and then gave way, not in a single rush but in fragments, as regiment after regiment came unhinged. They made one stand, in a heavy growth of cane along a creekbank they had passed on their way in, but Smith's Westerners came after them with a roar, delivering point-blank volleys and finally closing with clubbed muskets; whereupon the gray withdrawal, already touched with panic, degenerated abruptly into a rout. Now it was the Federals doing the whooping and the crowing, and the Confederates doing the running, as the counterattack grew into a grand right wheel, pivoting irresistibly on the retaken village of Pleasant Hill, so recently overrun by gray attackers.

Taylor saw and tried to forestall the sudden reverse, but Walker had just been carried from the field with a bullet in his groin, Green was intent on maneuvering to cut off the expected blue retreat, and Polignac could not come up through the gathering dusk in time for anything more than a try at discouraging

★

the exultant pursuit. This he managed to do, holding a line two miles from the scene of the break, while the other three divisions fell back another four miles to the nearest water. The battle was over and Taylor had lost it, along with three guns abandoned when his flankers were themselves outflanked and thrown into sudden retreat. With some 12,500 men engaged, the Confederates had suffered a total of 1626 casualties, while the Federals, with about the same number on the field, had lost 1369. Though it was by no means as great as yesterday's, when fortune had smiled on the other side and blood had flowed more freely, Banks knew whom to thank for this disparity, along with much else. When the firing stopped and the rebels had passed out of sight in the pines and darkness, he rode over to A. J. Smith and took him gratefully by the hand. "God bless you, General," he said. "You have saved the army."

Tremendously set up by the sudden conversion of near-certain defeat to absolute victory, he was more anxious than ever to get back on the track to Shreveport, and he not only said as much to Smith while shaking his hand; he also sent a message instructing Albert Lee, who was riding escort, to turn the wagon train around and come back to Pleasant Hill. However, when he returned to headquarters to confer with Franklin and two of his brigadiers, William H. Emory and William Dwight — both had commanded divisions under Banks for more than a year, and both had always given him dependable advice — he found all three West Pointers opposed to resuming the offensive, especially in the precipitous manner he proposed. Franklin and Emory favored an eastward march across Bayou Pierre to Blair's Landing on the Red, there to reunite with Kilby Smith, secure a safe supply line, and regain the protection of the fleet, whereas Dwight urged a return to Grand Ecore for the same purpose. This last was much the safest course, and Banks, his enthusiasm quenched by this dash of cold water from the high-ranking trio of professionals, decided to adopt it. Orders went out for an immediate resumption of the retreat.

When word of this reached A. J. Smith he went at once to protest what seemed to him a loss of backbone. Banks refused to reconsider his decision, citing his lack of supplies, his loss in the past two days of just over 3600 men, and the advice of all his other generals. Smith then asked for time at least to bury his dead and finish gathering up his wounded, but Banks declined that too. Furious, the bespectacled Pennsylvanian, his gray-streaked whiskers bristling with indignation, went to Franklin, whom he found enjoying a cup of coffee, and proposed that, as second in command, he put Banks in arrest and take charge of the army for a rapid advance on Shreveport. Franklin stirred and sipped his coffee, nursed his injured shin, and said quietly: "Smith, don't you know this is mutiny?" That ended the protest, if not the anger. In the small hours after midnight, leaving their non-walking wounded behind — the train had left that morning with all the wagons: including, through some mixup, those containing the army's medical supplies — the weary bluecoats formed ranks and slogged away from the scene of their victory, down the road to Grand Ecore.

Ten miles in the opposite direction, up the Mansfield road at Carroll's Mill, Taylor was wakened from his badly needed sleep at 10 o'clock that night by Kirby Smith, who had learned of the Sabine Crossroads fight at 4 o'clock that morning and left Shreveport at once to join his army in the field, only to find at the end of his sixty-mile horseback ride that still a second unauthorized battle had been fought. What was worse, even though this one had been lost, Taylor seemed intent on provoking a third — with any number of others to follow, so long as his blood was up and anything blue remained within his reach. It was more or less clear to Smith by now that if the Louisianian was left to his own devices he would use up the army entirely, leaving him nothing with which to defend his Transmississippi headquarters and supply base from an amphibious

assault by Porter, whose gunboats and gorilla-laden transports were at Loggy Bayou, within pouncing distance of Shreveport, and/or an overland attack by Steele, whose troops had crossed the Little Missouri five days ago, brushing Price's horsemen casually aside, and by now might well be closer to their goal than its supposed defenders were at Carroll's Mill. Informed of this, Taylor increased his chief's dismay by proposing to ignore that double threat in order to keep the heat on Banks; both Porter and Steele would withdraw of their own accord, he argued, as soon as they learned that the main Federal column had pulled back. Smith would not hear of taking such a risk, even though Taylor kept insisting that, with Banks on the run and Porter likely to be stranded by low water, "we had but to strike vigorously to capture or destroy both." Finally the department commander ended the discussion with a peremptory order for the infantry to take up the march for Shreveport the following day. If the danger

A battery with infantry support repulses the Confederate attack at Pleasant Hill. Despite the Federal victory, Banks ordered a retreat to Grand Ecore.

there was as slight as Taylor claimed, he could return and try his hand at the destruction he had in mind downriver.

The result next morning was a rather unusual tactical situation wherein two armies, having met and fought, retreated in opposite directions from the field for which they had presumably been contending. It was made even more unusual, perhaps, by the fact that the victors were unhappier than the losers, and this was especially true of the two commanders. Disgruntled though Taylor was at having been overruled by his superior, Banks was put through the worse ordeal of being sneered at by his military inferiors, all the way down to the privates in the ranks. Taking their cue from Franklin, who avoided such blame as came his way by letting it be known that he would never have recommended a withdrawal if the army had had a competent general at its head, even regimental commanders looked askance at Banks as he rode by them, doubling the column. The men themselves did more than exchange sly glances. Angry because some four hundred of their wounded comrades had been left behind to be nursed and imprisoned by the rebels, they began the march in a mutinous frame of mind, muttering imprecations. But presently the company clowns took over. After the manner of all soldiers everywhere, in all ages, they began to ridicule their plight and mock at the man who had caused it, inventing new words for old songs which they chanted as they slogged. For example, in remembrance of Bull Run:

> *In eighteen hundred and sixty-one*
>
> *We all skedaddled to Washington.*
>
> *In eighteen hundred and sixty-four*
>
> *We all skedaddled to Grand Ecore.*
>
> *Napoleon P. Banks!*

This last — "Napoleon P. Banks!" — was shouted for good measure as the general rode past, and recurred as a refrain in all the parodies they sang. Nor were such high jinks limited, as before, to A. J. Smith's irreverent gorillas. Banks's own men, whom he had commanded at Port Hudson and through the easy-living months in New Orleans, took up the songs and bawled them as he passed along the roadside, trailing a kite tail of smirking officers from his staff.

Fortunately, they had nothing worse to contend with, in the way of opposition on the march, than butternut cavalry which mainly limited its attention to stragglers until near the end of the second day, April 11, when it made a cut-and-slash attack that drove the rear brigade into Grand Ecore on the run. Once there, their prime concern was to protect themselves from the vengeful

★

Taylor, who was reported to be hard on their heels with 25,000 effectives. They themselves would not have that many on hand until Franklin's fourth division came up the Red from Alexandria and A. J. Smith's third division returned from Loggy Bayou with the fleet, whose heavy guns they presently heard booming in the distance, apparently involved in some kind of trouble far upstream. Meantime they kept busy constructing a semicircular line of intrenchments around the landward side of the high-sited village on its bluff. They worked hard and well, incorporating the trunks and tops of large trees which they felled for use as breastworks and abatis. Not only did they require no urging from their officers in this work; they kept at it after they were told that they could stop.

"You don't need any protection. We can whip them easily here," Franklin chided a detail of diggers as he rode on a tour of inspection.

But they remembered Sabine Crossroads and the hilltop they had lost to a savage rebel charge: the result, they now believed, of having trusted their security to generals like this one. They kept digging.

"We have been defeated once," a spokesman replied, leaning on his shovel, "and we think we will look out for ourselves."

In point of fact they were by no means in such danger as they feared. Far from closing on their heels, Taylor's four divisions of infantry were fifty muddy miles away at Mansfield, marched there against his wishes in order to have them within supporting distance of Shreveport. And even when it turned out that the withdrawal had been unnecessary because his prediction was fulfilled — Steele veered from his southwest course on April 12 for an eastward strike at Camden, which would put him as far from Shreveport as he had been when he crossed the Little Missouri a week ago, and Porter not only ventured no farther up the Red, he was even now bumping his way downstream in an effort to rejoin Banks — Taylor constituted no real threat to the Federals intrenched at Grand Ecore, even though he was free at last to move against them, since he had by then a good deal less than one fourth the number of soldiers his adversary believed he was about to use in an all-out assault on the blufftop citadel. Convinced by captured dispatches that Banks would soon be obliged to withdraw if he was to get Sherman's troops across the Mississippi within the little time remaining, Kirby Smith believed there would be small profit in pursuing him through a region exhausted of supplies. Instead, he decided to go in person after Steele, who was still a threat, and for this purpose he took from Taylor not only Churchill's Arkansans and Missourians, who had been lent to help in stopping Banks, but also Walker's Texans, who would now return the favor by helping to stop Steele. That left the Louisiana commander with barely 5000 men in all: Polignac's infantry, bled down to fewer than 2000 effectives, and Green's cavalry, which numbered only a little above 3000, including a small brigade that had just arrived. In any case, however few they were, on April 14 he started them southward for Grand Ecore, where the bluecoats had obligingly penned themselves up, as if in a stockyard, awaiting slaughter.

Taylor himself went up to Shreveport next day, on the outside chance that he could persuade his chief to countermand the orders which he believed would deprive him of a golden opportunity. "Should the remainder of Banks' army escape me I shall deserve to wear a fool's cap for a helmet," he had said the week before, but now that his force had been reduced by more than half he was less confident of the outcome: especially when he learned that Tom Green, while attempting to add to the problems of the Union fleet in its withdrawal down the still-falling Red, had been killed two days ago in an exchange of fire with the gunboats at Blair's Landing, twenty miles above Grand Ecore. A veteran of the Texas war for independence, the Mexican War, the horrendous New Mexico expedition of early 1862, and the retaking of Galveston, the fifty-year-old Hero of Valverde had been Taylor's most dependable lieutenant in last year's fighting on the Teche and the Atchafalaya, as well as in the campaign still in progress down the Red. His loss was nearly as heavy a blow as the loss of the three divisions about to set out for Arkansas, and caused Taylor to redouble his efforts to have them returned while there was still a chance to overtake and destroy the invaders of Louisiana, afloat and ashore. But Kirby Smith was not to be dissuaded; Steele was the major danger now, and he intended to go after him in strength. "Should you move below and Steele's small column push on and accomplish what Banks has failed in, and destroy our shops at Jefferson and Marshall," he told Taylor, "we will not only be disgraced, but irreparably deprived of our means and resources."

Accordingly, he left Shreveport on April 16, taking Walker and Churchill with him. Taylor stayed on for two more days, arranging for the shipment of supplies, and then set out on the 19th to join what he called "my little force near Grand Ecore." He was still hopeful that the Federals could be bagged, despite the disparity in numbers, and he counted on using deception to that end. Compelled, as he said, "to eke out the lion's skin with the fox's hide," he had instructed his unit commanders to keep Banks on edge, and deceived as to their strength, "by sending drummers to beat calls, lighting campfires, blowing bugles, and rolling empty wagons over fence rails."

All this they had done, and more, with such effect that when Taylor dismounted near Grand Ecore on the evening of April 21, ending his ninety-mile ride, he found that the Federals had begun to pull out of the place that afternoon. The head of their column was already beyond Natchitoches, slogging south in an apparent attempt to take up a safer position at Alexandria, if not to get away entirely. Determined not to permit this, Taylor set about planning how to intercept the retiring bluecoats and, if possible, bring them to battle, although they outnumbered him five to one, exclusive of their heavily gunned flotilla. Their march was down the narrow "island" lying between Cane River and the Red, and it was his hope to force them into a strung-out halt that would give him a chance to go to work on them piecemeal. With this in mind, he sent Bee's brigade of cavalry on a fast ride south to Monett's Ferry, forty miles away at the far end of the island, with instructions to block the crossing of the Cane at that point, so that the rest of his troops could be thrown upon some vulnerable segment of the blue column stalled between there and Natchitoches. This was an ambitious undertaking for some 5000 men opposed by 25,000, but Taylor undertook it gladly, anticipating the Cannae he had been seeking all along.

Confederate General Thomas Green was killed at Blair's Landing twenty miles above Grand Ecore.

Banks anticipated much the same thing, and moved rapidly to avoid it if he could. He was by now, as a result of the strain of the past ten days, about as edgy as even Taylor could have wished, and this edginess had been provoked by more than the various nerve-jangling ruses those "22,000 to 25,000" gray-backs had been practicing in the woods beyond his semicircular line. For one, there was a growing sense of failure. He still had spasms and flickers of hope, during which he planned to go back over to the offensive, but these grew fewer and weaker as the days wore on, until finally they stopped. For another, he had found waiting for him at Grand Ecore a message from Sherman, notifying him that his lease on A. J. Smith's three divisions had expired and ordering their immediate return. This could be ignored or countermanded because of the exigencies of the situation, which plainly would permit no such detachment; but a few days later, on April 18, he received from Grant a follow-up letter of instructions that had for him, in his present hemmed-in state, a sound of hollow mockery not so easily dismissed. Written at the end of March, it set forth in some detail the procedure he was to follow, once Shreveport had been taken, in moving without delay against Mobile. "You cannot start too soon," the letter ended. "All I would now add is that you commence the concentration of your force at once. Preserve a profound secrecy of what you intend doing, and start at the earliest possible moment."

That was perhaps the cruelest blow; Grant had written as if in fervid haste, lest time be wasted between the fall of Shreveport, apparently expected momentarily, and the arrival of his letter urging Banks to be quick in taking the road to glory, which led from Shreveport to the White House, by way of Mobile, Atlanta, and Richmond. Contrasting what was with what might have been — for the road's only entrance, for him, was Shreveport, and he could not get there to take it — the former Bay State governor was correspondingly depressed. He relieved his spleen to some degree, however, with a pair of summary dismissals. One was of Stone, his chief of staff (Stone took no further part in the war, though afterwards he served the Khedive of Egypt in the same capacity for thirteen years, with the rank of lieutenant general, and then returned to act as chief engineer in the construction of the pedestal for the Statue of Liberty); Banks let him go because he found him "very weak," and the same might have been said of young Albert Lee, whom he relieved of duty as cavalry commander and sent back to New Orleans, although not without regret. He testified later that Lee had been "active, willing, and brave," if not skillful, and had "suffered, more or less unjustly, as all of us did, for being connected with that affair."

Such administrative corrections had little effect on a tactical situation which seemed to be growing increasingly grim as the rebels out in the brush continued to beat drums, build a myriad of campfires, blow bugles, and bring up what sounded like thousands of wagonloads of supplies and ammunition. For what purpose all this was being done Banks could only guess, but with every passing hour he was brought closer to the inevitable conclusion that if he could not go forward, as was obviously the case, then he would do well not to postpone going back. This applied most of all to Porter's gunboats, for the river was still falling: was already down, in fact, to half the seven-foot depth required to float them over the double falls at Alexandria. The thing to do was get back there as soon as possible, before the river took another perverse drop, for a close-up look at what was reported to be an impossible situation. So the admiral advised, although the temptation was strong to remain where he was, under the friendly bluff at Grand Ecore, his recent trip to Loggy Bayou having given him all too graphic a preview of what to expect in the course of his return to the Mississippi, down those more than three hundred winding miles of the Red. "It is easy to die here, and there are many ways of doing it," a sailor diarist had observed en route. In addition to the more or less normal dangers involved in descending a swift and crooked river at the speed required to maintain steerage — staved-in bows, unshipped rudders, broken wheels, and punctured hulls, all brought on by collisions with other boats, with underwater snags, with the iron-hard red clay bottom — there were the rebels to contend with, fast-firing marksmen who shot at passing or stalled vessels from hidden positions along both banks. At Blair's Landing, for example, where Tom Green was killed by a blast of canister, the fleet was exposed to what one veteran skipper called "the heaviest and most concentrated fire of musketry I have ever witnessed." As a

*B*rigadier General
*Albert L. Lee was relieved
of his Federal cavalry
command and sent to
New Orleans after the
battles at Sabine Cross-
roads and Pleasant Hill.*

result of this and other such nightmare encounters at places with names like
Campti and Coushatta Chute, the thirty-boat flotilla got back from its ten-day
upstream excursion sadly altered in appearance: especially the vessels loaded with
Kilby Smith's gorillas, to which the butternut riflemen and cannoneers had
given their particular attention. "The sides of some of the transports are half
shot away," a soldier noted in his diary on April 15, after watching them come
in, "and their smokestacks look like huge pepper boxes."

Porter recommended an immediate return to Alexandria, but Banks
was not quite ready to make so frank an admission of defeat. That took him another
four days, two of which he used to compose a letter to Grant, explaining that his
retrograde movement from Mansfield had been due more to a shortage of water
and the nonarrival of Steele than to resistance by the enemy — though he
added, rather ingeniously, that the stubborn quality of the latter had proved the
campaign to be "of greater importance than was generally anticipated at its com-
mencement," and asked therefore that he be allowed to continue it beyond
schedule, but only a bit, since "immediate success, with a concentration of our
forces, is within our reach." Knowing Grant's low tolerance for failure, however
skillfully disguised, he did not have much hope that his request would be granted,
and he had even less hope, in case it was, that he would be continued in command. At the end of the four days (April 19: the day Taylor set out on his
ninety-mile ride from Shreveport) Banks issued orders for a withdrawal to
Alexandria. It got under way two days later, after A. J. Smith moved out and
occupied Natchitoches, from which point he would cover the retreat by protecting
the flanks of the column as it passed, then follow to serve as rear guard on the
long march down the "island" between the two rivers, Cane and Red.

★

*On its way to Alexandria, Porter's Federal flotilla
suffered attacks at Blair's Landing, Campti, and
Coushatta Chute along the Red River.*

★

Whatever shortcomings the invaders had shown in the past forty days, they demonstrated conclusively, in the course of the next two, that their ability to cover ground at a fairly dazzling rate of speed not only had not been impaired, but in fact had been considerably improved by the events of the past two weeks. The march began at 5 o'clock in the afternoon, and by the time the tail of the column left Grand Ecore at 3 o'clock next morning, April 22, the men at the head were twenty miles away, taking their first rest while waiting for the others to close up. Before nightfall, the entire command had cleared Cloutierville, thirty-two miles from the starting point. Not even then was the blistering pace relaxed; Banks had learned that the rebels intended to contest his crossing of the Cane at Monett's Ferry, another dozen miles southeast, and he pressed on, determined to get off this jungly island and past the last natural obstacle between him and Alexandria, where he would recover the protection of the fleet and his army could once more break out its shovels and throw up dirt between itself and the danger of assault.

So far, its performance had been highly commendable from the logistics point of view; nor had it permitted haste to interfere unduly with the exercise of its various other talents. A. J. Smith's irrepressible campaigners, while holding off pursuers with one hand, so to speak, still found time for more than their usual quota of vandalism and destruction with the other. Grand Ecore had gone up in flames at the outset, along with the surplus goods the army left behind; then Natchitoches, whose old-world French and Spanish charm had been admired by many of its blue-clad visitors, was put to the torch as a farewell gesture. Gray cavalry came up in time to turn fire-fighters and save the latter place, as well as Cloutierville the following day, far down the island. But Smith's troops made up for this double disappointment with the amount of damage they inflicted on barns and houses along the road between the two, including even the cabins of the Negroes who turned out to welcome them. "At night the burning buildings mark our pathway," a marcher recorded. "As far as the eye can reach, we see in front new fires breaking out, and in the rear the dying embers tell the tale of war."

Close in their rear with Polignac, while his cavalry harassed their flanks and rode hard to get into position in their front, Taylor was finding it "difficult to restrain one's inclination to punish the ruffians engaged in this work." He meant that the prisoners were a temptation in that regard — blue-clad stragglers picked up along the roadside, blown and blistered or drunk on looted whiskey, unable to hold the pace Banks was setting them in his eagerness to attain the safety Alexandria would afford — but there was also the temptation for the pursuers to strike before the tactical iron was hot. Too quick a blow, delivered before the Federals had been brought to a disjointed halt on unfavorable terrain, would merely hasten their march and inflict only superficial damage, not to mention that it would be likely to disclose the smallness of

Taylor's command; whereas if he waited till their path was blocked he might be able to bag the lot by tricking them (much as Bedford Forrest had tricked Abel Streight, about this time last year in Alabama) into surrendering to the "superior force" Banks believed was breathing down his neck. However, the Louisianian soon had cause to regret that he had stayed his hand, forgoing a leaner in hope of a fatter prize. Brigadier General Richard Arnold, Lee's replacement as chief of the Union cavalry — a thirty-six-year-old West Pointer, son of a former governor of Rhode Island and descendant of a distinguished New England family that included the notorious Benedict — had come upon Bee's dismounted brigade in a stout defensive position overlooking, from the opposite bank, the approaches to the Cane at Monett's Ferry. Instead of attempting the suicidal attack Bee expected, head-on down the road, Arnold located an upstream crossing for the infantry to use while he kept up a show of force in front and probed industriously below, as if in search of another crossing a couple of miles down-river, to attract Bee's attention in that direction.

It was neatly done. Emory's division, coming up at the head of the Federal main body on the morning of April 23, crossed the river two miles above the ferry and struck in force at the upstream rebel flank, while a second arriving division added its weight to the frontal demonstration and the downstream feint. This last was so well carried out, indeed, that Bee — a Charleston-born adoptive Texan whose younger brother had given T. J. Jackson his nom-de-guerre at First Manassas, but who himself had been a desk soldier until the present campaign — believed he was swamped on the right as well as the left, though in fact he had managed to inflict rather heavy casualties on the attackers from upstream. "The critical moment had come," he later reported; "the position turned on both flanks and a large force close in front ready to spring on the center." He counted himself fortunate to get away — "in good order at a walk," he noted — with a loss of "about 50 men and 1 artillery wagon . . . while the enemy lost full 400 killed and wounded," and he complained that, with fewer than 2000 men in all, he had been expected to block the path of "an army of 25,000 marching at their leisure on the main road to Alexandria." Yet that was exactly what had been expected of him, and Taylor was no more inclined to be charitable in such cases than was the man Bee's brother had caused to be nicknamed Stonewall. The fact remained that Banks had made his getaway, avoiding the destruction planned for him, and Bee had let the escape hatch be slammed ajar with a loss to himself of only "about 50 men and 1 artillery wagon." Nor was the disparity of losses any mitigation of the offense. "He displayed great personal gallantry, but no generalship," Taylor said of the South Carolinian, and ordered his removal from command.

Into the clear at last, though greatly relieved to be out of a jungle whose gloom seemed made for ambuscades, Banks did not slacken the pace for his foot-sore troops. He was still not half way to his goal, and he covered the last fifty

R̄ichard Arnold (above) succeeded Albert L. Lee as chief of the Union cavalry in the West.

miles with something of the hard-breathing urgency of a long-distance runner entering the stretch and catching sight of the tape drawn taut across the finish line, ready to be breasted. All through what was left of that day and the next, molested by nothing worse than small clusters of Confederate horsemen taking pot shots at the column from off in the pines, he kept going hard and fast, his over-all casualties now increased to about 4000, more than half of them captured or missing in battle and on the march. On the third day, April 25 — the fifth since he left Grand Ecore — the lead division slogged into Alexandria, followed next day by the others. There they promptly got to work with their shovels, heaving dirt, despite the recovered protection of Porter's fleet: what was left of it, at any rate, after an equally strenuous five days of fighting rebels and the river.

The admiral had suffered woes beyond a landsman's comprehension, including the loss of his finest ironclad, the 700-ton *Eastport*. Sunk by a torpedo eight miles below Grand Ecore, she was patched and raised with the help of two pump boats hastily summoned upriver, and continued on her way — only to ground again in the shallow water forty miles below. Porter unshipped her four 9-inch guns, along with her other four 50- and 100-pounder Dahlgren and Parrott rifles, loading them onto a flat behind the light-draft gunboat *Cricket*, and thus got her afloat; at least for a time. She had only gone a few more miles, bumping bottom as she went, when she ran full tilt into a pile of snags, and there she stuck and settled. After three days' work by her crew and skipper, Lieutenant Commander Ledyard Phelps, who could not bear to lose "the pride of the western waters," Porter, having observed that such efforts to haul her off only made her stick the harder, gave orders for her destruction. A ton and a half of powder was distributed about her machinery and hold. When the electrical detonator failed to work, Phelps himself, in accordance with the tradition requiring the captain to be the last to abandon ship, applied a "slow match," then went over the side and into a waiting launch. The match was almost not slow enough, however. When the *Eastport* blew, Phelps was only a short way off and barely avoided being crushed by one of the dory-sized fragments from the 280-foot iron hull that came hurtling down and raised huge red geysers all around the launch.

★

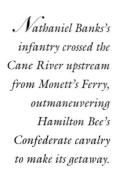

Nathaniel Banks's infantry crossed the Cane River upstream from Monett's Ferry, outmaneuvering Hamilton Bee's Confederate cavalry to make its getaway.

Porter had a double reason for ordering the ironclad's destruction. One was that further delay seemed likely to cost him not only the *Eastport* — which, in point of fact, had been Confederate at the outset, captured uncompleted up the Tennessee River near the Mississippi town that gave her her name, just after the fall of Fort Henry in early 1862 — but his other boats as well. While the attempted salvage work was in progress, enemy marksmen were gathering on both hostile banks of the river and adding to his discomfort by sniping at the

flotilla. Small-arms fire, though deadly enough, was only part of the danger; for presently, emboldened by the absence of the infantry escort now on the march with Banks, they brought up batteries of horse artillery and opened fire from masked positions. So intense and accurate was this, Porter lost one of his unarmored pump boats that afternoon and the other the following morning, together with all but five of about 175 Negroes, mostly fieldhands taken aboard from surrounding plantations, who were scalded to death by steam from a punctured boiler. The gunboats *Juliet* and *Fort Hindman* lost 22 men between them in the course of the downstream run, along with their stacks and most of their upper works. Hardest hit of all, though, was the *Cricket,* now serving as the flagship. Rounding a bend, she came upon a rebel battery cleverly sited atop a bluff, and took 38 hits within the five minutes she was exposed to its plunging fire. Out of her crew of fifty, 31 were casualties, including a dozen killed. "Every shot [went] through and through us, clearing all our decks in a moment," according to the admiral, who had to take the wheel himself when he ran up to the pilot house and found the helmsman badly wounded.

This was the firing the soldiers heard at the end of their long march from Grand Ecore, and when Porter reached Alexandria next morning, April 27, he saw at close range the validity of his other reason for having abandoned the deep-draft ironclad far upstream: which was that, even if he had managed to get her this far down, he would not have been able to get her one mile farther. The Red had dwindled by now to a depth of three feet four inches over the falls — two inches less than half the draft of his heavier gunboats — and there still was no sign that the river was going to rise at all this spring, if indeed it ever stopped falling. In fact, it was becoming more evident every day that the fate of the *Eastport* was likely to be the fate of every warship in the fleet; that is, if they were to be kept out of enemy hands. And now there was added to the admiral's woes, as if this last was not enough, the apprehension that he was about to be left on his own by the army. Banks came aboard the badly shot-up *Cricket* with a ten-day-old letter just arrived from the general-in-chief, peremptorily ordering him to desist from any activity that might cause him to be "detained one day after the 1st of May in commencing your movement east of the Mississippi." Today was Wednesday; May Day was Sunday, barely four days off. "No matter what you may have in contemplation," Grant had added by way of emphasis, "commence your concentration, to be followed without delay by your advance on Mobile."

Knowing how eager the Massachusetts general was to engage in the very campaign Grant's letter not only authorized but *ordered* him to undertake at once, Porter had a nightmare vision of the fleet — or anyhow the dozen vessels trapped above the falls — being left stranded high and dry, unprotected from heavy-caliber snipers or highly explosive underwater devices, its fate restricted to a choice between capture and self-destruction. If the former was unthinkable, involving as it well might do the loss of all the navy had won in the past two years on western rivers, the latter choice was only a bit less so, since either would mean professional ruin for the admiral himself. Partly his apprehension was based on his contempt for Banks, which encouraged him to think the worst of the one-time politician, especially in regard to his feeling any obligation to a man who he knew despised him, who was of a rival and often high-handed

★

Finding the falls at Alexandria at only a depth of about three feet, Admiral David Dixon Porter feared that his fleet would be trapped on the Red River.

branch of the service, and whom he could protect only by disregarding a direct order from a superior famed for sternness in such matters.

But in this the admiral did the general wrong. Banks quickly made it clear that he had no more intention of abandoning the navy here at Alexandria than he had had at Grand Ecore the week before, and for much the same reasons. One was that it was not his way, no matter what Porter might think of him, to desert an associate in distress. Another was that he still had nearly a hundred downriver miles to go before he would be out of the Red River country, and he wanted naval protection all the way. Still another, which would require the navy's continued support even more, was that he had not completely given up the notion that he could retrieve his reputation in the region where he had lost it. Whether he would get that chance depended on Grant's reply to the letter sent ten days ago from Grand Ecore, suggesting a return to the recently abandoned upriver offensive, provided he could secure "a concentration of our forces." That meant Steele, who was long since overdue, but about whose progress Banks knew little except for a disconcerting rumor that the Arkansas commander had turned aside from his southwest march on Shreveport for an eastward lunge at Camden, 165 air-line miles due north of Alexandria and almost twice that far by the few roads.

Meantime, while waiting to hear again from Grant and finally from Steele, Banks and Porter — despite their mutual distaste for striking, even figuratively, so intimate an attitude — put their heads together in an attempt to solve the apparently insoluble problem of how to get armored gunboats, drawing seven feet of water, down a still-falling river whose rocky bottom was in places only three feet four inches below its russet surface.

★ ★ ★ *S*teele had been at Camden, just as Kirby Smith had been informed and Banks had chanced to hear. In fact, he had been there for the past twelve days, penned up like his supposed partner at Grand Ecore, behind intrenchments. But he was there no longer. He had pulled out during the small hours of this same April 27 — headed not for the Red, as Banks expected and Smith intended to prevent, but back toward Little Rock, the headquarters he had left five weeks ago today. In the course of the first three of these he had crossed the Saline, the Ouachita, the Little Missouri, then the Ouachita once more, along with a number of lesser streams in a region as wet as the upper Red was dry; now he was hard on the march for the Saline again, fifty air-line miles to the north, hoping to put that river between him and his pursuers, a superior force dead bent on his destruction, and thus bring an end to what a Saint Louis newsman would presently call "a campaign of forty days in which nothing has been gained but defeat, hard blows, and poor fare."

Although he seemed on the face of it to have done even worse than Banks — who, in all conscience, had done poorly enough by almost any standards, not excluding Pleasant Hill, which amounted to little more than a pause in his flight before inferior numbers — it could at least be said of Steele, by way of extenuation, that he had never had a moment's belief that anything good was going to come of an undertaking he had protested being involved in from the start. Unlike the former Massachusetts governor, whose inveterate optimism was inclined to feed on straws, he had not been lured by cotton or dazzled by stars in a political firmament which for him did not exist. Yet he had certain other disadvantages. For one, while Banks merely believed he was outnumbered, Steele actually was outnumbered, at any rate in the final stage, when Kirby Smith came after him with all but a handful of the infantry Dick Taylor had used to drive the larger Federal column pell-mell down the Red, ironclads and all. The Arkansas commander's losses, though so far only half as great as those in

Louisiana, stood a dismal chance of being considerably greater in the end. Banks had lost some 4000 men to date, but at least he had found sanctuary within the Alexandria intrenchments: whereas Steele, in northward flight for Little Rock with hordes of exultant graybacks hot on his trail across the hundred miles of intervening hinterland, was in grievous danger of losing about three times that many, the only limit being that that was all he had. Still, for whatever consolation it was worth, the outcome could scarcely be direr than he had predicted in response to Halleck's original suggestion that he move on Shreveport in coöperation with Banks's ascent of the Red. He could only do so, he wired back, "against my own judgment and that of the best-informed people here. The roads are most if not quite impracticable; the country is destitute of provision." Moreover, he added, if he marched south the butternut guerillas were likely to hold carnival in North Arkansas and Southwest Missouri, with predictable results. "If they should form in my rear in considerable force I should be obliged to fall

Grant might or might not approve of this Transmississippi undertaking, . . . but it was clear he wanted it over and done with in the shortest possible time . . .

back to save my depots, &c." He thought it best not to go at all, in any case not in earnest. A feint at Arkadelphia or Hot Springs was the most he could recommend as a means of discouraging a rebel concentration against Banks, and having said as much — this was March 12, ten days past the time Old Brains had wanted him to set out southward — he remained at Little Rock, awaiting a reply. It came within three days, but not from Washington and not from Halleck. A brief telegram signed *U. S. Grant Lieutenant General* arrived from Nashville on March 15: "Move your force in full coöperation with General N. P. Banks' attack on Shreveport. A mere demonstration will not be sufficient."

That was that. Grant might or might not approve of this Transmississippi undertaking, conceived before his appointment as director of the nation's military effort, but it was clear he wanted it over and done with in the shortest possible time, and it was equally clear that to achieve this he intended to employ his accustomed method of bringing everything available to bear: including Steele. Accordingly, the Arkansas commander wasted no more energy on appeals which might have influenced Halleck but would obviously — as he knew from past experience, first as a classmate at West Point, then as a division commander in the Vicksburg campaign — do nothing but anger the new general-in-chief and probably bring on his own dismissal. Rather, he spent the next eight days preparing to move (an election of delegates to a constitutional convention, requiring the presence of his troops as poll watchers to protect the reconverted "loyal" ten percent of the state's voters from as many of the irreconcilable ninety percent as were not already in the field with Price, had been held the day before, March 14, with predictably satisfactory results) and then on March 23, midway through Holy Week, he set out.

Originally he had intended to proceed due south down the Ouachita, by way of Monroe, for a meeting with Banks at Alexandria. By now, though, it was too late for that; Alexandria had been taken, and he would scarcely be helping Banks by making him wait for him that far down the Red. So he chose instead to march southwest, through Arkadelphia and Washington to reach the upper Red, which he would then descend for a combination, near Shreveport, with the amphibious column moving northwest up that river toward that goal. An epicure and a sportsman, a breeder and racer of horses, forty-five years old, high-voiced and dandified in dress — "a velvet-collared esthete," one observer called him — Fred Steele was rumored by his enemies to live in the style of an Oriental prince, surrounded by silk-clad servants and pedigreed lapdogs, although this alleged limp-wristed aspect was considerably at odds with a lifetime habit of blasphemy, a full if silky beard, and a combat infantry record going back to the Mexican War, in which he had won two brevets for gallantry as an officer of the line. He had under him, for service in the campaign now beginning, some 14,000 effectives of all arms. Of these, a column including a little more than half — 5000 infantry and artillery, 3000 cavalry — left Little Rock under his immediate supervision, while another containing 4000 — the so-called Frontier Division, in occupation of Indian Territory — marched from Fort Smith under Brigadier General John M. Thayer, who had orders to join the main body at Arkadelphia by April 1. A third force of about 2000, mostly cavalry and therefore highly mobile, was based on Pine Bluff, with instructions to divert attention in that direction, away from the column on the march to the southwest, and keep a close watch on the rebel garrison at Camden, one of the places where Sterling Price had had his headquarters since his loss of all the northern portion of the state in the fall of the previous year.

A warm-up march of nine miles on the first day flexed muscles used but scantly during months of easy duty. But next morning — Holy Thursday, and the weather remained clear — the men turned out of their blankets in the chill pre-dawn to find themselves involved in the full panoply of war. "Bugles rang out as we had never heard them before," an Iowa soldier would recall. "If an enemy had been in hearing distance, he must have thought we were at least a hundred thousand men, to raise such a wide-spread din." On the near bank of the Saline River by nightfall, still with no evidence that a single rebel was within earshot, they were informed that they would be on half-rations for the balance of the march. Digesting this as best they could, they woke to find it raining, which made for a hard Good Friday on soft roads. The same was true the next day and the next, Easter Sunday, when they crossed the Ouachita. The going was slow, especially across the frequent bottoms, which had to be corduroyed to get the wagons through. They did not reach Arkadelphia until March 29, having covered only seventy miles in a solid week of marching.

The worst of it, though, was that there was no sign at the rendezvous of the column from Fort Smith, and no word of its whereabouts came back from scouts sent out to find it. A three-day wait, while welcome as a rest, reduced the dwindling supply of food and forage in the trains, and still there was no message from Thayer, whose division was known to

An epicure and a sportsman, a breeder and racer of horses, forty-five years old, high-voiced and dandified in dress . . . Fred Steele was rumored by his enemies to live in the style of an Oriental prince . . .

have left Fort Smith two days before the main body left Little Rock. The earth might have swallowed him up: or the rebels, none of whom seemed to be lurking in this direction. On April 1, after three days of marking time and further depleting his supplies, Steele decided he could wait no longer. He ordered the southwest march resumed down the old military road that led to Washington, thirty miles beyond the Little Missouri, which lay twenty-five miles ahead. On that day — April Fools' — the marchers encountered their first opposition, in the form of slashing attacks by mounted graybacks who struck them flank and rear.

They encountered only cavalry because that was all Price had to send against them. His two small divisions of infantry, summoned to Louisiana to help Taylor go for Banks, had reached Kirby Smith at Shreveport on the day Steele set out from Little Rock with the same goal in mind; so that, however much this might benefit him tactically by reducing the type and number of troops he would encounter on his march through Arkansas, the Federal commander had no sooner gotten started than he failed in his main purpose, which was to keep the Transmississippi Confederates from ganging up on Banks. In any case, having accomplished this much without the firing of a shot, Price was left with only five brigades of cavalry, some 5000 effectives in all, badly scattered about the state. Two of these, combined in a division under Brigadier General James Fagan, were stationed east of the Saline to counter a possible Union advance from Pine Bluff, while two of the remaining three were posted at Camden, on the lower Ouachita, and the third was just west of Washington, on the upper Red. These three were under Brigadier General John S. Marmaduke and contained about 3200 troopers, veterans of many fights and raids, particularly those in Brigadier General J. O. Shelby's brigade, hard-bitten Missourians who asked for nothing better than a chance to come to grips with the bluecoats on the march. Two more brigades were said to be on the way from Indian Territory under Brigadier General Samuel B. Maxey, freed by Thayer's withdrawal to Fort Smith for his share in the Arkansas offensive, but Price had no way of knowing when they would arrive. "Retard the enemy's advance," Smith urged him in an Easter dispatch. "Operate on their communications if practicable. Time is everything with us." This aggressiveness was somewhat modified, however, by a warning not unlike the ones that were stretching Taylor's patience thin at the same time: "Do not risk a general action unless with advantage to yourself. You fall back toward reinforcements." Accordingly, Price held Fagan where he was, shielding Camden from attack by the bristly Pine Bluff garrison, and turned Marmaduke loose on Steele with instructions to deal as roughly with him as the disparity in numbers would allow. Marmaduke ordered a concentration of two brigades in the path of the Federal advance, intending to give ground as slowly as conditions would permit, while the third brigade — Jo Shelby's — set out on a circuitous march to get into position to harass the flanks and rear of the enemy slogging through Arkadelphia. Which Shelby did: beginning with the slashing attack he launched on All Fools' Day against just those tender parts of the blue column.

Steele came on, skirmishing front and rear, still not knowing what had become of Thayer or whether his division still existed. Sizeable clashes at Hollywood, a few miles out of Arkadelphia, and then next day at Spoonville and Antoine, along Terre Noir Creek, cost him more in time than they did in men. Time was what he could least afford, however, obliged as he was to balance his consumption of rations against his dwindling supply, already reduced by about three fourths though

John M. Thayer (above) was ordered to join Frederick Steele for a concentration of forces at Arkadelphia.

he was still a good deal short of halfway to his goal. On April 3, while the head of the column moved into the valley of the Little Missouri, diverging from the Washington road to secure a crossing at Elkin's Ferry, off to the south, Marmaduke launched a concerted attack on the main body, back at Okolona. Steele had to call a halt to fight him off, losing still more time and consuming still more rations. At this rate, he perceived, he was never going to make it; Shreveport might as well have been on the Gulf of Mexico or the back side of the moon. Still he pressed on, and next day, having secured a bridgehead at the ferry, he began to cross the river, still under attack from several directions. Then on April 6, with most of his men across, word came from Thayer. He had been delayed by poor roads; he had had to change his route; he would arrive from Hot Springs in a day or two or three. Steele cursed, shrill-voiced and blasphemous, and kept his troops at work corduroying the soggy bottoms for the passage of his and Thayer's trains. Finally, on April 9 — one day short of three weeks on the march — the Frontier Division came up and began to cross the Little Missouri. For Steele and his men, marking time on the south bank, the meeting with the frontiersmen was a let-down. "While we lay here," one recorded in disgust, "the long-looked-for and much-talked-of reinforcement of 'Thayer's command' arrived, from Fort Smith. A nondescript style of reinforcement it was too, numbering almost every kind of soldier, including Indians, and accompanied by multitudinous vehicles, of all descriptions, which had been picked up along the roads."

Worst of all, from Steele's point of view, though the buggies and carriages and buckboards were heavily loaded with plunder, they had little in them in the way of food. What Thayer had mainly brought him was another 4000 mouths to feed, reducing still further any chance Steele had of getting to Shreveport before he starved. There was nothing for it, he decided, but to send back word to department headquarters for a train to be made up and dispatched to him at once, "using, if necessary, every wagon and mule at Little Rock," with a thirty-day supply of "one-half rations of hard bread, one-quarter rations of bacon, and full rations of salt and coffee for 15,000 men." Whether he could survive in the barrens surrounding Elkin's Ferry until the supplies arrived, and whether they had any chance of getting through the rebel-infested region he had just traversed with so much fret, Steele did not know. Nor did he intend to find out, on either count. "Leaving here," he informed his adjutant in Little Rock, thereby giving the destination for the train, "I shall proceed directly to Camden with the whole force."

Nothing Confederate was any longer there to dispute its seizure; Price had evaluated Camden and joined Marmaduke two days ago, bringing Fagan's two brigades along to get in on the action. That raised the total to half a dozen gray brigades, one of Maxey's having ridden in the day before from Indian Territory, so that Price now had about half as many troops as Steele and Thayer, who had 12,000 between them. The Virginia-born former Missouri governor, white-haired in his middle fifties and weighing close to three hundred pounds, mild-mannered despite his imposing bulk and much beloved by his soldiers — although he and they had won no solid victory since Wilson's Creek and Lexington, back in the early days of the war in his home state — had intended to use all six brigades to contest a crossing at Elkin's Ferry; but when he arrived to find the Federals established in their bridgehead he revised his plan to take advantage of a line of shallow earthworks already dug along the near side of the Prairie d'Ane, a gently rolling stretch of meadowland affording his horsemen an excellent field for maneuver, five to ten miles back from the river and about midway between Arkadelphia and Spring Hill. The latter place he now thought was Steele's immediate objective, and the earthworks blocked the way there.

Preliminary skirmishing continued through April 8 and 9 (Banks had left Natchitoches two days before, and while Thayer was crossing the Little Missouri the Louisiana commander was falling back from Sabine Crossroads and Pleasant Hill) and then on April 10 Steele moved against Price across the undulating prairie. All morning and into the late afternoon (while Banks was intrenching feverishly at Grand Ecore and Tom Green was riding toward Blair's Landing, where he would encounter Porter and the naval gun that killed him) the skirmishing continued, gradually building almost to battle proportions — including a noisy exchange of long-range artillery fire which accomplished little except to demoralize a pet bear named Postlewait, the mascot of a rebel battery — until it faded and died away. The following day was much the same, long blue lines of skirmishers moving forward only to recede, and so was the next. On April 13 Maxey's other brigade arrived, Choctaw riders led by Colonel Tandy Walker, eager to use their scalping knives on Thayer's men, who had been despoiling their homes for the past year out in the Territory. But that was not to be: at least not yet. Under cover of these impressive demonstrations, it soon developed, Steele had been preparing, not for a mass assault, but for a withdrawal, a tangential march due east to Camden, forty miles away.

It was neatly done, and in the course of it Steele's soldiers gave a good account of themselves. Left holding the bag on the Prairie d'Ane, Price sent Marmaduke on a cross-country ride to block the road ahead, while Fagan and Maxey set out to overtake the bluecoats who had camped the night before on Terre Rouge Creek, well to the east. Both gray forces were able to get in position for their work, front and rear, but neither had the strength to carry it out. Thayer, whose division served as rear guard, managed to hold off his attackers through a two-day running fight, and German-born Brigadier General Frederick Salomon, commanding the advance division, repulsed Marmaduke in a hotly contested two-hour engagement, fourteen miles from Camden, on the morning of April 15. Just before dark of that same day Steele's lead brigade marched into

After sending reinforcements to Taylor, Sterling "Pap" Price (left) had only five brigades of cavalry to employ against Steele's Federals in Arkansas.

the town, followed that night and next morning by all the others. While the Federals got to work improving the Confederate-dug intrenchments, semicircular in design and anchored at both ends to the Ouachita, above and below, Price came up and made a leisurely investment of the place. Steele was besieged: besieged by greatly inferior numbers: *self*-besieged, so to speak. Rare as this was in military annals, the situation was not unlike the one that obtained at the same time at Grand Ecore, 125 air-line miles to the south, with the difference that Steele had only a two-to-one advantage, while Banks had better than twice that.

Another difference, far more stringent and constricting, was that the Louisiana Federals had a fleet to bring supplies up the river they were based on, whereas those in Arkansas had to depend on foraging expeditions, highly vulnerable to ambush and assault by the enemy waiting just outside their lines for just such opportunities. Steele had managed to get his wagons through, but there was little in them that was edible. "Our supplies were nearly exhausted, and so was the country," he wrote Halleck on April 17, explaining his perpendicular divergence. "We were obliged to forage from five to fifteen miles on either side of the road to keep our stock alive." The same was true at Camden, however, and next day he received a double shock, half of which provided a graphic demonstration of the risk attendant on venturing outside his fortifications, although the only alternative was starvation. Fifteen miles out the Washington road there was a settlement with an ominous name: Poison Spring. Returning from a successful hunt for food in that direction, a train of 198 heavily loaded wagons, escorted by a mixed command of 1100 infantry, cavalry, and artillery with four guns, was jumped by Marmaduke and Maxey, who had better than 3000 troops between them. The slaughter was heavy, the rebel success almost complete. All four guns were taken, together with 170 of the wagons and their teams, the rest being burned. According to one of the captors, the train was "laden with corn, bacon, stolen bed quilts, women's and children's clothing, hogs, geese, and all the *et ceteras* of unscrupulous plunder." This helped to explain the heavy losses of the escort, nearly one third of whom were killed or captured by the infuriated attackers: particularly by Tandy Walker's Choctaws, who whooped with delight at finding the 1st Kansas (Colored) to their front. This was one of Thayer's outfits, well known for its ransack activities in the past, and the troopers unsheathed their knives for bloody work. According to the regimental commander, the high death rate among his casualties, 117 out of 182, was due to the fact that a number of the wounded were "murdered on the spot" by the vengeful red men. Confederate losses totaled 115, many of them only slightly hurt. The Federals lost 301, mostly killed or missing, plus all their guns and wagons.

By the time the survivors came stumbling back from Poison Spring that afternoon, Steele had been profoundly shaken by the other half of the double shock to his nervous system. It had been given him by a scout sent out the week before to get some news of Banks. Returning with word that the Louisiana commander had been thrown into reverse, first at Sabine Crossroads and then again at Pleasant Hill, the messenger reported that he had left him at Grand Ecore, three days back, though where he might be now he did not know. Steele was quick to perceive the dangers of noncoöperation, now that they were directed at himself. If his supposed partner were to pull out, every rebel in the Transmississippi would be free to concentrate against Camden and its hungry garrison, with results no doubt as grisly as those at Poison Spring this morning. He thought this over for four days, wincing at the prospect — which was in fact more likely than he yet knew; Banks left Grand Ecore on the third of these days, beginning another withdrawal, this time to Alexandria, another ninety miles downriver — and then appealed to his superiors not to allow him to be swamped and slaughtered because an adjoining commander lost his army or his nerve. "Although I believe we can beat Price," he protested, "I do not expect to meet successfully the whole force which Kirby Smith could send against me, if Banks should let him go."

Next day, April 23, he heard at last from Banks himself, who proposed, in a dispatch written a week ago at Grand Ecore, before he decided to withdraw farther down the river, that Steele march south at once to join him on the Red for a resumption of the advance upriver. "If you can join us on this line," Banks told him, "I am confident we can move to Shreveport without material delay, and that we shall have an opportunity of destroying the only organized rebel army west of the Mississippi."

Steele wanted no part of such an operation, and frankly said as much that same day in his reply. "Owing to contingencies," he wrote, "it is impossible for me to say definitely that I will join you at any point on Red River within a given time." Among the contingencies, he was careful to say, was Price's army, which was not only highly "organized," whatever Banks might imply to the contrary, but had recently been "very much encouraged by an order of General E. K. Smith, detailing his success against your command." He wished Banks well in whatever he might undertake of an offensive nature down in Louisiana, but as for himself, he had his hands full where he was; "I desire to coöperate with you in the best manner possible, at the same time covering Arkansas until Shreveport shall be ours." Moreover, he informed the man he held responsible for a large part of the woes he now saw looming, "We have been receiving yesterday and today rumors of reinforcements sent by Kirby Smith to Price at this point, and of a contemplated attack. It is said that 8000 infantry have arrived." Interrupted by the jar of guns, he set his pen aside to look into the cause of the disturbance, then took it up again with something of the perverse satisfaction of a prophet watching his gloomiest fears materialize in fact. "They have just opened upon my outposts with artillery," he continued. "This may be to get as near our lines as possible tonight, preparatory to a general attack tomorrow morning."

He was wrong about the attack next morning. Rather than a prelude to assault, the boom of guns was part of a design to frighten him into retreat. But he was altogether right about the rebel reinforcements and his adversary's intention to make bloody use of them. Kirby Smith had arrived three days ago from Shreveport, accompanied by three divisions of infantry flushed with pride for their recent victory over Banks, and he had it in mind to bag the Camden garrison entirely: in which case, he said later, "the prize would have been the Arkansas Valley and the fortifications of Little Rock," to be used in turn, quite possibly, as a base from which to recover the offensive in Missouri. Before this ambitious program for reversing the tide of war could be placed in execution, however, Steele would have to be disposed of, and Smith had no intention of trying to do so by attacking him in his intrenchments, either at Camden or at Little Rock. He preferred to catch him out in the open, between the two, after frightening or forcing him into attempting a retreat across the intervening barrens, where the blue column could be intercepted and cut to pieces by the now superior gray force. The infantry-artillery demonstration of April 23 having resulted only in causing the Federals to button themselves more tightly in their works, Smith intensified his efforts to smoke them out by disrupting their supply lines, particularly those beyond the Ouachita, which Price had not felt strong enough to threaten up to now. Accordingly, while the Camden demonstration was in progress, Fagan crossed the river at Eldorado Landing, twenty miles downstream, with instructions to use his division, reinforced to a strength of more than 3000 by the addition of Shelby's brigade, to strike at logistical targets along the Saline and the Arkansas, as well as along the roads that ran between and across them, from Little Rock and Pine Bluff, down to Camden. The result was not long in coming, and when it came it was as decisive, on a larger scale, as the rout at Poison Spring.

Crossing the Ouachita on the morning of April 24, Fagan was informed by Shelby's scouts, who had ridden ahead, that a large train, heavily guarded, had left Camden two days ago, sent by Steele to Pine Bluff for supplies. Determined to intercept the Federals before they got across the Saline at Mount Elba, he led his troopers on a forced march of forty-five miles to halt at midnight near Marks Mill, where the road he had taken from Eldorado Landing joined the one connecting Camden and Pine Bluff, five miles short of the river. He was pleased to learn that the blue train, delayed by muddy going on cut-up roads, had made camp at nightfall on the near side of Moro Bottom, a few miles to the west, and he was also pleased to hear that the prize was quite as plump as he had hoped: 240 government wagons, together with a number of other vehicles belonging to "cotton speculators, refugees, sutlers, and other army followers," escorted by three regiments of infantry, one of cavalry, and a six-gun battery — in effect, a reinforced brigade, whose strength of 1440 effectives was less than half his own. Anticipating a larger reward than Marmaduke and Maxey had won at Poison Spring, a week ago tomorrow, Fagan instructed Shelby to use his Missourians to block the road between Marks Mill and Mount Elba, thus to prevent an escape across the Saline, and posted his other brigades near Marks Mill itself, with orders to assail the flank and rear of the slow-grinding column as soon as it came up next morning.

Confederate cavalrymen under Samuel B. Maxey routed a Federal wagon train at Poison Spring.

It came up shortly after dawn and the action went as planned, except for a more determined resistance by the Iowa, Ohio, and Indiana infantrymen than had been expected. Alarmed by the sudden attack, they panicked, then rallied and counterattacked. Fagan used his superior numbers with skill, however, and after about four hours of hard fighting, some of it hand to hand — especially when Shelby came back and forced the issue; "I determined to charge them first, last, and all the time," he later reported — the blue regiments surrendered one by one, in different quarters of the field. "Less than 150 of the brigade escaped from the conflict," the Federal commander admitted, "the balance, including the wounded, being made prisoners." Himself among them, these totaled 1300, excluding the civilian hangers-on, whose captured vehicles brought the haul to more than 300 wagons, together with their teams. All were taken, along with the six guns and the four regimental standards, and Fagan, whose own loss of more than 300 killed and wounded testified to the savagery of the fighting, rode off northward, mindful of Kirby Smith's instructions for him to maneuver in the region between Camden and Little Rock, not only in order to continue his depredations, but also in order to be in position to intercept the retreat of Steele, which was expected any day now.

Even so, it came sooner than either side had anticipated before hearing of Fagan's coup. Informed of the disaster that night by the handful of fugitives who made it back to Camden from Marks Mill, Steele called an immediate council of war to ponder what had better be done to meet this latest crisis. The choice seemed limited to starvation, surrender, or flight. Without exception, his chief subordinates — Salomon, Thayer, and Brigadier General Eugene Carr, his cavalry commander — advised the last, and after a day of feverish preparations, including the destruction of such goods as there was no room for in the depleted train, issued what scant rations were left to his alerted troops, which in some cases consisted of two crackers of hardtack and half a pint of cornmeal, together with a warning that this was likely to be all they would get until they had covered a considerable portion of the hundred-mile trek to Little Rock. All day (while Porter was blowing up the *Eastport* and Banks was getting resettled in Alexandria, which the tail of his column had reached that morning) they worked from dawn to dark to complete their preparations for departure, loading wagons, rolling packs, destroying unneeded equipment with a minimum of noise and smoke, lest the rebels in their camps across the way become aware that they were leaving. By way of adding to the deception, and thereby lengthening the head start, drums beat a noisy tattoo at 8 o'clock, followed an hour later by taps, which was sounded on a far-carrying bass drum. Meantime the loaded wagons were rolling slowly across the Ouachita on the pontoon bridge. By midnight all were over and the infantry followed, breaking step to muffle the hollow sound of their crossing. In the small hours of April 27, with Camden lying silent and empty behind them, dark except for a few scattered lamps left burning to encourage the illusion that the army was still there, the engineers silently took up the bridge, knowing that it would be needed when and if they reached the Saline, then hurried after the column, which had been halted several miles beyond the river to give the troops some rest for the ordeal that lay ahead.

Back at Camden, the Confederates did not discover until well after sunrise that they were besieging an empty town. It was midmorning before they marched in, and even then the infantry could not take out after the departed garrison until some way was found for them to cross the bridgeless Ouachita. While Marmaduke's troopers were swimming their mounts across, and Maxey's were preparing for an unexpected return to Indian Territory in response to a report of a threatened invasion from Missouri — Kirby Smith made them a speech of thanks for their Arkansas service before they set out on their long ride home — Price began the construction of a "floating bridge," to be used in ferrying Churchill's and Walker's three divisions over the swollen river. Building and then using the raft, which had a limited capacity, was an all-afternoon, all-night affair; it was daylight, April 28, before the pursuit began in earnest. As a result of the loss of Maxey and the recent detachment of Fagan, who had done excellent work at Marks Mill but now was somewhere off to the north and west, unaware that Camden had been evacuated or that a race to the death was in progress in his rear, Smith was down to about 10,000 effectives. Although this amounted to nothing like the preponderance he might have enjoyed, he

It was here, in this "sea of mud" . . . that fleers and pursuers . . . fought the Battle of Jenkins Ferry, a miry nightmare of confusion and fatigue.

pressed them hard in the wake of the fleeing Federals — whose trail was marked by abandoned equipment, including personal effects, foundered mules, and wagons buried axle-deep in mud — knowing only too well that if he did not overtake them before they crossed the Saline he might as well give up hope of coming to grips with them anywhere short of Little Rock; which meant, in effect, that he would not be able to come to grips with them at all, since there they would have the advantage of intrenchments and could summon reinforcements from other departments roundabout.

Steele was down to roughly the same number of troops as Smith, having suffered 2000 casualties in the past month without inflicting half as many. What was worse, his men had been on short rations all this time, which tended to make them trembly in the legs and short on endurance. However, he had not only gained them a full day's head start in the race for the Arkansas capital, he had also managed to coax or prod them into making good time on the way there. Shortly after noon on this second day out of Camden, the head of the column reached the town of Princeton, in whose streets his rear guard bivouacked that night, two thirds of the distance to the Saline, which in turn was halfway to his goal. He had chosen this nearly barren route to Little Rock, rather than the more accustomed one through Pine Bluff, in order to avoid the

Moro swamps, where the train that fell to Fagan had been so grievously delayed; but presently, as rain began to patter on the marchers and the road, he began to doubt that he had chosen wisely. The mud deepened, slowing the pace of his soldiers as they slogged along in the ankle-twisting ruts of the wagons up ahead, and the rain came down harder every hour. Before nightfall, rebel troopers — Marmaduke's amphibious horsemen — were shooting and slashing at the bedraggled tail of the column. By that time, though, the van had reached the Saline at Jenkins Ferry, and the engineers were getting their pontoons launched and linked and floored, while other details worked at corduroying the two-mile-long approach across the bottoms giving down upon the river, beyond which there stretched another just as long and just as mean. Such labor was too heavy for troops in their condition, faint for sleep as well as food. While they strained at cutting and placing timbers, Steele's chief engineer afterwards reported, "wagons settled to the axles and mules floundered about without a resting place for their feet." After dark, he added, the work continued by the light of fires, and "every exertion [was] made to push the impedimenta across before daylight, it being evident that the enemy was in force in our rear. But we failed. The rain came down in torrents, putting out many of the fires, the men became exhausted, and both they and the animals sank down in the mud and mire, wherever they were, to seek a few hours' repose."

It was here, in this "sea of mud," as the engineer called it, that fleers and pursuers — blue and gray, though both would be dun before the thing was over — fought the Battle of Jenkins Ferry, a miry nightmare of confusion and fatigue. This last applied as much to one side as the other; for if the Confederates had no foundered mules and shipwrecked wagons to haul along or strain at, they had to make a faster march, with fewer halts, in order to overcome the substantial Union lead. North of Princeton by nightfall, they took a four-hour rest, then moved out again at midnight. By 7.30 next morning, April 30, the lead brigade had come up to where Marmaduke's dismounted troopers were skirmishing with blue infantry posted astride the road leading down to the ferry, two miles in its rear. Price committed his troops as fast as they arrived, first Churchill's own and then its companion division, led by Brigadier General Mosby Parsons. They made little headway, for the Federals were crouched behind stout log breastworks, in a position whose access was restricted on the left and right by Toxie Creek and an impenetrable swamp. Moreover, this narrow, alley-like approach not only afforded the charging infantry no cover, it was for the most part slathered over with a spongy, knee-deep layer of mud and brim-full pools of standing water. Their only protection was a blanket of fog, thickened presently by gunsmoke, which lay so heavily over the field that marksmen had to stoop to take aim under it or else do their shooting blind. In point of fact, however, this was more of an advantage for the defenders, who were already lying low, than it

After his success at Marks Mill, James F. Fagan arrived too late to join the fight at Jenkins Ferry.

was for the attackers toiling heavy-footed toward them through the mire. Besides, fog stopped no bullets: as the rebels soon found out, encountering fire that was no less murderous for being blind. They fell back, abandoning three guns in the process, and failed to recover them when Price, after giving the blown attackers time to catch their breath, ordered the assault renewed.

Kirby Smith was on the field by then, coming up with Walker, who insisted on remaining with his men despite his unhealed Louisiana wound, suffered three weeks ago today at Pleasant Hill. Committed just after Churchill and Parsons were thrown back the second time, his Texans attacked with such fury and persistence that all three of their brigade commanders were wounded, two of them mortally. But they did no better, in the end, than the Arkansans and Missourians had done before them. The bluecoats were unshaken behind their breastworks, apparently ready to welcome another attempt to budge them, although the Confederates were not disposed to try it, having lost no fewer than 1000 casualties in the effort, as compared to about 700 for the defenders, including stragglers who had fallen by the wayside on the three-day march from Camden. It was past noon; the last Federal wagon had passed over the river an hour ago, escorted by the cavalry, and now the infantry followed, unmolested by the former owners of the three captured guns they took along. Once on the far side of the Saline, they cut the bridge loose from the south bank and set it afire, partly because they had no further use for it, having no

★

more rivers to cross, and partly because their mules were too weary to haul it. Bridgeless, the rebels could do nothing but let them go, even if they had been of a mind to stop them; which they no longer were, having tried.

Fagan came up soon afterward from over near Arkadelphia, where he had gone for supplies after proceeding north, then west and south, from the scene of his coup five days ago at Marks Mill, less than thirty miles downstream from the battle fought today. Though he made good time on his thirty-four-mile ride from the Ouachita to the Saline, which began at dawn when he learned that Steele was on the march for Little Rock by way of Jenkins Ferry, he not only arrived too late for his 3000 troopers to have a share in the fighting, he was also on the wrong side of the river for them to undertake pursuit. Kirby Smith saw in his failure to intercept and impede the Federals one of the might-have-beens of the war, saying later that if Fagan had "thrown himself on the enemy's front on his march from Camden, Steele would have been brought to battle and his command utterly destroyed long before he reached the Saline." Dismissing this, however, as "one of those accidents which are likely to befall the best of officers," the even-tempered Floridian was more inclined to count his gains than to bemoan lost opportunities. He had, after all, frustrated both Union attempts to seize his Shreveport base and drive him from his department, and though Banks at Alexandria was still to be reckoned with as a menace, the Arkansas column was no longer even the semblance of a threat, at least for the present, to the region it had set out forty days ago to conquer. At a cost to himself of about 2000 casualties, a good portion of whom had already returned to his ranks, Smith had inflicted nearly 3000, two thirds of them killed or captured and therefore permanent subtractions. Losing three guns he had taken ten, all told, in a campaign that had cost the invaders 635 wagons surrendered or destroyed, according to the Federal quartermaster's own report, along with no less than 2500 mules. The list of captured matériel was long, including weapons of all types, complete with ammunition, not to mention sutler goods, rare medical supplies, and enough horses to mount a brigade of cavalry. But the major gain, as Smith himself declared, was that he had "succeeded in driving Steele from the valley of the Ouachita . . . and left myself free to move my entire force to the support of Taylor."

That was clearly the next order of business. With one prong of the two-pronged Union offensive — Steele — now definitely snapped off, it was time to attend to the other — Banks — already severely bent. After giving the divisions of Churchill, Parsons, and Walker two days of badly needed rest, Smith issued orders on May 3 for them to return at once to Camden and proceed from there "by the most direct route to Louisiana."

Steele's men returned on the same day to Little Rock near exhaustion, having found the going even more arduous on the north side of the Saline than on the south. Partly this was because they were one day hungrier and one battle wearier, but it was also because the mud was deeper and timber scarce. As a result of this shortage of corduroy material, they had a much harder time trying to keep the wagons rolling. When one stuck beyond redemption, as many did, it was burned to keep it from falling into rebel hands, and when teams grew too weak to be led, as many did, they were set free: all of which added greatly to the army's loss of equipment and supplies. From dawn of May Day to 4 a.m. the next, out of the soggy bottoms at last, the infantry slogged in a daze that was intensified that night by the lurid flicker of roadside fires the cavalry had kindled to light their way through the darkness. "A strange, wild time," one marcher was to term it, recalling that hardtack sold for two dollars a cracker, while in one instance two were swapped for a silver watch. Late the second afternoon a shout went up from the head of the column, announcing that a train had come out from the capital with provisions. They made camp for the night, wolfing their rations before turning in, and were off again at sunrise. When the fortifications of Little Rock came into sight, around midmorning of May 3, they halted to dress their tattered ranks and thus present as decent an appearance as they could manage, then proceeded into town, giving a prominent place in the column to the three captured guns that were all they had to show, in the way of trophies, for their forty-two days of campaigning.

"The Camden Expedition," Steele called the unhappy affair, as if Shreveport had never been part of his calculations. But the men themselves, being rather in agreement with the Saint Louis journalist that all they had gained for their pains was "defeat, hard blows, and poor fare," were not deceived. They had failed to reach their assigned objective, whatever their silky-whiskered commander might claim to the contrary, and they knew only too well what the failure had cost them: not to mention what it might cost Banks, who seemed likely to lose a great deal more, now that Steele had left the rebels free to shift their full attention to matters in Louisiana.

★ ★ ★   **A**ll would now depend on speed in that direction: speed for the three divisions on the way to Taylor, speed for him in bringing them to bear, and speed for Banks and Porter in solving, before that happened, the problem of how to get ten gunboats, some of which drew seven feet of water, down and past a mile-long stretch of river less than half that deep. It was in that sense a race, with the odds very much in favor of the Confederates. So far at least as the concentration went, they had only to do in Louisiana what they had just finished doing in

Arkansas; whereas the Federals were confronted with a problem that seemed, on the face of it, insoluble. Yet by now, before they even knew that Steele had back-tracked and a race was therefore on, the blue commanders had found a way to win it. Or in any case they had found a man who believed he knew a way to win it, if they would only let him try.

On April 29 — while Marmaduke was closing on Steele near Jenkins Ferry and opening the action that would swell to battle proportions tomorrow morning — Lieutenant Colonel Joseph Bailey, Franklin's chief of engineers, came to Banks with a plan for raising the level of the river by installing, above Alexandria, a system of wing dams that would constrict and thereby deepen the channel leading down to and over the falls. A former Northwest lumberman, thirty-nine years old this week, he had used such methods to get logs down sluggish Wisconsin streams, and he was convinced they would work here, too, on a larger scale and for a larger purpose. "I wish I was as sure of heaven as I am that I can save the fleet," he said. Banks needed little persuading, not only because he was desperate enough by now to try almost anything, but also because the young engineer had demonstrated his ability along those lines the previous summer at Port Hudson, where he had salvaged, by damming a shallow creek to float them free, a pair of transports the rebels had left lying on their sides in the mud. The general took him that evening to present his plan to Porter. Contemplating the loss of his gunboats and the wreck of his career, the admiral was in an unaccustomed state of dejection; "This fatal campaign has upset everything," he had recently complained to Welles in a dispatch designed to prepare the Secretary for darker ones to follow. His first reaction to Bailey's proposal was to scoff at it. "If damning would get the fleet off, we would have been afloat long ago," he broke in, brightening a bit at this evidence that his sense of humor, such as it was, was still in working order. When it was explained to him further that the navy would have little to do but stand by and watch the army sweat and strain, he declared that he was willing on those terms. Accordingly, Banks issued orders on the last day of April for the thing to be tried, and Bailey, given 3000 soldiers to use as he saw fit in getting it done, put them to work without delay on May Day morning.

His plan was to construct above the lower falls, where the Red was 758 feet wide, a pair of wing dams, each extending about three hundred feet out into the river, then sink high-sided barges filled with brick across the remaining gap. The north-bank dam was to be formed of large trees laid with the current, their branches interlocked and their trunks cross-tied with heavy timbers on the downstream side; while the one on the south bank, where trees were scarce, would consist of huge cribs, pushed out and sunk and anchored in place with rubble of all kinds. Most of the left-bank work was done by a Maine regiment of highly skilled axmen and loggers, the rest being left to three regiments of New

Yorkers, experienced in tearing down old buildings — one was the military academy of which Sherman had been superintendent just before the war — for bricks and stone, to be used to hold the sunken cribs and barges in position against the force of the nine-knot current. They worked day and night, under a broiling sun and by the light of bonfires, much of the time up to their necks in the swift, rust-colored water.

At the outset they provoked more jeers than cheers from the sailors and off-duty soldiers looking on, but as the ends of the two dams drew closer together, day by day and hour by hour, interest mounted and skepticism lessened among the spectators on the gunboats and both banks, who now began to tell each other that Bailey's notion might just be practicable, after all. The sailors, especially those aboard the "teakettles," as the ironclads were called, were pleased to be afforded this diversion, now that rising temperatures had added physical discomfort to their boredom. "During the day," an officer recorded, "the iron on the decks would get so hot that the hand could barely rest upon it. At night, sleep was impossible. The decks were kept wetted down, and the men

*W*orkers fill wooden cribs to form a dam on the Red
River to raise the water level enough for Porter's
Federal fleet to pass the rapids at Alexandria.

lay on them, getting, toward the morning hours when the hulls had cooled down, such sleep as could be secured." Nor were excursions ashore of much help in this regard, involving, as they sometimes did, another form of torture which southern women, then and later, were adept at inflicting. "Saw quite a number of ladies from Pine Village opposite Alexandria," a sailor wrote in his diary after one such visit. "Two in particular were out on display promenade, one of whom had a beautiful black squirrel which ran all over her, up her dress sleeves and under her lace cape into her bosom, with a familiarity that made me envy the little favorite and sent a thrill that did not feel very bad through all the little veins in my body."

Still, being bored or titillated, painful though they were in their different ways, was better than getting shot at: as a good many soldiers and sailors could testify from experience while the dams were being built. If Taylor lacked the strength to interfere with the work going on behind the Federal intrenchments, he could at least make life hectic for the troops who manned them, and he could do considerably worse to those who ventured outside them, on foot or afloat. On the day Bailey started construction, the transport *Emma* was captured at David's Ferry, thirty miles below Alexandria, her captain and crew looking on as prisoners while the rebels burned her. Three days later another, the *City Belle*, was served in much the same fashion a few miles farther down, this time with a 700-man Ohio regiment aboard. More than a third of the soldiers were captured — 276 by Taylor's count — while the rest went over the side, escaped ashore, and eventually made their way back through the lines. Next day, May 5, saw the gravest loss of all. The transport *Warner*, escorted by the gunboats *Covington* and *Signal* while taking another regiment of Ohioans downriver to begin their reënlistment furloughs, came under fire from a masked battery as she rounded a bend near the mouth of Dunn's Bayou. Disabled by an unlucky shot in her rudder, she spun with the current, absorbing heavy punishment from riflemen posted along the high south bank, and when the two warships tried to come to her assistance by bringing their seventeen guns to bear on the rebel four, they were given the same treatment in short order. *Covington*, hulled repeatedly, went aground and was set afire by her skipper, who got away into the woods with 32 of his crew of 74, leaving the rest to the mercy of the gray marksmen who by then were at work on *Signal*. They cut her up so badly that the captain, prevented from destroying her by the fact that there was no time for removing the wounded, struck his colors and surrendered his 54 survivors, together with some 125 killed and wounded left strewn about the decks of the *Warner* when she and they were abandoned by her crew and their fellow soldiers. That brought the total for the past five days to better than 600 amphibious Federals killed or captured, together with three transports and two gunboats, at a cost to the Confederates of little more than the ammunition they expended. Worst of all, from the point of view of the soldiers and sailors cooped up in Alexandria or marooned above the falls, the Red was emphatically closed to Union shipping. They had to subsist on what they had, which by now was very little, or starve; or leave.

Along with everyone else in blue, Banks preferred the last of these three alternatives, although it appeared about as unlikely as the first. At this stage, the choice seemed narrowed to the second — starvation — which was scarcely a choice at all. As of May Day, he computed that he could subsist his army for three weeks on half-rations out of what he had on hand. That might or might not be enough, depending on whether the work begun on the dams that day could be completed within that span, but there seemed little doubt, at best, that he would lose his train for lack of animals to haul the wagons. Forage was so short already that Taylor was complaining, and exulting, that the horses he captured were little more than skeletons. Pitiable as they were, he intended to be still harder on them in the immediate future, as a means of being harder on the men who rode or drove them. On May 7, after claiming that his downstream successes near Dunn's Bayou had converted the lower Red, formerly a broad Federal highway of invasion, into "a *mare clausum*," he reported to Kirby Smith: "Forage and subsistence of every kind have been removed beyond the enemy's reach. Rigid orders are given to destroy everything useful that can fall into his hands. We will play the game the Russians played in the retreat from Moscow."

So he intended, gazing all the while back over his shoulder for some sign of the approach of the troops from Arkansas, without whom he lacked the strength to come to earnest grips with the beleaguered Unionists. All he could do was pray that they would arrive before the bluecoats started the downstream march that would increase the distance his reinforcements would have to cover before they could be brought to bear.

In point of fact, the race was closer than he knew. Faith had replaced skepticism in the attitude of the watchers at the dam site. "Before God, what won't the Yankees do next!" a gray-haired contraband cried in amazement at his first sight of the week-old work in progress, now rapidly nearing completion. Crews of the largest of the ten warships above the falls, having caught the spirit of the workers in the water, were busy lightening their vessels by stripping off side armor, which they dumped in a five-fathom hole upstream to keep it out of rebel hands, and unloading such heavy materials as commandeered cotton, anchors, chains, ammunition, and most of the guns, which — all but eleven old 32-pounders, spiked and sunk, like the iron plating, to forestall salvage — were to be carted below on wagons for reloading in deep water beyond the falls. By the following day, May 8, the river had risen enough to allow

★

The Federal transport Warner trades fire with a battery near Dunn's Bayou. Her captain and survivors abandoned the badly damaged ship and surrendered.

three of the lighter-draft boats, the tinclad *Fort Hindman* and the broad-bottomed monitors *Osage* and *Neosho,* to pass the upper falls and take station just above the dam, awaiting the further rise that would enable them to make their run. That would not take long, apparently, for now that the dam was finished and the rubble-laden barges sunk to plug the gap between the wings, the river was rising so swiftly that it deepened more than a foot between sunset and midnight, increasing the midstream depth to a full six feet. Another foot would do it, the engineers said. As the depth increased, however, so did the speed of the current and the resultant pressure on the dam, which mounted in ratio to both. Banks, for one, began to fear that the whole affair would be swept away in short order. Arriving for an inspection by the light of bonfires late that night, he sent Porter a message expressing hope that the flotilla would be ready to move down at a moment's notice, since it seemed to him unlikely that the dam, already trembling under the weight of all that water, could survive past dawn.

He was wrong by about one hour. It held all night, then blew at 5.30 next morning when two of the barges shifted, first tentatively, then with a rush, and went with the boom and froth of current through the re-created gap.

Porter was on the scene. He had paid Banks's warning no mind last evening, but now that its validity was being demonstrated so cataclysmically, he reacted in a hurry by leaping astride a horse for a fast ride upstream to order the boats above the upper falls to start their run before the water, rushing Niagara-like between the unplugged wings of the dam, fell too low for them to try it. All but *Lexington*, the oldest vessel with the fleet — one of the three original "timberclads," she was a veteran of practically all the river fights since Belmont, where Grant got his start, and had harassed the Confederates trying to get some sleep in the captured Federal camps after the first day's fight at Shiloh — were unready for action of any kind, moored to bank with their steam down and all but their anchor watches taking it easy about the decks. *Lexington* got under way at once, passing scantly over the rocks of the upper falls, and headed straight for the 66-foot opening between the two remaining barges. The admiral, one of the thousands of soldiers and sailors who lined both banks of the Red to watch her go, later reported her progress and the reaction, afloat and ashore: "She entered the gap with a full head of steam on, pitched down the roaring current, made two or three spasmodic rolls, hung for a moment on the rocks below, and then was swept into deep water by the current and rounded to, safely into the bank. Thirty thousand voices rose in one deafening cheer, and universal joy seemed to pervade the face of every man present."

Encouraged by *Lexington*'s example, the skippers of the three boats that had crossed the upper falls the previous day decided to try their hand at completing the run before the mass of water drained away and left them stranded in the shallows of the rapids. *Neosho* led off, advancing bravely under a full head of steam. At the last minute, however, just as she was about to enter the gorge, the pilot lost his nerve and signaled for the engine to be stopped. It was, but not the monitor herself. She went with the sucking rush of the current, out of control; her low hull plunged from sight beneath the spume as she went into the gap, careening through at an angle so steep it was nearly a dive, and struck bottom with an iron clang, loud against the bated silence on both banks; then reappeared at last below, taking cheers from the watchers and water through the hole the stones had punched along her keel. This last was slight and soon repaired — a small price to pay for deliverance from a month's captivity, not to mention the risk of self-destruction or surrender. The other two warships, *Osage* and *Hindman*, made it through in a more conservative style, with less excitement for the troops on shore but also with less damage to themselves. Four boats were now below the double falls, assured of freedom and continuing careers in their old allegiance. But the remaining six were trapped as completely as before, the water having fallen too low for them to cross the upper falls by the time they got up steam enough to risk the run.

Banks was more or less unstrung by the fulfillment of his prediction that the dam was about to go. He foresaw indefinite postponement of the departure which just last night had seemed so near, and he was correspondingly cast down, having seen the effects of starvation only too clearly last summer at Port Hudson when the scarecrow garrison lined up for surrender. "We have exhausted the country," he told Porter that afternoon, "and with the march that is before us it will be perilous to remain more than another day."

The admiral, perhaps because he had put less faith in the dam as a means of deliverance, reacted less despairingly to the mishap. After all, he had saved four of his boats already — four less than he had feared he well might lose — and he believed he could save the other half dozen as well, if the army would only stand fast until the dam could be replugged. But there was the rub. Banks, in his depression, was giving what seemed to Porter signs that he was about to pull out, bag and baggage, workers and all, and leave the stranded warships to the mercy of butternut marksmen who had demonstrated at Dunn's Bayou, four days ago, their skill at naval demolition when there was no army standing by to hold them off. On May 11, when Banks displayed further jumpiness by sending a staff officer to complain that the navy seemed unmindful of the need for utmost haste, Porter did what he could to calm him down. "Now, General," he replied soothingly, "I really see nothing that should make us despond. You have a fine

The Federal ironclad Neosho glides along the Red River on her way to the dams constructed by Joseph Bailey to raise the water level in the river.

★

army, and I shall have a strong fleet of gunboats to drive away an inferior force in our front." Up to now, he artfully pointed out, the press had been highly critical of the conduct of the campaign; but think what a glorious finish the salvation of the flotilla would afford the journalists for the stories yet to be filed. And having thus appealed to the former governor's political sensibilities, the admiral closed with an exhortation designed to stiffen his resolution. "I hope, Sir, you will not let anything divert you from the attempt to get these vessels all through safely, even if we have to stay here and eat mule meat."

No blue-clad soldier or sailor had yet been reduced to such a diet; nor would one be here, though Banks was quick to reply that he had no intention of leaving the navy in the lurch. The reason again was Bailey, who once more solved a difficult engineering problem in short order. Instead of attempting to plug the swift-running gap between the still-intact wings of the dam just above the lower falls, he decided instead to construct another at the upper falls, similar to the first, and thus not try any longer to sustain the weight of all that water with one dam. It was done with such dispatch, his thousand-man detail being thoroughly experienced in such work by now, that within three days — that is, before sunset of the day Porter urged Banks to stand by him "even if we have to stay here and eat mule meat" — three more vessels completed their runs down the mile-long rapids and over the two sets of falls. These were the veteran Eads gunboats *Mound City, Pittsburg*, and *Carondelet*. Next day, May 12, the remaining three — the armored steamer *Chillicothe*, the fourth Eads gunboat *Louisville*, and finally the third monitor *Ozark*, successor to the *Eastport* as the pride of the river fleet — did the same. Porter and his precious warships were delivered, thanks to Bailey, to whom he presented, as a personal gift, a $700 sword. The engineer also received, as tokens of appreciation, a $1600 silver vase from the navy, a vote of thanks from Congress, and in time a two-step promotion to brigadier general. None of this was a whit too much, according to Porter, who said of the former Wisconsin logger in his report: "Words are inadequate to express the admiration I feel for the abilities of Lieutenant Colonel Bailey. This is without doubt the best engineering feat ever performed. Under the best circumstances a private company would not have completed this work under one year, and to an ordinary mind the whole thing would have appeared an utter impossibility."

He might have added that his own mind seemed to fit in that category, since he had prejudged the attempt in just that way. But for the present, steaming down the lower Red, where the going was deep and easy because of backwater from the swollen Mississippi, he was altogether occupied with savoring his freedom, his narrow delivery from ruin. "I am clear of my troubles," he wrote home to his mother that week, though he was not so far clear of them that he forgot to add: "I have had a hard and anxious time of it."

★

★ ★ ★   *S*o had Banks had a hard and anxious time of it, and so was he still, along with the slogging troops under his command. Leaving Alexandria on May 13, the day after Porter completed his run, they had another sixty hostile miles to cover before they would return to their starting point, Simsport on the Atchafalaya, where Sherman's men had opened the campaign, just one day more than two full months ago. In point of fact, except as a location on the map, the town no longer existed; A. J. Smith's gorillas had burned it at the outset. And now, looking back over their shoulders as they set out, they had a similar satisfaction — similar not only to Simsport, but also to Grand Ecore, three weeks ago, as well as to a number of lesser hamlets in their path, before and since — of seeing Alexandria aflame. It burned briskly under a long, wind-tattered plume of greasy smoke, while over the levee and down by the bank of the river, as one Federal would recall, "thousands of people, mostly women, children, and old men, were wringing their hands as they stood by the little piles of what was left of all their worldly possessions." They had been driven there by the sudden press of heat from a score of fires that quickly merged after starting simultaneously with the help of a mixture of turpentine and camphene, which the soldiers slopped on houses and stores with mops and brooms. Experience had greatly improved their incendiary technique. "Hurrah, boys! This looks like war!" Smith shouted by way of encouragement as he rode through the streets, rounding up his men for departure.

They had their usual assignment as rear guard, the post of honor on retreat, while the Easterners took the lead. Banks rode with the more congenial troops up front, commanded now by Emory; Franklin, after recommending that his chief engineer's proposal for saving the fleet be tried, had left on May Day, still fretted by his shin wound, which seemed to require more skilled attention than the Transmississippi doctors were able to furnish, and by disgust and bitterness at having been prominently connected with still another large-scale defeat. Banks of course had that fret too, without the red-badge distraction of a physical injury, but he felt better, all in all, than he had done at any time in the past horrendous month. For one thing, the salvation of the flotilla had given journalists the upbeat ending Porter had dangled as bait for prolonging the army's stay in Alexandria, and for another his casualties had been replaced, before the end of April, by reinforcements who arrived from Pass Cavallo, Texas, under Major General John A. McClernand, resurrected from his Grant-enforced retirement in Springfield, Illinois, and put in command of the lower Texas coast by his old friend and fellow townsman Abraham Lincoln. That brought the army's total strength to 31,000 effectives up the Red, more than Banks had had directly under him so far in the campaign. Even though there was no compensation for the loss of twenty guns, two hundred wagons, and something over a thousand mules, this added strength brought added confidence; which, aside from military skill, had been the thing most lacking at headquarters since the crossroads confrontation short of Mansfield, five weeks ago today. Moreover, there was the relief of having the end at last in sight, whatever disappointments had occurred along the way, and of discovering that Taylor, for all his bluster in the course of the Alexandria siege, seemed considerably less a menace now that the cooped-up bluecoats were out in the open, inviting the attack he formerly had seemed anxious but now seemed strangely reluctant to deliver.

At any rate that appeared to be the case throughout the first three days of the march downriver. Crossing the Choctaw Bayou swamps on the second day out of smouldering Alexandria, the Federals occupied Marksville on the evening of the third. That was May 15; they had covered forty miles by then, molested by nothing worse than grayback cavalry, which failed in its attempts to get at the wagons drawn by scarecrow mules, and were a good two thirds of their way to the sanctuary a crossing of the Atchafalaya would afford them.

"Like 'Sister Ann' from her watch tower, day after day we strained our eyes to see the dust of our approaching comrades. . . . Vain, indeed, were our hopes."

— Richard Taylor

Banks tempered his optimism, however, by reminding himself that the tactical situation resembled the one that had obtained, or had seemed to obtain, on the march from Natchitoches to within three miles of Mansfield, where it ended in disarray. The resemblance was altogether too close for comfort, let alone for premature self-congratulation; Taylor might well be planning a repeat of that performance at another crossroads, somewhere up ahead. And sure enough, advancing next morning across the Avoyelles Prairie, five miles south of Marksville, Banks found the Confederates disposed in force athwart his path, much as they had been at Sabine Crossroads, except that here the terrain was open and gave him a sobering view of what he faced. Their line of battle extending east and west of the village of Mansura, they had thirty-odd pieces of artillery — more than half of them had been his own, up to the time of the previous confrontation just short of Mansfield, which this one so uncomfortably resembled — unlimbered and ready to take him under fire as soon as he ventured within range. Their numbers in infantry and cavalry were hard to estimate, masked as their center was by the town, but Banks did not decline the challenge. He shook out his skirmishers, put his own guns in position — as many of the remaining seventy, in any case, as he could find room for on the three-mile width of prairie — formed his infantry for attack with cavalry posted neatly on both flanks, and then went forward, blue flags rippling in the breeze.

The result, as the troops began to move and the guns to growl, was enough to make observers in both armies, each of which had a full view of the other, catch their breath in admiration. Advancing across the lush and level prairie — "smooth as a billiard table," Taylor was to say of it in his report — the Union host was "resplendent in steel and brass," according to one of its members, a Connecticut infantryman who afterward tried his hand at a word sketch of the scene, including "miles of lines and columns; the cavalry gliding over the ground in the distance with a delicate, nimble lightness of innumerable twinkling feet; a few batteries enveloped in smoke and incessantly thundering, others dashing swiftly to salient positions; division and corps commanders with their staff officers clustering about them, watching through their glasses the hostile army; couriers riding swiftly from wing to wing; everywhere the beautiful silken flags; and the scene ever changing with the involutions and evolutions of the vast host." It was, in short, that seldom-encountered thing, picture-book war — which it also resembled, as events developed, in its paucity of bloodshed. Though the armies remained in approximate confrontation for four hours, the action was practically limited to artillery exchanges, since neither commander seemed willing to venture within point-blank range of the other's guns. When at last Banks brought A. J. Smith's Westerners forward for an attack on the rebel left, Taylor withdrew in that direction, south and west, and the Federals resumed their march to the south and east, through Mansura, then on to Bayou de Glaise, on whose banks they stopped for the night. Next day, May 17, after skirmishing warmly with enemy horsemen on both sides of Moreauville, they pushed on to Yellow Bayou, within five miles of Simsport and the Atchafalaya, which would shield them from further pursuit once they were across it.

If Banks had known the extent of the odds in his favor, he not only would have been less surprised at the sidelong rebel withdrawal from Mansura, he would also have been considerably less concerned for the safety of his army, which in fact enjoyed a five-to-one numerical advantage over the force attempting to waylay and impede it. Taylor fairly ached for some sign of the three divisions on the march from Arkansas; to no avail. "Like 'Sister Ann' from her watch tower," he was to write, "day after day we strained our eyes to see the dust of our approaching comrades. . . . Vain, indeed, were our hopes. The commander of the 'Trans-Mississippi Department' had the power to destroy the last hope of the Confederate cause, and exercised it with all the success of Bazaine at Metz. 'The affairs of mice and men aft gang aglee,' from sheer stupidity and pig-headed obstinacy." And lest his meaning be clouded by his fondness for religious and historical allusions and poetic misquotations, he made the charge specific and identified by name the man he held responsible for his woes: "From first to last, General Kirby Smith seemed determined to throw a protecting shield around the Federal army and fleet."

This bitterness would grow; would in time become obsessive. But for the present the Louisiana general directed most of his attention to a search for some way, despite the odds, to inflict more vengeful damage on the spoilers of his homeland before they fled beyond his reach. The side-step at Mansura, allowing them to press on south and east, had been as necessary as it was painful; for if Taylor was to preserve his little army for future use, he could not afford to take on the blue host without a tactical advantage totally lacking on the open prairie. Then next day he received, as if from Providence, what he believed might be the chance for which he prayed. Pushing on through Moreauville, the Federal main body reached Yellow Bayou only to learn from its scouts, who had ridden ahead, that backwater from the Mississippi had swollen the Atchafalaya to a width too great for spanning by all the pontoons the engineers had on hand. Without a bridge, the crossing would be at best a slow affair, involving the use of transports as ferries. Penned up with its back to the river, as it had been at Grand Ecore and Alexandria, the blue mass would grow more vulnerable as it shrank, regiment by regiment, until at last a gray assault could be launched against the remnant — perhaps with the help, by then, of the slow-moving troops from Arkansas — extracting payment in blood for the vandalism of the past nine weeks. Taylor brightened at the prospect, and next morning, May 18, moved his infantry up to join his cavalry on Yellow Bayou, intending to advance from there and establish a semicircular, close-up line of intrenchments from which to observe the dwindling Union army, held under siege amid the ashes of what had once been Simsport.

Looking out across the unbridgeable 600-yard expanse of the Atchafalaya, a swollen barrier to the safety his army could only attain by reaching the far side, Banks foresaw an outcome all too similar to the one his adversary was moving to effect. Still, his despair was not so deep as to keep him from doing all he could to ward it off. When he was informed, around midmorning, that Taylor had moved up to Yellow Bayou, close in his rear, he instructed A. J. Smith to countermarch and drive him back. Smith returned to the Bayou, crossed three brigades, and pitched without delay into the rebel skirmish line, throwing it back on the main body, which then attacked and drove him back in turn. It went that way for a couple of hours, first one side gaining ground and then the other — each had about 5000 men engaged — until at last the underbrush caught fire and both withdrew in opposite directions, choked and scorched, from the crackling barricade of smoke and flame. That ended the action. Unresolved and indecisive as it was, Smith's gorillas once more had proved their worth as fighters as well as burners, losing about 350 to inflict a total of 608 casualties on Taylor.

Nothing daunted, the Louisianian prepared to return to the offensive next day, May 19. But that was not to be. The back-and-forth engagement on the west side of Yellow Bayou turned out to be the last of the campaign — for the simple reason that presently no blue-clad troops remained within his reach. Banks by then had bridged the unbridgeable Atchafalaya.

Once more the *deus ex machina* was Joe Bailey. Handed the problem by Banks, the engineering colonel promptly solved it by mooring all the available riverboats and transports side by side across the near-half-mile width of the stream, like oversized pontoons, and bolting them together with timbers which then served as stringers for planks laid crosswise on them to form a roadbed. Soon after midday, though the varying heights of the boats on which it rested gave it something of the crazy, up-and-down aspect of a roller coaster, Banks had the bridge he needed to reach the sanctuary beyond the river.

Colonel Joseph Bailey engineered the dams at Alexandria and a bridge for Banks to cross the Atchafalaya.

The wagon train began to cross at once, followed that night by the guns and ambulances; next morning, May 20, the troops themselves were marched across and the makeshift bridge dismantled in their rear. Two days later — a solid month past the time when they had been scheduled to rejoin Sherman in far-off Georgia — Smith's three divisions filed back aboard their transports and set out for Vicksburg. Banks meantime was as full of praise for Bailey, here on the Atchafalaya, as Porter had been the week before, back up the Red. "This work was not of the same magnitude, but was as important to the army as the dam at Alexandria was to the navy," he said of the improvised bridge in his final report, and repeated his recommendation that the former logger be promoted to brigadier as a reward for his resourcefulness under pressure.

Another upbeat flourish had been provided, but so had additions been made to the list of casualties — more than fifteen hundred of them, all told, since the return to Alexandria in late April. Army losses for the campaign now stood at 5245 killed, wounded, and missing, and to this were added some three hundred naval casualties, suffered in the course of the subtraction from the flotilla of an ironclad, two tinclads, three transports, a pair of pump boats, and 28 guns of various calibers, captured or spiked and abandoned up the Red. This Federal total of about 5500 exceeded by well over a thousand the Confederate total of 4275. Losses in matériel were of course even more disproportionate, not only because the rebels had lost much less in battle, but also because they had had a great deal less to lose: aside, that is, from civilian property, the destruction of which, if included, would doubtless swing the balance the other way. But perhaps the greatest contrast lay in what a member of Banks's official family called "the great and bitter crop of quarrels" raised in the northern ranks by what he referred to as "this unhappy campaign." If on the Confederate side there were arguments in the scramble to divide the glory, on the Union side there were hotter ones involved in the distribution of the blame. Looking back over the events of the past seventy days, the staffer noted that feelings had been severely ruffled and several lofty reputations quite undone. "Franklin quitted the department in disgust," he recalled; "Stone was replaced by Dwight as chief of staff, and Lee as chief of cavalry by Arnold; A. J. Smith departed more in anger than in sorrow; while between the admiral and the general commanding, recriminations were exchanged in language well up to the limits of 'parliamentary' privilege."

Now still another illustrious name was added to the list: Banks's own. Not that he was relieved outright or shunted into obscurity, as so many others had been in the doleful course of the past six weeks. This was an election year, and too much rode on the outcome for the authorities to risk alienating a man with as many votes as the one-time Speaker of the House controlled. Lincoln and Halleck put their heads together and came up with the answer. Major General Edward R. S. Canby, a forty-six-year-old Kentucky-born West Pointer, had come east after the New Mexico campaign of 1862, in which he had managed to save the Far West for the Union, and had since been involved in administrative matters, including the reëstablishment of law and order in New York after the draft riots of 1863. In all these positions his outstanding characteristic had been his prudence, a rare quality nowadays in the Transmississippi; Lincoln and Halleck, with Grant's concurrence — Canby had been another of his classmates at the Point — decided to send him there to supply it, not as Banks's replacement, but rather as his superior, by placing him in charge of the newly created "Military Division of West Mississippi," which stretched from Missouri to the Gulf and from Florida to Texas. Banks's unquestioned abilities as an administrator, honest amid corruption, were thus preserved for the government's use, along with his political support, while his military ineptness was set aside by depriving him of any further independence — or, as it turned out, service — in the field.

Canby was waiting for him with the necessary papers at Simsport, and accompanied him on the final leg of the retreat, another hundred miles downriver to Donaldsonville, where the campaign formally ended on May 26, seventy-five days after its start and more than a month beyond its scheduled finish. An Iowa soldier wrote in his diary that Banks looked "dejected and worn" at that stage, and small wonder. More had ended and more had been lost, for him, than the campaign. The former governor, whose reduction of Port Hudson had opened the Mississippi to northern trade throughout its length, was now the mere desk-bound head of a subdepartment in an organization commanded by a man almost two years his junior in age and three full years behind him in date of rank. That came hard, but that was by no means the worst of it for Banks, who was taunted not only by the thought of what he had lost but also by the thought of what he had failed to gain. Mobile might someday be attacked and taken, but not by him, and along with much else that had gone with the winds of war — including all those hundreds of thousands of bales of cotton, which were to have put the national effort on a pay-as-you-go basis, but which instead had tainted it with scandal — were his hopes for the highest political office. All that had ended up the Red. He not only had been defeated by his enemies up that river, he had been oversloughed by his superiors on his return: "a fit sequel," the Saint Louis *Republican* asserted, "to a scheme conceived in politics and brought forth in iniquity."

If contention was less widespread on the Confederate side, where there was more credit than blame to be divided, such contention as there was only flared the higher on that account. Taylor's distress in reaction to his fear that the Federals were going to escape — the result, he claimed, of "sheer stupidity and pig-headed obstinacy" on the part of the high command at Shreveport — was mild compared to the frustration he felt when the bluecoats did in fact improvise an Atchafalaya crossing before the arrival of the Arkansas reinforcements enabled him to exact the retribution he felt they owed. Though his pride in his outnumbered army was as boundless as his contempt for the invaders ("Long will the accursed race remember the great river of Texas and Louisiana," he said of the latter in a congratulatory order

Edward R. S. Canby became commander of the new Federal Military Division of West Mississippi.

he issued to his troops on May 23. "The characteristic hue of its turbid waters has a darker tinge from the liberal admixture of Yankee blood. The cruel alligator and the ravenous garfish wax fat on rich food, and our native vulture holds high revelry over many a festering corpse") his wrath had mounted with each passing day of the unimpeded blue retreat. Moving up to Yellow Bayou five days ago, he had taken time to communicate his chagrin at having been obliged to step aside, just when he had the vandals within his grasp, for lack of strength to stand his ground at Mansura. "I feel bitterly about this," he protested in a dispatch to Kirby Smith's adjutant, "because my army has been robbed of the just measure of its glory and the country of the most brilliant and complete success of the war."

The further it receded into the past, the more "brilliant and complete" that missed victory became. Indeed, within a week or so, Taylor had come to believe that his superior's military ineptness, which had obliged him to forgo a certain triumph, might well have cost the South its one best chance to win its independence. What was more, he said as much to Kirby Smith himself on June 5, in a letter combining indignation and despair. "In truth," he wrote, quite as if he had a corner on that rare commodity, "the campaign as a whole has been a hideous failure. The fruits of Mansfield have turned to dust and ashes. Louisiana, from Natchitoches to the Gulf, is a howling wilderness and her people are starving. Arkansas is probably as great a sufferer. In both States abolition conventions are sitting to overthrow their system of labor. The remains of Banks' army have already gone to join Grant or Sherman, and may turn the scale against our overmatched brethren in Virginia and Georgia." What made the hot-tempered Louisianian angriest was the contrast between this and the situation that might have obtained if his chief had not rejected his advice on how to go about disposing of the invaders, which he was certain would have led to their destruction and the reversal of the tide of war. "The roads to Saint Louis and New Orleans should now be open to us. Your strategy has riveted the fetters on both." The more he wrote — and he wrote at length, including a full critique of the campaign, with emphasis on the mismanagement of events beyond his reach, both here and in Arkansas — the angrier he grew: until finally, as he drew to a close, his wrath approached incandescence. "The same regard for duty which led me to throw myself between you and popular indignation, and quietly take the blame for your errors," he wound up, "compels me to tell you the truth, however objectionable to you. The grave errors you have committed in the recent campaign may be repeated if the unhappy consequences are not kept before you. After the desire to serve my country, I have none more ardent than to be relieved from longer serving under your command."

Thus Taylor, whose rage had made him as blind to the virtues of others as he was perceptive of their faults. To refer to the just-ended campaign as "a hideous failure," simply because it had not yielded all that he had hoped for, was to overlook its fruits, which in fact were far from slight. Inflicting more than 8000 casualties on Steele and Banks, at a cost to Price and Taylor of 6500, Smith had captured or caused the destruction of 57 pieces of artillery, nearly half of them naval, along with about a thousand wagons, most of them loaded with valuable supplies, and more than 3500 mules and horses. This was a considerable tactical haul, by almost any standards, and yet the strategic gains were even greater. Despite the hot-tempered Louisianian's claim to the contrary, the campaign had cost Sherman the use of 10,000 veterans in North Georgia; which meant that he moved with that many fewer against Joe Johnston, while Johnston's own army was enlarged by nearly twice that number because the upset of Banks's schedule had ruled out an early movement against Mobile, leaving Polk free to shift from Demopolis toward Dalton with some 20,000 troops who otherwise would have been drawn in the opposite direction by the threat to coastal Alabama. The greatest effect of the campaign up Red River thus was felt in northern Georgia, where a net difference of 30,000 men was registered in favor of the defenders of Atlanta. If the South was going to lose the war, then this would no doubt prolong the conflict. On the other hand, this might just narrow the long odds enough for the South to win it.

That of course remained to be seen. In the meantime, there was nothing Kirby Smith could do, despite his disinclination in such matters, but act on Taylor's insubordinate letter. Appointing Walker as his successor, he ordered him to Natchitoches, there to await instructions from their superiors, and forwarded the correspondence to Richmond with a covering letter to his friend the President. The good of the service required that he or Taylor be removed from command, the mild-mannered Floridian declared, adding that if Davis thought it best — as he well might do; Smith freely acknowledged the Louisianian's "merits as a soldier" — "I will willingly, with no feeling of envy or abatement of interest in the service of my country, turn over my arduous duties and responsibilities to a successor."

It made a sorry end, this falling-out by the victors, after all the glory that had been garnered up the Red and on the Saline; Dick Taylor was afterwards far from proud of his conduct in the quarrel, and set it down as the result of overwork and nervous strain. For the present, though, he was not unhappy to be reunited with his wife and children in Natchitoches, the lovely old French-Spanish town he recently had saved from Sherman's burners, there to await the judgment of his presidential brother-in-law.

★   ★   ★

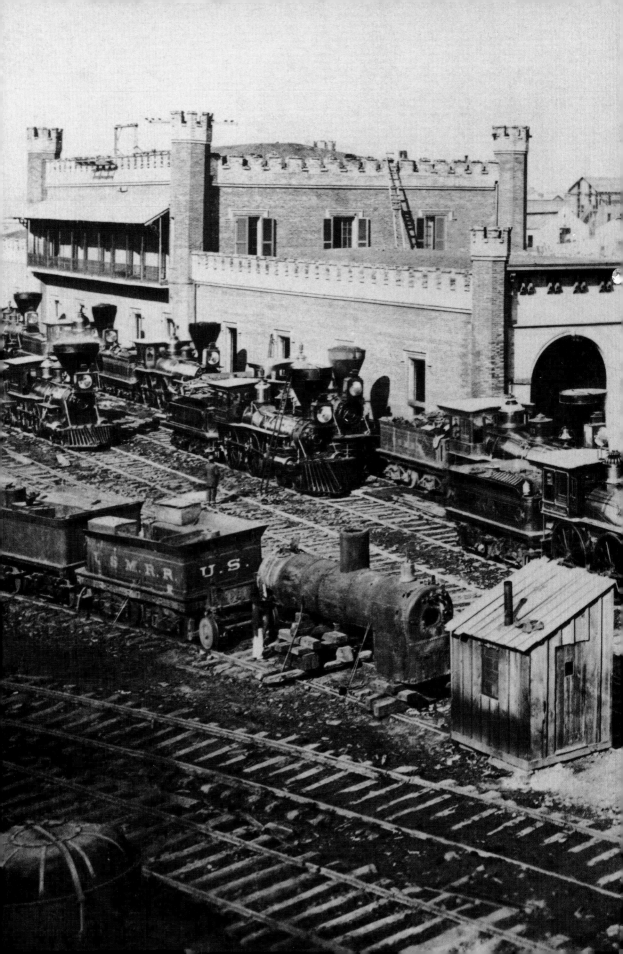

*U*nion forces in Chattanooga
and Knoxville depended on
Nashville's busy depot, which became
a model of efficiency in carrying
men and supplies to the front.

T H R E E

Paducah, Fort Pillow; Plymouth

1864 ★ ★ ★ ★ ★ ★ **D**avis **had troubles enough by then,** and differences enough to attempt to compose, without the added problem of trying to heal this latest split between two of his friends, one of whom was among the nation's ranking field commanders, responsible for the conduct of affairs in the largest of all its military departments, while the other was his first wife's younger brother. Down in Georgia, for example, on March 10 — the day A. J. Smith's gorillas left Vicksburg, beginning the ten-week campaign that would take them up and down Red River, and the day before Grant left Washington for the meeting with Sherman in Nashville, where they would begin to plan the campaign designed to bring Georgia to its knees and the Confederacy to extinction — Governor Joseph E. Brown addressed the state legislature, which he had called into special session to hear some things he had to say on the subject of the war. What he had to say, in essence, was that the war had been a failure. This was not only because it was now to be waged on his doorstep, so to speak, but also because, as he saw it, the authorities in Richmond had abandoned the principles embodied in the Declaration of Independence, including "all self-government and the sovereignty of the States."

Brown's solution, as set forth in his address, was for the Confederacy to dissolve itself into its components, thus calling a halt to discord and bloodshed:

★

after which, in an atmosphere of peace and fellowship, a convention of northern and southern governors would assemble at Baltimore or Memphis, Montreal or the Bermuda Islands, and each state, North as well as South, would "determine for herself what shall be her future connection, and who her future allies." In other words, he would stop and start anew, this time without taking so many wrong turnings in the pursuit of happiness along the path that led to independence. Brown was careful, in the course of his speech, not to propose that Georgia rejoin the Union. That would have amounted to outright treason. He proposed, rather, that the Union rejoin Georgia, and he favored "negotiation" as the means of achieving this end. "In a crisis like the present," he maintained, "Statesmanship is ever more important than Generalship. Generals can never stop a war, though it may last twenty years till one has been able to conquer the other. Statesmen terminate wars by negotiation."

Praised for its acumen or condemned as disloyal, the address pleased some of its hearers and outraged others, depending largely on their predilections. Politically, an observer remarked, "Georgia was rent asunder." Among the governor's firmest supporters, though he was not in Milledgeville to hear him, was Alexander H. Stephens, Vice President of the Confederacy. Stephens not only gave the speech his full approval — as well he might; "I advised it from stem to stern," he admitted privately — but arrived in person six days later from Liberty Hall, his estate at nearby Crawfordville, to reinforce it with one of his own, twice as long and twice as bitter, in which he lashed out at the national authorities for their betrayal of the secessionist cause by adopting conscription and suspending the writ of habeas corpus. "Better, in my judgment," he declared, "that Richmond should fall and that the enemy's armies should sweep our whole country from the Potomac to the Gulf than that our people should submissively yield to one of these edicts." A small, pale-faced man with burning eyes and a shrill voice, weighing less than a hundred pounds in the voluminous overcoat he wore against the chill he felt in all but the hottest weather, he spoke for three full hours, in the course of which he sustained at several points a critic's charge that his alarm "had long ago vaulted into the hysterical." Where personal freedom was concerned Stephens rejected all arguments as to expediency. "Away with the idea of getting our independence first, and looking after liberty afterward!" he cried. "Our liberties, once lost, may be lost forever." If he had to be ruled by a despot, he said darkly, he preferred that it be a northern one, and he closed on a dramatic note, quite as if he expected to be clapped in arrest by government agents as soon as he came down off the rostrum. "I do not know that I shall ever address you again, or see you again," he told the legislators filling the chamber, row on row, from wall to wall. "As for myself," he added by way of farewell — though he knew, as Patrick Henry had not known before him, that the authority he assailed would not dare call him to account —

"give me liberty as secured in the Constitution, amongst which is the sovereignty of Georgia, or give me death!"

He proceeded not to the dungeon he had seemed to predict, but back to Liberty Hall, where he continued to fulminate, in letters and interviews, against the government of which he was nominally a part and the man whose place he would take in case of death or the impeachment he appeared to recommend. Reproached by a constituent for having "allowed your antipathy to Davis to mislead your judgment," Stephens denied that he harbored any such enmity in his bosom. "I have regarded him as a man of good intentions," he replied, "weak and vacillating, petulant, peevish, obstinate but not firm." Having gone so far, however, he then revoked the disclaimer by adding: "Am now beginning to doubt his good intentions." Meantime, back in Milledgeville, Brown's managers were steering through the legislature a double set of resolutions introduced by Little Aleck's younger brother Linton, one condemning the Richmond authorities

"Better, in my judgment that Richmond should fall and that the enemy's armies should sweep our whole country from the Potomac to the Gulf than that our people should submissively yield to one of these edicts."

— Alexander Hamilton Stephens

for having overridden the Constitution, the other defining Georgia's terms for peace as a return, North and South, to the "principles of 1776." This took three days; the governor had to threaten to hold the legislators in special session "indefinitely" in order to ram the resolutions through; then on March 19 they passed them and were permitted to adjourn. Brown had his and the Vice President's addresses printed in full, together with Linton Stephens's resolutions, and distributed copies to all the Georgia soldiers in the armies of Lee and Johnston.

Stephens and Brown were two of the more unpleasant facts of Confederate life that had to be faced in Richmond by officials trying to get on with a long-odds war amid runaway inflation and spreading disaffection. Others were nearer at hand. In North Carolina, for example — that "vale of humility," a native called the state, "nestled between two humps of pride," Virginia and South Carolina — the yearning for peace had grown in ratio to a general disenchantment with "glory," of which the war, according to Governor Zebulon Vance, had afforded the Old North State too meager a share. Less bitter than Joe

North Carolina Governor Zebulon Baird Vance criticized the Confederate government for appointing out-of-state officers to command North Carolina troops.

Brown — of whom a fellow Georgian was saying this spring, "Wherever you meet a growling, complaining, sore-headed man, hostile to the government and denunciatory of its measures and policy, or a croaking, despondent dyspeptic who sees no hope for the country, but, whipped himself, is trying to make everybody else feel as badly as himself, you will invariably find a friend, admirer, and defender of Governor Brown" — Vance was an unrelenting critic of the ways things were done or left undone at Richmond, and his correspondence was heavy with complaints, made directly to the President, that Carolinians were constantly being slighted in the distribution of promotions and appointments. Late in March, Davis lost patience and sought to break off the exchange, protesting that Vance had "so far infringed the proprieties of official intercourse as to preclude the possibility of reply. In order that I may not again be subjected to the necessity of making so unpleasant a remark, I must beg that a correspondence so unprofitable in its character, and which was not initiated by me, may here end, and that your future communications be restricted to such matters as may require official action." But Vance, a self-made man from old Buncombe County, had long since learned the political value of persistence; he was not so easily restrained. Scarcely a mail arrived from Raleigh that did not include a protest by the governor that some worthy Tarheel had been snubbed or overlooked in the passing out of favors, military as well as civil. Davis could only read and sigh, thankful at least that Vance kept his distance, even though it was not so great as the distance Brown and Stephens kept.

That was by no means the case with Edward A. Pollard, who was not only very much at hand as associate editor of the Richmond *Examiner*, but also took the trouble to let the authorities know it daily. He often seemed to despise the Confederacy to its roots, and seldom relaxed in his efforts to impale its chief executive on what was agreed to be the sharpest pen in the journalistic South. Invective was his specialty, and when he got on his favorite subject — Jefferson Davis — he sometimes raised this specialty to an art. "Serene upon the frigid heights of infallible egotism," the Kentucky-born Mississippian was "affable, kind, and subservient to his enemies" but "haughty, austere, and unbending to his friends," and though he assumed "the superior dignity of a satrap," he was in fact, behind the rigid mask, "an amalgam of malice and mediocrity." Future historians of various persuasions were to take their cue from this carving-up of a man on his wrong side; it was small wonder that Pollard, who spoke with the gadfly rancor of Thersites, found many who nodded in gleeful agreement as they read his jabs and jibes. They read him, in this fourth and gloomiest spring of a war they had begun to believe they could not win, to find relief from a frustration which grew, like his own, in ratio to the dwindling of their hopes.

Thoroughly familiar with the American proclivity for blaming national woes on the national leader, Davis had engaged in the practice too often himself not to expect it to be turned against him. He viewed it as an occupational hazard, one that more or less went with his job, and he spoke of it as a man might speak of any natural phenomenon — gravity, say, or atmospheric pressure — which could not be abolished simply because it bore within it the seeds of possible disaster. "Opposition in any form can only disturb me inasmuch as it may endanger the public welfare," he had said. Moreover, no one could sympathize more with the people who felt this fourth-spring frustration, for no one was in a position to know as well how soundly based the feeling was. Such blame as he attached to men like Stephens and Brown and Pollard was not for entertaining, but rather for giving vent to their defeatist conclusions, since by so doing they betrayed their high positions, converting them to rostrums for the spreading of despair, and did indeed "endanger the public welfare." As for the frustration itself, Davis not only sympathized with, he shared it. However much he might condemn those who gave way under pressure, he knew only too well how great that pressure was: especially for those who saw the problem, as he did, from within. Wherever he looked he perceived that the Confederacy's efforts to "conquer a peace" were doomed to failure. And this applied most obviously to the three most obvious fields for aggressive endeavor, whereby the South might attempt to force its will upon its mortal adversary: 1) by entering upon negotiations with representatives from the North to obtain acceptable peace terms, 2) by mounting and sustaining a military offensive which would end with the imposition of such terms, or 3) by securing the foreign recognition and assistance which would afford the moral and physical strength now lacking to achieve the other two.

As for the first of these, Davis had pointed out the difficulty, if not the impossibility, of pursuing this line of endeavor three months ago in response to a letter from Governor Vance, in which the Carolinian urged that attempts be made to negotiate with the enemy, not only because such an expression of willingness on the part of the South to stop shooting and start talking would "convince the humblest of our citizens . . . that the government is tender of their lives and happiness, and would not prolong their sufferings unnecessarily one moment," but also because the rejection by the North of such an offer would "tend greatly to strengthen and intensify the war feeling [of our people] and will rally all classes to a more cordial support of the government." Davis replied that while such results were highly desirable, "insuperable objections" stood in the way of their being achieved. One was that, by the simple northern device of refusing to confer with "rebel" envoys, all such offers — except to the extent that they were "received as proof that we are ready for submission" — had been rejected out of hand. He himself had seldom neglected an opportunity, in his public addresses and messages to Congress, to inform the enemy and the world that "All we ask is to be let alone." Nothing had come of this, in or out of official channels, and it was becoming increasingly clear that to continue such efforts was "to invite insult and contumely, and to subject ourselves to indignity, without the slightest chance of being listened to."

Suppose, though, that they did somehow manage to break through the barrier of silence. What would that do, Davis asked, but confront them with another barrier, still more "insuperable" than the first? "It is with Lincoln alone that we could confer," he reminded Vance, "and his own partisans at the North avow unequivocally that his purpose in his message and proclamation [of Amnesty and Reconstruction] was to shut out all hope that he would *ever* treat with us, on *any* terms." The northern President himself had made this clear and certain, according to Davis. "Have we not been apprised by that despot that we can only expect his gracious pardon by emancipating all our slaves, swearing obedience to him and his proclamation, and becoming in point of fact the slaves of our own Negroes?" In the light of this, he asked further, "can there be in North Carolina one citizen so fallen beneath the dignity of his ancestors as to accept or enter into conference on the basis of these terms? That there are a few traitors in the state who would be willing to betray their fellow citizens to such a degraded condition, in hope of being rewarded for their treachery by an escape from the common doom, may be true. But I do not believe that the vilest wretch would accept such terms for himself."

Having gone so far — for the letter was a long one, written in the days before he sought to break off corresponding with the Tarheel governor — Davis then proceeded to the inevitable conclusion that peace, if it was to come at all, would have to be won by force of arms. "To obtain the sole terms to which you or I could listen," he told Vance, "this struggle must continue until the enemy is beaten out of his vain confidence in our subjugation. Then and not till then will it be possible to treat of peace."

That brought him to the second, and much the bloodiest, of his three aggressive choices: the launching of an offensive that would not stop short of the table across which peace terms would be dictated to an enemy obliged to accept them as a condition of survival in defeat. Pleasant though this was to contemplate as a fitting end to slaughter and privation, it amounted to little more than an exercise in the realm of fantasy. If three blood-drenched years of war, and three aborted invasions of the North, had taught anything, they had taught that, however the conflict was going to end, it was not going to end this way. Davis, for one, never stopped hoping that it might, and even now was urging a course of action on Joe Johnston, down in Georgia, designed to bring about just such a closing scene. That the general declined to march all-out

> *"To obtain the sole terms to which you or I could listen, this struggle must continue until the enemy is beaten out of his vain confidence in our subjugation. Then and not till then will it be possible to treat of peace."*
>
> — Jefferson Davis

against the Union center was not surprising; Johnston had always bridled at cut-and-slash urgings or suggestions, and in this case, outnumbered and out-gunned as he was, he protested with ample cause. Nor was he the only one to demonstrate reluctance. "Our role must be a defensive policy," Kirby Smith was warning his impetuous lieutenants out in the Transmississippi; while nearer at hand, and weightiest by far in that regard, the nation's ranking field commander was tendering much the same advice to his superior in Richmond. The most aggressive of all the Confederate military chieftains — indeed, one of the most aggressive soldiers of all time, of whom a subordinate had declared, quite accurately, on the occasion of his appointment to head the Virginia army, just under two years ago: "His name might be Audacity. He will take more chances, and take them quicker, than any other general in this country, North or South" — R. E. Lee had taken care, well before the occasion could arise, to forestall even the suggestion that he attempt another large-scale offensive when the present "mud truce" ended in the East. Back in early February, in response to a presidential request for counsel, he said flatly: "We are not in a condition, and never have been, in my opinion, to invade the enemy's country with a prospect of permanent benefit."

There Davis had it. For though Lee added characteristically that he hoped, by a limited show of force, to "alarm and embarrass [the enemy] to some extent, and thus prevent his undertaking anything of magnitude against us," this was no real modification of his implied opinion that past efforts to end the war on northern soil — his own two, which had broken in blood along Sharpsburg ridge and across the stony fields of Gettysburg, as well as Bragg's, which had gone into reverse at Perryville — had been errors of judgment, serving, if for nothing else, to demonstrate the folly of any attempt at repetition of them. Such a statement, from such a source, was practically irrefutable, especially since it was echoed by the commanders of the other two major theaters, Smith and Johnston. The war, if it was to be won at all by southern arms, would have to be won on southern ground.

Third and last of these choices, the securing of foreign recognition and assistance, had long been the cherished hope of Confederate statesmen: especially Davis, who had uttered scarcely a public word through the first twenty months of the war that did not look toward intervention by one or another of the European powers. However, as time wore on and it became clearer that nothing was going to come of such efforts and expectations — Russia had been pro-Union from the start, and France, whatever her true desires might be, could not act without England, where the Liberals in power took their cue from voters who were predominantly anti-slavery and therefore, in accordance with Lincoln's persuasions, anti-Confederate — the southern President, smarting under the snubs his unacknowledged envoys suffered, grew increasingly petulant and less guarded in his reaction. Fifteen months ago, addressing his home-state legislature on the first of his western journeys to revive confidence and bolster morale, he lost patience for the first time in public. "'Put not your trust in princes,'" he advised, "and rest not your hopes on foreign nations. This war is ours; we must fight it out ourselves." The applause this drew, plus the growing conviction that nothing any Confederate said or did had any effect whatever on the outcome in Europe, encouraged further remarks along this line. Nor was his reaction limited to remarks. In June of 1863, with Lee on the march for Gettysburg and Vicksburg soon to fall, the exequatur of the British consul at Richmond was revoked. The presence of such consuls had long been irksome, not only because they sought to interfere in such matters as the conscription of British nationals and the collection of British debts, but also because they were accredited to a foreign power, the United States, rather than to the country in which they operated, the Confederate States, whose very existence their government denied except as a "belligerent." The strain increased. In August, James M. Mason, the still unreceived

★

ambassador to England, was told to consider his mission at an end, and before the following month was out he gave up his London residence and removed the diplomatic archives to Paris. In October the final strings were cut. Declaring their continued presence at Charleston, Savannah, and Mobile "an unwarranted assumption of jurisdiction," as well as "an offensive encroachment," Davis expelled all British consular agents from the South.

In Paris, Mason found the position of his fellow ambassador, John Slidell, highly enviable at first glance. Fluent in New Orleans French, the urbane Louisianian had practically free — though, alas, unofficial — access to Napoleon and Eugénie, both of whom were sympathetic to his cause; or so they kept assuring him, although nothing tangible in the way of help had so far proceeded from their concern. In many ways, the situation in Paris was more frustrating than the one in London, where Mason's non-reception at least had not built up hopes that came to nothing every time. By now, as a result of such recurrent disappointments, Slidell had become convinced that he was being led along for some purpose he could not fathom, but which he suspected would be of little benefit, in the end, either to him personally or to the government he represented. Disenchanted with the postcard Emperor, he was turning bitter in his attitude toward his job. "I find it very difficult to keep my temper amidst all this double dealing," he informed his friend and chief, Secretary of State Judah P. Benjamin. In point of fact, his experiences at court seemed to have jaundiced him entirely, for he added, by way of general observation: "This is a rascally world, and it is most hard to say who can be trusted."

What it came down to, in the end as in the beginning, whether Slidell was right or wrong about Napoleon and his motives, was that France could not act without England. And now, as the war moved into its fourth critical spring, Davis could not resist lodging a protest which, in effect, burned the last bridge that might have led to a rapprochement with that all-important power. The trouble stemmed from British acceptance of evidence supplied by U.S. Ambassador Charles Francis Adams that certain warships under construction by the Lairds of Liverpool, ostensibly for the Viceroy of Egypt, were in fact to be sold to the Confederacy, which intended to use

Charles Francis Adams (above) served as U.S. Minister to England in Lincoln's administration.

these powerful steam rams to shatter the Union blockade. "It would be superfluous in me to point out to your lordship that this is war," Adams informed Foreign Secretary Lord John Russell. It was indeed superfluous, since Russell, already alarmed by Seward's tail-twisting threats along that line, had previously taken steps to prevent delivery of the vessels by detaining them. That was in September, six months ago, and as if this was not enough to placate Seward there arrived in Richmond on April 1 — not through regular diplomatic channels, but by special courier under a flag of truce, as between belligerents — a message for Jefferson Davis from Lord Richard Lyons, the British minister in Washington, containing an extract from a dispatch lately sent by Russell protesting "against the efforts of the authorities of the so-called Confederate States to build war vessels within Her Majesty's dominions to be employed against the Government of the United States."

Jeff Davis was angered by the British position on neutrality, reported by Lord Richard Lyons (above).

Davis bristled. Hard as this governmental decision was to take — for the matter was still in litigation in the British courts, and he hoped for a favorable outcome there — the phrase "so-called" cut deeper, adding insult to injury as it did. Never one to accept a slight, let alone a snub, the Mississippian summoned his secretary and dictated a third-person reply. "The President desires me to say to your Lordship, that . . . it would be inconsistent with the dignity of the position he fills, as Chief Magistrate of a nation comprising a population of more than twelve millions, occupying a territory many times larger than the United Kingdom . . . to allow the attempt of Earl Russell to ignore the actual existence of the Confederate States, and to contumeliously style them 'so-called,' to pass without a protest and a remonstrance. The President, therefore, does protest and remonstrate against this studied insult, and he instructs me to say that in future any document in which it may be repeated will be returned unanswered and unnoticed." Lyons had not used diplomatic channels for delivery of his message; Davis, stung in his national pride, did not use diplomacy at all in his response. Warming as he dictated, he termed British neutrality "a cover for treacherous, malignant hostility," and closed with an icy pretense of indifference. "As for the specious arguments on the subject of the rams . . . while those questions are still before the highest legal tribune of the kingdom . . . the

President himself will not condescend to notice them." The signature read, "Burton N. Harrison, Private Secretary."

Such satisfaction as Davis got from thus berating the Foreign Secretary for his government's "persistent persecution of the Confederate States at the beck and bidding of officers of the United States" was small recompense for the knowledge that the South, engaged in what its people liked to think of as the Second American Revolution, would have no help from Europe in its struggle for independence. And what made this especially bitter to accept was a general historical agreement that in the original Revolution, with the Colonists in much the same position the Confederates were in now — unable, on the face of it, either to enforce or to negotiate a peace — such help had made the difference between victory and defeat. "This war is ours; we must fight it out ourselves," Davis had warned, by way of prelude to a year of hard reverses, and though the words were bravely spoken and loudly applauded at the time, there was sadness in the afterthought of what they meant in terms of the lengthening odds against success or even survival. Militarily, the handwriting on the wall was all too clear. In late November, within five months of the staggering midsummer news from Gettysburg and Vicksburg that Lee's army had been crippled and Pemberton's abolished, Bragg's army was flung bodily off Lookout Mountain and Missionary Ridge, impregnable though both positions had been said to be, and harried southward into Georgia. With these defeats in mind, it was no wonder that every Sunday at Saint Paul's in Richmond — the obvious goal of the huge offensive the North was about to launch as a follow-up of its triumphs, east and west, over the three main armies on which the Confederacy had depended for existence — the congregation recited the Litany with special fervor when it reached the words, "From battle and murder, and from sudden death, good Lord, deliver us."

The good Lord might, at that. For though military logic showed that the South could not win an offensive war, fought beyond the Potomac or the Ohio, there was still a chance that it could win a defensive one, fought on its own territory. It could win, in short, because the North could lose. In his letter to Vance, defining the conditions for peace under "the sole terms to which you or I could listen," Davis had not simply declared that the enemy must be beaten, period. He had said that the enemy must be "beaten out of his vain confidence in our subjugation," which was quite another thing. What he was saying was that for the North, committed by necessity to achieving an unconditional surrender, to settle for anything less than total conquest would amount to giving the South the victory by default. Lincoln knew this as well as Davis did, of course, and was not likely to coöperate in the dismemberment he had pledged himself to prevent. Yet the whole say-so would not be Lincoln's. Beyond the looming figure of the northern leader were the northern soldiers, and behind them were the northern people. If either became discouraged enough, soldiers or civilians, the war would end on terms not only acceptable but welcome to the South. The problem was how to get at them, beyond the loom of their leader, in order to influence their outlook and their choice. Davis saw cause for hope in both directions — tactical on one hand, political on the other — if certain requirements could be met.

Paradoxically, the tactical hope resulted from past Confederate defeats. Davis saw in every loss of mere territory — Nashville and Middle Tennessee, New Orleans, even Vicksburg and the Mississippi and the amputation of all that lay beyond — a corresponding gain, not only because what had been lost no longer required a dispersal of the country's limited strength for its protection, but also because the resultant contraction allowed a more compact defense of what remained. What remained now was the heartland, an 800-mile-wide triangle roughly defined by lines connecting Richmond, Savannah, and Mobile. Agriculturally and industrially, as well as geographically, this was the irreducible hard core of the nation, containing within it the resources and facilities to support a war of infinite length and intensity, so long as it and its people's will to fight remained intact. How long that would have to be, not in theory but in fact, depended on the validity of the companion political hope, according to which it would only be until November — specifically, the first Tuesday after the first Monday in that month — or, at worst, until early the following March — specifically, Inauguration Day. For this was a presidential election year in the North. The northern people, restrained by an iron hand these past three years, would finally have the chance to speak their minds on the question of war or peace, and the southern leader did not doubt that if his tactical hope was fulfilled — if no great Union victory, worth the agony to the army and the sorrow on the home front, was scored within that eight-month span by the blue drive on the heartland — his political hope would be fulfilled in turn. Weary of profitless bloodshed, the northern people would vote to end the war by turning Lincoln out of office and replacing him with a man who preferred to see half the nation depart in peace, as the saying went, rather than to continue the aimless destruction the two halves would have been visiting on each other for nearly three years. That was the prospect Davis had referred to, four months ago, when he declared in his State of the Nation address, opening the fourth session of Congress: "We now know that the only reliable hope for peace is in the vigor of our resistance, while the cessation of hostility [on the part of our adversaries] is only to be expected from the pressure of their necessities."

In brief, the problem between now and November was how to add to the North's war weariness, already believed to be substantial in certain regions where Copperheads were rampant, without at the same time increasing the South's disconsolation beyond the point of no return. This might or might not be possible, in light of the long odds, but in any case the prerequisite was that the northern people were to be denied the tonic of a large-scale victory within the triangular confines of the secessionist heartland — especially a tonic of the spirit-lifting kind that had come with the celebration of such victories as Vicksburg and Missionary Ridge, which had seemed to show beyond denial that a blue army could rout or capture a gray one as the result of a confrontation wherein Federal generalship was up to the standard set by the Confederates in the first two years of the war. Moreover, the general who had designed and directed both of those triumphs was now in over-all command of the Union forces, presumably chafing for the mud truce to end so he could get his armies headed south. Given the conditions that obtained in regard to numbers and equipment, plus the lightweight boxer's need for yielding ground in order to stay free to bob and weave and thus avoid a slugging match with his heavyweight opponent, there were bound to be southern losses and northern gains in the months immediately ahead; but that was not in itself a ruinous concession by the South, provided the losses and gains could be kept respectively minor and high-priced. In fact, such losses would serve admirably to drive home to the North the point that the prize was by no means worth the effort. The object was to make each gain so costly in blood and tears that the expense would be clearly disproportionate to the profit — if not in the judgment of the Federal

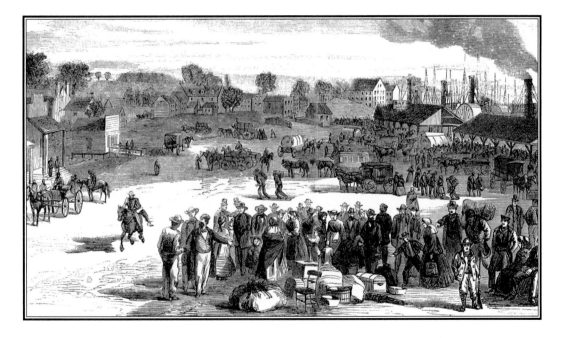

*R*ichmond, shown here, along with Mobile
and Savannah were the three points that defined
the triangular Confederate heartland.

Jefferson Davis pinned his hopes for the Confederacy on the election of 1864 in which Lincoln was opposed by men who preferred negotiation to continued warfare.

high command, whose political or professional survival depended on continuing the conflict, then at any rate in the minds of those who would be casting their ballots in November, many of whom had an intensely personal interest in the casualty lists, future as well as past, and who might therefore be persuaded that their survival, unlike their leaders', depended on bringing the conflict to a close. Thus the South would be waging war not only on its own terrain (an advantage from which it had profited largely in the past) but also in the minds of northern voters who would be going to the polls, under what Davis termed "the pressure of their necessities" some seven months from now, to register a decision as to whether sustaining Lincoln's resolution that the rebels not be allowed to depart in peace was worth the continuing loss of their blue-clad sons and brothers and nephews and grandsons down in Georgia and Virginia.

★ ★ ★ **T**ime and time alone would provide the answer to the question of survival; Patrick Henry's "liberty or death" applied quite literally to Confederate hopes and fears, which had between them no middle ground a man could stand on, patriot or traitor. Give or take a week or two, depending on the weather, the six months that would follow the end of large-scale inactivity in Georgia and Virginia, where the major forces lay mud-bound in their camps, would decide the issue, since Lincoln's appeal on that all-important Tuesday in November was likely to be in ratio to the progress of his soldiers in the field. Meantime, though, while the outsized armies on both sides took their ease and prepared as best they could for the shock to come, lesser forces had not been idle, east or west. And for the most part, when the military balance sheet was struck, the result of these out-of-season confrontations was encouraging to the hopes of the South for continuing its resistance to the superior weight the North could bring to bear.

Of these several upbeat Confederate successes — for though it was by far the most remote (Shreveport and Richmond were a thousand air-line miles apart; communication between them was necessarily slow and at best uncertain) it was not only the largest in numbers engaged, it was also achieved against the longest odds — the most encouraging was Kirby Smith's frustration of the double-pronged offensive designed by the Federals for completion of their conquest of the Transmississippi. All through the last half of March and the first half of April, the news from Louisiana and Arkansas had been gloomy; Banks and Steele appeared unstoppable in their respective penetrations, across the width and down the length of those two states, with Texas obviously next on the inexorable blue list. Then came word of Mansfield and Pleasant Hill, of Prairie d'Ane and Poison Spring; Steele and Banks were in full retreat from Price and Taylor, and Porter's dreaded ironclads were in flight from probable capture or destruction, bumping their bottoms as they scurried down the Red. It was incredible, and Camden and Jenkins Ferry, like Mansura and Yellow Bayou, only added to the glory and the uplift when news of them reached Richmond across those thousand embattled air-line miles. Other successes had preceded this, and others were to follow. Down in Florida, for example, an all-out Union effort to return that scantly defended state to its old allegiance, in accordance with Lincoln's recent proclamation, had been thrown into sudden reverse by Brigadier General Joseph Finegan's decisive late-February victory at Olustee, which drove the disarrayed invaders all the way back to the banks of the Saint Johns River. About the same time, westward in Mississippi, Sherman was slogging practically unopposed from Vicksburg to Meridian, where he was to be joined by a heavy cavalry column from Memphis for a hundred-mile extension of the march to Selma, a major industrial center whose destruction would do much to weaken the South's ability to sustain its armies in the field. This went by the board, however, when he learned that no cavalry column was any longer moving toward him; Nathan Bedford Forrest, lately promoted to major general with authority to raise a cavalry force of his own in the region the blue troopers would traverse, had whipped them soundly at Okolona, despite their two-to-one numerical advantage, and sent them staggering back to Memphis, part afoot and the rest on mounts so winded that two thirds of them were presently judged unfit for service. Sherman, left marking time, had to be content with wrecking what he held. "Meridian, with its depots, storehouses, arsenals, hospitals, offices, hotels, and cantonments, no longer exists," he reported as his wreckers, having done their worst, fell in for the march back to Vicksburg. But Selma still existed, together with all that Sherman listed and still more — including its vital cannon foundry, which, thanks to Forrest and his green command, continued to forge the heavy-caliber guns that would tear the ranks of other columns of invasion in other quarters of the South. Similarly the following week, as March came in, a raid by 3500 horsemen under Brigadier General Judson Kilpatrick, intended to achieve the liberation of an equal number of prisoners held in Richmond, was turned back at the city limits by old men and boys, home guardsmen serving worn-out artillery pieces long since replaced by new ones, captured or manufactured, in the batteries with Lee on the Rapidan. Soon regular graybacks arrived from there, overtaking the raiders who had slipped past them two nights ago, and harried the survivors into the Union lines, well down the York-James peninsula. Like March itself, Kilpatrick (called "Kill Cavalry" now) had come in like a lion and gone out like a lamb, and Richmonders were proud of their scratch resistance in the emergency that prevailed until the regulars came up.

Olustee and Okolona, like the improvised action that marked the limit of Kilpatrick's penetration, were primarily defensive victories, counterpunches landed solidly in response to Federal leads. But now, between mid-March and mid-April, there followed two exploits that were even more encouraging to Confederate hopes, though admittedly on a limited scale, because they proved that the South could still defy the lengthening odds by mounting and being successful in offensive operations. One was eastern, necessarily amphibious since it occurred in the region giving down upon the North Carolina sounds, while the other was western, staged throughout the length of the critical geographical corridor that lay between the Tennessee River and the Mississippi and extended all the way north to Kentucky's upper border, the Ohio, whose waters no uniformed Confederate had gazed upon since John Morgan's troopers crossed it, ten months ago, on the ill-fated raid from which the colorful brigadier himself had returned only by breaking out of prison.

Forrest, in command of what he called "the Cavalry Department of West Tennessee and North Mississippi," had never stopped thinking of this river-bound, 100-mile-wide, 200-mile-long stretch of land as belonging to him, particularly as a recruiting area, although all of it lay well beyond the Union lines and had done so in fact for nearly two years now. For him, as for most of his men — North Mississippians, West Tennesseans, and Kentuckians — the region was home, and he and they looked forward to returning there, if only on a visit. Indeed, he had already done so twice since it passed into northern hands, once at the beginning and once at the end of the year just past, and now he was going back for the third time. Accordingly, after disposing of Sherman's troopers by chasing them pell-mell into Memphis, he reorganized his own, grown to a strength of about 5000 and seasoned by their recent victory, into

Judson Kilpatrick (fourth from left), known as "Kill Cavalry," and his staff pose for a photograph after their 3500-man raid on Richmond in March 1864.

two divisions, commanded by Brigadier Generals Abraham Buford and James R. Chalmers, and set out northward with one of them — Buford's — on March 15 from his headquarters at Columbus, Mississippi. There were, he said, some 3000 recruits still available in West Tennessee, and he intended to have them, along with much else that was there in the way of horses and equipment which now were U.S. Army property.

The alarm went out at once to Federal garrisons in all three states bordering the Mississippi south of the Ohio; Forrest was much feared, his unorthodox methods and slashing attacks, often delivered in utter disregard of the odds and the tactics manuals, having led one blue opponent to protest that he was "constantly doing the unexpected at all times and places." Nor did all the complaints have their origin beyond the enemy lines. Some Southerners had their objections, too, although these were primarily social. A former Memphis alderman and planter, a self-made millionaire before the war, the forty-two-year-old Forrest had not only been "in trade"; the trade had been in slaves. And though some Southerners might fight for the peculiar institution, or send

★

their sons to fight for its preservation, they would not willingly associate with others who made, or once had made, a living from it. "The dog's dead," a young Mississippi aristocrat wrote in his diary this winter. "Finally we are under N. Bedford Forrest. . . . I must express my distaste to being commanded by a man having no pretension to gentility — a negro trader, gambler — an ambitious man, careless of the lives of his men so long as preferment be *en prospectu*. Forrest may be, and no doubt is, the best cavalry officer in the West, but I object to a tyrannical, hot-headed vulgarian's commanding me."

In Jackson, Tennessee, on March 20 — presumably with the disgruntled young grandee in tow — Forrest sent word for Chalmers to take up the march, feinting at Memphis en route to add to the confusion in his rear, and detached a regiment to move against Union City, up in the northwest corner of the state. This was the 7th Tennessee Cavalry, Confederate, and by coincidence the town was garrisoned by the 7th Tennessee Cavalry, Union, whose surrender

> *"If you surrender you shall be treated as prisoners of war, but if I have to storm your works you may expect no quarter."*
>
> — Nathan Bedford Forrest

was accomplished in short order four days later, March 24, by a pretense of overwhelming strength, including the use of wheeled logs in place of guns (actually, there were fewer troops outside than there were inside, while the outer 7th had no guns at all) and a blood-curdling note, sent forward under a flag of truce, which ended: "If you persist in defense, you must take the consequences. N. B. Forrest, Major General, Commanding." The Union colonel decided not to persist. Instead he surrendered his 481 men, together with 300 horses and a quantity of arms and stores — all, as the colonel who had signed the general's name declared, "almost without the loss of blood or the smell of powder." Sending his prisoners south, where Chalmers was bristling as if on the verge of clattering into Memphis, he rode hard to catch up with the main column, which Forrest had led northward through Trenton two days ago, then across the Kentucky line near Fulton, to descend on Paducah in the early afternoon of the following day, March 25, having covered the final muddy hundred miles in fifty hours.

Paducah, strategically located at the confluence of the Tennessee and the Ohio, was an important Union supply base, and it was supplies the general was after, not the garrison, which retired posthaste into a stoutly fortified earthwork supported by two gunboats patrolling the river in its rear. While sending in his usual demand for an unconditional surrender — "If you surrender you shall be treated as prisoners of war, but if I have to storm your works you may expect no quarter" — Forrest put his troopers to work on the unprotected depot, gleaning what he later reported to be "a large amount of clothing, several hundred horses, and a large lot of medical stores," along with about fifty prisoners who had not made it into the fort before the gates were shut. Inside, the blue commander declined to capitulate despite continued threats and demonstrations, including one all-out attack that was launched by a Kentucky regiment whose colonel, a native of Paducah, disobeyed restraining orders, apparently in an excess of pride and joy at being home again, and led a charge in which he and some two dozen of his men were killed or wounded. These were the only Confederate casualties, although the town itself was badly damaged by shells thrown into it from the gunboats and the fort. At midnight, having gathered up everything portable and destroyed much that was not — a government steamboat found in dry dock, for example, and a number of bales of precious cotton awaiting shipment on the landing — Forrest withdrew in the direction from which he had appeared, eight hours before. At Mayfield, a dozen miles southwest, he halted to give his captives a head start south and to furlough his three Kentucky regiments, with instructions to go to their nearby homes for a week, there to secure new clothes and mounts, at the end of which time they would reassemble at Trenton, fifty miles south of the Tennessee line. This they did, on schedule and to a man, many of them accompanied by recruits, fellow Kentuckians anxious for service under "the Wizard of the Saddle," as Forrest was beginning to be called.

He was by then in Jackson, planning another strike before he ended what was afterward referred to as his "occupation" of West Tennessee. His losses so far, including those of Chalmers, who had been skirmishing much of the time near Memphis, amounted to 15 killed and 42 wounded, as compared to Federal losses of 79 killed, 102 wounded, and 612 captured. This was a clear gain, but there was more. While planning a sudden enlargement of these figures, he did not neglect the normal intelligence-gathering duties of cavalry on the prowl. In fact, from his vantage point well within the enemy lines — even as Grant was at work on the details in Washington, Cincinnati, Culpeper, and elsewhere — Forrest not only saw through the latest Union "grand design" for the conquest of the South, he also recommended a method by which he believed it could be frustrated, if not shattered, at least in the western theater. "I am of the opinion," he wrote Joe Johnston on April 6, "that everything available is being concentrated against General Lee and yourself. Am also of opinion that if all the cavalry in this and your own department could be moved against Nashville that the enemy's communication could be broken up." What would come of this plea that he be turned loose on Sherman's life line remained to be seen. For the present, however, he had a lesser blow in mind, one that he had mentioned two days earlier in a report to Polk, whereby he intended to mount and equip his growing number of recruits: "There is a Federal force of 500 or 600 at Fort Pillow which I shall attend to in a day or two, as they have horses and supplies which we need."

Fort Pillow, established originally by the Confederates atop a bluff overlooking the Mississippi forty miles above Memphis, had been in enemy hands for nearly two years, ever since the evacuation of Corinth following Shiloh, and was garrisoned by a force of about 550. Half were Negroes, former slaves who had volunteered for service in the army that freed them in the course of its occupation of the plantations they had worked on, while the other half were Union-loyal whites; "Tennessee Tories" and "Homemade Yankees," their since-departed neighbors, many of whom now rode with Forrest, contemptuously styled the latter. This was the place and these were the men Forrest had said he

Confederate cavalry commander Nathan Bedford Forrest begged Joe Johnston for permission to strike Sherman's supply line, including this railroad bridge.

★

would "attend to," and accordingly, by way of creating a diversion, he sent Buford with one brigade to menace Columbus and ride back into Paducah, where newspapers were boasting that he had overlooked 140 fine government horses kept hidden in an old rolling mill throughout the recent raid. Buford's instructions were to get those horses and, in the process, draw the enemy's attention northward, away from Pillow, which would be attacked by his other brigade and one from Chalmers, who was told to come along and take command of both — 1500 men in all — for the march, which got under way on April 10, and the investment, which began at daylight two days later. Northward, on the Mississippi and the Ohio, Buford carried out his assignment to the letter, detaching a couple of companies to menace Columbus while he rode with the main body into Paducah at noon on April 14. There, as before, the defenders fell back to their fortified position, and the raiders gathered up the horses they had missed three weeks ago. Returning south across the Tennessee line next day, they found that Chalmers too had carried out his assignment to the letter: so zealously so, in fact, that he and his men and Forrest, who was in over-all command, were already being widely accused of having committed *the* atrocity of the war. "The Fort Pillow Massacre," it was called, then and thereafter, in the North.

Arriving at dawn of April 12 Chalmers had the fort invested by the time Forrest came up at midmorning and took over. Pillow's original trace, some two miles long and an average 600 yards in depth, had been reduced to about half that by the Confederates before their evacuation, and now the Federals had contracted it still farther into a single earthwork, 125 yards in length, perched on the lip of the bluff and surrounded on three sides by a ditch six feet deep and twelve feet wide. Parapets four feet thick at the top and eight feet tall added greatly to the sense of security when the defenders were driven in from their outer line of rifle pits, although they presently found a drawback to this massiveness which the attackers were quick to exploit. "The width or thickness of the works across the top," a rebel captain afterwards explained, "prevented the garrison from firing down on us, as it could only be done by mounting and exposing themselves to the unerring fire of our sharpshooters, posted behind stumps and logs on all the neighboring hills." Their six guns were similarly disadvantaged, since the cannoneers could not depress them enough to fire at the attackers at close range. "So far as safety was concerned," the captain summed up, "we were as well fortified as they were; the only difference was that they were on one side and we were on the other of the same fortification." In partial compensation, the Federals had a gunboat in support, which flung a total of 282 rounds of shell, shrapnel, and canister at the dodging graybacks in the course of the fight. Also, there was the reassuring thought of what half a dozen double-shotted guns could do in the way of execution if any mass of rebels tried to scale those high dirt walls and poke their heads above that flat-topped parapet.

★

Forrest was thinking of that too, of course, but he did not let it deter him any more than he did the loss of three horses shot from under him in the course of the five hours he spent maneuvering for a closer hug and waiting for the arrival of his ammunition train to refill the nearly empty cartridge boxes of his rapid-firing troopers. Shortly after 3 o'clock the train arrived, and the general sent forward under a flag of truce his usual grisly ultimatum. "Should my demand be refused," the note closed, "I cannot be responsible for the fate of your command." By way of reply, the Union commander requested "one hour for consultation with my officers and the officers of the gunboat." But Forrest by now had spotted a steamer "apparently crowded with troops" approaching, as well as "the smoke of three other boats ascending the river." Believing that the Federals were stalling for time in which to gain reinforcements and additional naval support, he replied that he would give them twenty minutes and no more; "If at the expiration of that time the fort is not surrendered, I shall assault it." Either because he considered this a bluff, or else because he believed an assault was bound to fail — his soldiers, white and black, apparently were of the same conviction, for they had been taunting the rebels gleefully and profanely from the parapets throughout the cease-fire that attended the exchange — the Union commander replied succinctly, "I will not surrender." Forrest had no sooner read the note than he turned to his bugler and had him sound the charge.

The assault was brief and furious, practically bloodless up to a point, and proceeded according to plan. While the sharpshooters back on the hillsides kept up a harassing fire that skimmed the parapet, the first wave of attackers rushed forward, leaped into the slippery six-foot ditch, and crouched in the mud at the bottom, presenting their backs to the men of the second wave, who thus were able to use them as stepping-blocks to gain the narrow ledge between the ditch and the embankment just beyond, then lean down and hoist their first-wave comrades up beside them. It was as neatly done as if it had been rehearsed for weeks, and in all this time not a shot had been fired except from the hillsides and around on the flanks, where Forrest had other marksmen at work on the gunboat. "Shoot at everything blue betwixt wind and water," he had told them: with the result that the vessel, which had closed to canister range, kept its ports tight shut to protect its gunners and took no part in attempting a repulse. By now the attackers were all on the narrow ledge, holding their unfired weapons at the ready and keeping their heads well down while the hillside snipers continued to kick dirt on the parapet, across whose width, although the graybacks were only a few feet away, flattened against the opposite side of the earthwork, no member of the garrison could fire without exposing two thirds of his body to instant perforation. At a signal, the sharpshooters held their fire and the men on the ledge went up and over the embankment, emptying their pistols and rifles into the blue mass of defenders, who fought briefly against panic, then broke rearward for a race to the

Forrest's cavalrymen storm Fort Pillow and offer no quarter to Federal defenders. More than 40 percent of the 557-man Federal garrison was killed.

landing at the foot of the bluff, where they had been told that the gunboat, in the unlikely event of a rebel breakthrough, would cover their withdrawal by pumping grape and canister into the ranks of their pursuers.

It did not work out that way, not only because the gunboat was shut up turtle-tight and took no part in the action, but also because the graybacks were too close on their heels for the naval gunners to have been able to fire without hitting their own men, even if they had tried. Flailed from the rear by heavy downhill volleys, the running bluecoats next were struck in the flanks by the troopers who had been shooting at the gunboat. Some kept going, right on into the river, where a number drowned and the swimmers became targets for marksmen on the bluff. Others, dropping their guns in terror, ran back toward the Confederates with their hands up, and of these some were spared as prisoners, while others were shot down in the act of surrender. "No quarter! No quarter!"

was being shouted at several points, and this was thought by some to be at Forrest's command, since he had predicted and even threatened that what was happening would happen. But the fact was, he had done and was doing all he could to end it, having ordered the firing stopped as soon as he saw his troopers swarm into the fort, even though its flag was still flying and a good part of the garrison was still trying to get away. He and others managed to put an end to the killing and sort out the captives, wounded and unwounded. Out of a total Federal force of 557, no less than 63 percent had been killed or wounded, and of these about two thirds — 221, or forty percent of the whole — had been killed. Forrest himself lost 14 killed and 86 wounded. Before nightfall, having seen to the burial of the dead by the survivors, he gathered up his spoils, including the six pieces of artillery, and moved off with 226 prisoners, twenty of whom were men so lightly wounded they could walk. Next morning he sent his adjutant, accompanied by a captured Union captain, back to signal another gunboat — which had resumed the shelling of the woods around the fort, unaware that there was no longer anything Confederate there to shoot at, only Federals — to put in, under a flag of truce, and take the more seriously wounded aboard for treatment downriver in Memphis. That ended the Fort Pillow operation.

But not the talk, the cultivated reaction which quickly mounted to a pitch of outraged intensity unsurpassed until "the Rape of Belgium" fifty years later, when propaganda methods were much improved by wider and faster means of disseminating "eyewitness" accounts of such "atrocities," true or false. Within six days a congressional committee — strictly speaking, a subcommittee of the feared and ruthless Joint Committee on the Conduct of the War — left Washington for Tennessee, having been appointed to gather "testimony in regard to the massacre at Fort Pillow," and within another three days was taking depositions from survivors, along with other interested parties, which resulted in a voluminous printed report that the rebels had engaged in "indiscriminate slaughter" of men, women, and children, white and black, and afterwards had not only set barracks and tents afire, roasting the wounded in their beds, but had also "buried some of the living with the dead," despite their piteous cries for mercy while dirt was being shoveled on their faces. "Many other instances of equally atrocious cruelty might be enumerated," the report concluded, "but your committee feels compelled to refrain from giving here more of the heart-sickening details." Southerners might protest that the document was "a tissue of lies from end to end," as indeed it largely was, but they could scarcely argue with the casualty figures, which indicated strongly that unnecessary killing had occurred, although it was in fact the opposite of "indiscriminate." For example, of the 262 Negro members of the garrison, only 58 — just over twenty percent — were marched away as prisoners; while of the 295 whites, 168 — just under sixty percent — were taken. The rest were either dead or in no shape for

General Ulysses S. Grant (above) urged
William T. Sherman to retaliate for the savage
murder of Federal troops at Fort Pillow.

walking. Here was discrimination with a vengeance, as well as support for a Confederate sergeant's testimony, given in a letter written home within a week of the affair, describing how "the poor, deluded negroes would run up to our men, fall upon their knees and with uplifted hands scream for mercy, but were ordered to their feet and then shot down." This was not to say that Forrest himself had not done all he could, first to prevent and then to end the unnecessary bloodshed. He had, and perhaps the strongest evidence of his forbearance came not from his friends but from his enemies of the highest rank. Within three days of the fall of the fort, when news of the "massacre" reached Washington, Lincoln told Stanton to investigate without delay "the alleged butchery of our troops." Stanton passed the word to Grant, who wired Sherman that same day: "If our men have been murdered after capture, retaliation must be resorted to promptly." Sherman undertook the investigation, as ordered, but made no such recommendation: proof in itself that none was justified, since no one doubted that otherwise, with Sherman in charge, retaliation would have been as prompt as even Grant could have desired.

As for Forrest, his mind was soon on other things, including the removal of his spoils and a stepped-up enforcement of the conscription laws throughout West Tennessee. His recruiting methods were as rigorous as they were thorough. "Sweep the country, bringing in every man between the ages of eighteen and forty-five," he told his agents. "Take no excuse, neither allow conscripts to go home for clothes or anything else; their friends can send them." Haste was required, for before he got back to Jackson, two days after Pillow fell,

---

"Sweep the country, bringing in every man between the ages of eighteen and forty-five. Take no excuse, neither allow conscripts to go home for clothes or anything else; their friends can send them."

— Nathan Bedford Forrest

---

he received a dispatch from Polk directing him to return promptly to Okolona, where his two divisions would combine with those under Major General Stephen D. Lee, Polk's chief of cavalry in the Department of Mississippi, Alabama, and East Louisiana, to meet an anticipated raid-in-force from Middle Tennessee, southward through Decatur, Alabama. Forrest replied that the order would of course be complied with, though in his opinion "no such raid will be made from Decatur or any point west of there." Events were to prove him right in this, but even if such a raid had been intended he believed that the best way to turn it back was by striking deep in its rear. He still had his eye on Sherman's life line. He wanted to hit it, and he wanted to hit it hard. This time, however, he presented his views not only to Polk and Johnston, who seemed unwilling or unable to act on them, but also to Jefferson Davis, addressing him directly. Stephen Lee had about 7000 cavalry, and he himself was approaching that strength by now. "With our forces united," he wrote Davis on April 15, "a move could be made into Middle Tennessee and Kentucky which would create a diversion of the enemy's forces and enable us to break up his plans." It was Sherman he meant — specifically, the long rail supply line reaching down from Louisville on the Ohio, through Nashville on the Cumberland, to Chattanooga on the Tennessee. That was a lot of track, and Forrest had long since shown what he could do to a railroad when he turned his troopers loose on one in earnest. Moreover, he assured the Commander in Chief lest the plan be considered an impractical hare-brained escapade like the one on which John Morgan had come to grief last summer, "such an expedition, managed with prudence and executed with rapidity, can be safely made."

★ ★ ★ *W*hatever merit there was in the proposal, for the present at least the authorities in Richmond were more interested in a project closer at hand, involving an attempt to recover the North Carolina coastal region, which got under way in earnest that same week, two days after Forrest wrote his letter. A Tarheel brigade under a native North Carolinian, Brigadier General Robert Hoke, had been detached from the Army of Northern Virginia to undertake the job in coöperation with an ironclad ram that had been under construction for the past year in a cornfield at Edwards Ferry, two thirds of the way up the Roanoke River to Weldon. General Braxton Bragg, assigned as the President's chief military adviser after his removal from command of the Army of Tennessee, had conceived the plan, secured the troops, and worked out the details, beginning with an amphibious assault on Plymouth at the point where the Roanoke flowed into Albemarle Sound. Occupied for more than two years by the Federals, who had fortified it stoutly, the town would have to be attacked by water as well as by land, since otherwise the heavy guns of the Union fleet, on station in support of the place, would drive the attackers out about as soon as they got in. Bragg had much confidence in Hoke, who was given large discretion after a detailed briefing on this opening phase of the campaign — a veteran, though not yet twenty-seven, he had fought with distinction in all the major eastern engagements from Big Bethel through Chancellorsville, where he was severely wounded — as well as in the ironclad successor to the *Virginia* and the *Arkansas,* both of glorious memory.

Christened *Albemarle,* she was launched from the riverside cornfield in which she had been built, mostly by local carpenters and blacksmiths, and set off downstream on the day she was commissioned, April 17, en route to her maiden engagement. Sheathed in two layers of two-inch iron and mounting a pair of 64-inch Brooke rifles pivoted fore and aft to fire through alternate portholes, she was just over 150 feet in length, 34 feet in the beam, and drew 9 feet of water. Because of the numerous twists and turns in the river this far up — which, incidentally, had served to protect her from interference by Federal gunboats during her construction — she set out stern-foremost, dragging a heavy chain from her bow to steer by. Fitters were still at work on her armor and machinery, and portable forges were brought along for emergency repairs. They soon were needed, first when the main driveshaft wrenched loose from its coupling, late that night, and next when the rudderhead broke off, early the following morning. Three miles from Plymouth the second night, and ten hours behind schedule because of time-out for repairs, she was stopped by reports that the river ahead was obstructed by hulks which the enemy, hearing rumors that the *Albemarle* was approaching completion, had sunk in the channel to tear out her bottom in case she ventured down. Aboard as a volunteer aide to her skipper, Commander James W. Cooke — another Tarheel and a veteran of more than thirty years in the old navy — was her builder, Gilbert Elliott, a native of nearby Elizabeth City, where he had learned his craft in his grandfather's shipyard. Elliott set out in the darkness in a small boat with a pilot and two men, taking a long pole for soundings, and presently returned to report that, thanks to the unusually high stage of the river this spring, "it was practicable to pass the obstructions provided the boat was kept in the middle of the stream."

Cooke by then had turned the ram around and cleared for action. He had no contact with Hoke ashore, but on being informed that a sporadic attack had been in progress against Plymouth most of the day and up until 9 o'clock that night, when the skirmishers withdrew — presumably because of the nonarrival of the *Albemarle*, without whose help the town could not be held under the frown of a quartet of gunboats just inside the mouth of the river — he weighed anchor and stood down to engage. It was close to 4 o'clock in the morning, April 19, when he passed safely over the sunken hulks, taking a few harmless heavy-caliber shots from the fort as he went by, and came in sight of the four Union warships. Warned of his approach, they were prepared to receive him. The two largest, *Miami* and *Southfield* — big, double-ended sidewheel steamers of a novel design, with rudders fore and aft for quick reversals — were lashed together, but not too tightly, in accordance with a plan to catch the *Albemarle* between them, thus making her useless as a ram, while they tossed explosives down her stack. Cooke avoided this by steering close to the south bank, then turning hard aport as he drew nearly abreast of the shackled gunboats, presenting his long, tapered bow to the nearer of the two. Both opened on him with solids at close range, bringing as many of their dozen guns into play as could be brought to bear, but with no more effect than if the shots had been tennis balls, except that they left spoon-shaped dents in the armor when they bounced. Closing fast, with the force of the current added to her thrust, the ironclad put her snout ten feet into *Southfield*'s flank, penetrating all the way to her fireroom, but then had trouble withdrawing it from so deep a wound. The two hung joined, the ram taking water into her forward port because of the weight of the rapidly sinking gunboat: seeing which, the captain of the *Miami* ran to one of his 9-inch Dahlgrens, depressed it quickly, and fired three explosive shells point-blank at the

James W. Cooke, commander of the ram Albemarle, was victorious in engagements with two Federal gunboats, the Miami and the Southfield, on the Roanoke River.

rebel monster. All three shattered against the iron casement, a scant twenty feet away. Pieces of the third, which was fired with a short fuze, flew back from the target and knocked down most of the gun crew, including the captain, who lay dead with the jagged fragments stuck deep in his chest and face.

Albemarle's captain was backing his engines hard to free the ram of the weight on her bow, but by the time he managed to do so, the *Miami* — called the "Miasma" by her crew, who had found duty aboard her boring up to now — cut loose from the sinking *Southfield* and ran with all her speed for open water. Followed out into Albemarle Sound by the other two gunboats, which had observed the action at long range, she wanted no more of a fight with an adversary impervious to shot and shell alike. Cooke attempted a brief pursuit, then broke off when he saw that it was fruitless, mainly because his engines were getting almost no draft through his badly shot-up smokestack, and turned back to give his full attention to the fort. Now it was the Federals' turn to learn what it was like to try to hold the place while under attack from the river as well as the land.

They found it hard indeed. Delaying only long enough to patch up his riddled stack and get in touch with the Confederates ashore, Cooke steamed back past Plymouth that afternoon and opened on the fort in conjunction with Hoke, whose batteries were skillfully disposed for converging fire and whose infantry returned to within small-arms range of the Federal ramparts. The result was altogether harrowing for the defenders, caught thus as it were between the devil and the deep blue sea, the landward attackers and the *Albemarle*, both of which kept up the pressure until well after sunset and resumed it at daylight with even greater fury. "This terrible fire had to be endured without reply, as no man could live at the guns," the fort's commander was to report. "The

★

breast-height was struck by solid shot on every side, fragments of shell sought almost every interior angle of the work, the whole extent of the parapet was swept by musketry, and men were killed and wounded even on the banquette slope. . . . This condition of affairs could not be long endured without a reckless sacrifice of life; no relief could be expected, and in compliance with the earnest desire of every officer I consented to hoist a white flag, and at 10 a.m. of April 20 I had the mortification of surrendering my post to the enemy with all it contained." This included 2834 soldiers, thirty guns, and a large haul of supplies, all secured at a cost to the attackers of less than 300 casualties, only one of whom

Crewmen abandon the Southfield after the Albemarle rammed the Federal warship on the Roanoke River during an amphibious strike on Plymouth, North Carolina.

was naval, a seaman hit by a pistol ball while the *Albemarle* had her snout in the sinking *Southfield*. "Heaven has crowned our efforts with success," a presidential aide-observer wired Davis, who replied directly to Hoke: "Accept my thanks and congratulations for the brilliant success which has attended your attack and capture of Plymouth. You are promoted to be a major general from that date."

Young Hoke was the hero of the hour, together with Cooke and the *Albemarle*, all down the eastern seaboard, and Bragg — though his basic planning went unnoticed amid the general praise for Hoke and Cooke — was hard at work, now that the ram had reversed the naval advantage, projecting exploits of a similar nature for the immediate future.

It was this the Federals feared. Unable to get an ironclad through any of the shallow inlets into Pamlico Sound, and with no time left in which to build one there, they saw no way to stop the apparently invulnerable, new-hatched monster before it returned the whole region to Confederate control. "The ram

will probably come down to Roanoke Island, Washington, and New Bern," the district commander, Major General John J. Peck, informed his department chief, Ben Butler, on the day Plymouth fell. "Unless we are immediately and heavily reinforced, both by the army and navy, North Carolina is inevitably lost." Butler shared the alarm, although belatedly. Two months earlier, when the navy had asked him to send troops up the Roanoke to destroy the rebel vessel on its stocks, he had replied: "I don't believe in the ironclad," and even now, in passing on to Halleck the news that the fort had been reduced in part by the guns of the nonexistent warship, he declined to accept a fraction of the blame, which he declared was all the navy's for having left the garrison's water flank exposed. "Perhaps this is intended as a diversion," he ended blandly. "Any instructions?"

In point of fact, New Bern was next on the *Albemarle*'s list, once she finished off the gunboats skittishly awaiting her emergence into the Sound

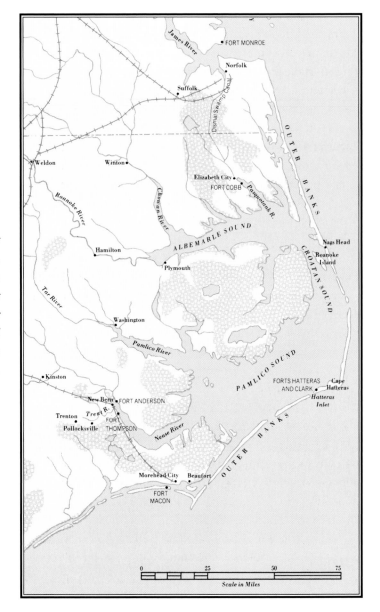

After the victorious assault on Plymouth, the Confederate ram Albemarle sailed out of the sound for which she was named toward Washington and New Bern.

from which she took her name, and Hoke was told to prepare for this, rather than for an early return to the Army of Northern Virginia, despite that army's commander's pleas that he and his brigade were needed to help meet the attack that was soon to be launched across the Rapidan. Whatever disappointment this might involve for Lee, outnumbered two to one by the bluecoats on the north side of the river, Plymouth made a fine addition to the list of late winter and early spring victories which the President was compiling for inclusion in the message he was preparing for delivery to Congress when it convened next week in Richmond.

★

"Recent events of the war are highly creditable to our troops," he wrote, "exhibiting energy and vigilance combined with the habitual gallantry which they have taught us to expect on all occasions. We have been cheered by important and valuable successes in Florida, northern Mississippi, western Tennessee and Kentucky, western Louisiana, and eastern North Carolina, reflecting the highest honor on the skill and conduct of our commanders and on the incomparable soldiers whom it is their privilege to lead. . . . The armies in northern Georgia and in northern Virginia," he added, by way of compensation for the fact that there had been no such recent, gloom-dispelling triumphs in either of those regions, "still oppose with unshaken front a formidable barrier to the progress of the invader, and our generals, armies, and people are animated by cheerful confidence."

★ ★ ★ *S*o he would say, and so Congress would be pleased to hear. But there were things he left unmentioned because to air them — involving, as they did, plans untried and expectations unfulfilled — would serve to deepen, rather than relieve, the nation's gloom regarding one of the two main armies on which it depended for survival. Davis's disappointment was not in Lee, who was fairly immobilized by the fact that a solid third of the Army of Northern Virginia had been detached for the past seven months; it was in Johnston, who had been given command of the Army of Tennessee with the understanding, at least on the part of the Richmond authorities, that he would go over to the offensive in an attempt to recover East and Middle Tennessee, lost by his predecessor in the course of the bloody, erratic, year-long retreat from Murfreesboro to Dalton. "You are desired to have all things in readiness at the earliest practicable moment for the movement indicated," the transplanted Virginian was reminded in early March. "The season is at hand and the time seems propitious."

Plans for such an offensive were quite explicit. Union forces now preparing at Chattanooga and Knoxville for a spring advance were dependent on uninterrupted communication with Nashville; if this supply line could be severed, both would be obliged to abandon what they held, with much attendant disruption of their plans. In line with this, Richmond's proposal was that Johnston be reinforced by Polk for a shift northeast to Kingston, forty miles west of Knoxville, where he would be joined by two divisions under Lieutenant General James Longstreet, detached from Lee and wintering near Greeneville, for an advance across the Tennessee River with a combined strength of more than 70,000 men. By such a move, the authorities assured him, "Knoxville [would be] isolated and Chattanooga threatened, with barely a possibility for the enemy to unite. Should he not then offer you battle outside of his entrenched lines, a rapid move across the mountains from Kingston to Sparta (a very practicable and easy route) would place you with a formidable army in a country full of resources, where it is supposed, with a good supply of ammunition, you may be entirely self-sustaining, and it is confidently believed that such a move would necessitate the withdrawal of the enemy to the line of the Cumberland." Bragg was the author of these suggestions, and he wrote from experience. In essence, they called for a repetition of the movement he himself had made soon after he assumed command of the army in the summer of 1862, whereby the western seat of war was shifted, practically overnight and practically without bloodshed, from Mississippi to North Georgia and from there all the way north to Kentucky. The Federals then had been obliged to give up, at least for a season, their designs on Chattanooga, and Bragg was of the opinion that if Johnston would only profit by his example the same results could be obtained in regard to their designs on Atlanta — provided, of course, that he advanced before his adversaries did. "To accomplish this," he was re-reminded in mid-March, "it is proposed that you move as soon as your means and force can be collected."

Johnston had many objections to the plan. Time had probably run out; he lacked supplies, as well as the mules and wagons needed to haul them; the Federals, in greatly superior numbers, would combine and jump him as soon as he got started, obliging him to fight at a disadvantage and with nothing to do, in case of defeat, but scatter his troops in the mountains. What he preferred, he told Bragg on March 18, was to stand where he was, letting the bluecoats crack their skulls against his works, then follow them up when they retreated. Meantime, he urged, the proffered reinforcements under Longstreet should be sent to him at Dalton for a share in the defensive battle, rather than have them wait in idleness to join him on the march. Bragg's reply, three days later, was curt and stiff: "Your dispatch . . . does not indicate an acceptance of the plan proposed. The troops can only be drawn from other points for an advance. Upon your decision of that point further action must depend." Alarmed at this evidence that he would not be reinforced on his own terms, Johnston was quick to assert that he had been misunderstood. "I expressly accept taking offensive," he wired back. "Only differ with you as to details. I assume that the enemy will be prepared for an advance before we are and will make it to our advantage. Therefore, I propose as necessary both for offensive and defensive to assemble our troops here immediately. Other preparations for advance are going on."

For two weeks there was no reply to this. The answer, when it came on April 7, was in a dispatch addressed not to Johnston but to Longstreet, who was told to prepare his two divisions for an immediate return to Virginia. Johnston was depressed by this lack of confidence, and outraged by reports that he had declined to move against the enemy. "I learn that it is given out," he wrote to a senator friend whose son was on his staff, "that it has been proposed to me to take the offensive with a large army & that I refused. Don't believe any such story." Besides,

*R*iverboats lie moored along the Tennessee River
after bringing supplies to Chattanooga. The Federals
were stockpiling matériel for a drive into Georgia.

he said, after outlining his objections to the plan he had rejected, Lee's army, not his, was the one that should have been ordered to advance. "It would have been much easier to take the offensive (excuse such frequent use of that expression) in Va. than here," he wrote, basing his statement on the erroneous double claim that Lee's army was not only larger than his but also had a smaller blue army to its front. However, he was not greatly surprised at the way things had gone. The authorities in Richmond — Davis himself, Secretary of War James A. Seddon, and now Bragg, his erstwhile friend — had about as low an opinion of him, apparently, as he had of them; which was low indeed. His consolation was in his men. "If this army thought of me and felt toward me as some of our high civil functionaries do," he closed his letter, "it would be necessary for me to leave the military service. But thank heaven, it is my true friend."

It was true the army was his friend; no general on either side, not even R. E. Lee or George McClellan, had more affection from the soldiers he commanded. "He was loved, respected, admired; yea, almost worshipped by his troops," a Tennessee veteran was to say. Richmond had taken this quality into account in sending him to Dalton to repair the shattered morale of an army which had recently been thrown off Missionary Ridge and chased southward into Georgia by the opponent it faced there now. And in this he had succeeded. "He restored the soldier's pride; he brought the manhood back to the private's

★

bosom," the same veteran declared. The drawback, according to those who had advised against his appointment, was that he was too defensive-minded for the tactical part of his assignment. He had only assumed the offensive once in the whole course of the war, and that had been at Seven Pines, which might well seem to him the exception that proved the unwisdom of attacking, since all it had got him was the wound that had cost him the command he most preferred, now held by Lee, and a subsequent transfer to the less congenial West. Those who had opposed his appointment in December, on grounds that he would never go forward as intended, were quick to point out now in April that their prediction had been fulfilled. In fact, they said, if he continued to follow his accustomed pattern of behavior, he would be likely to fall back from Dalton at the first bristly gesture by the Federals in his front. Davis and Seddon, who had favored his appointment — primarily, it was true, because no one could think of another candidate for the job — were obliged to admit the strength of this, as evidence

They had given up on Johnston, who would neither go forward nor refuse to go forward, and who they knew from past experience . . . would wind up doing exactly as he pleased in any case.

of what to expect, and so was Bragg after his exchanges with the general, by letter and wire, throughout the latter part of February and the first two thirds of March. It was then, on the heels of this admission by Davis and Seddon and Bragg, that the summons went to Longstreet for a quick return to Lee. They had given up on Johnston, who would neither go forward nor refuse to go forward, and who they knew from past experience (in northern Virginia, down on the York-James peninsula, outside beleaguered Vicksburg, and back in the piny woods of Mississippi) would wind up doing exactly as he pleased in any case. He always had. He always would. The only decision left was whether to keep him — and the fact was, they had no one to put in his place. So they kept him. And in keeping him, however regretfully, they committed the Army of Tennessee to the defensive and gave up all hope for a slash at the Union center as a means of disrupting at the outset the latest Grand Design for their subjugation.

Lee was committed to the defensive, too, though not by inclination or from choice. "At present my hands are tied," he confessed in a mid-April letter to Bragg. "If I was able to move . . . the enemy might be driven from the Rappahannock and obliged to look to the safety of his own capital instead of the assault upon ours." As it was, he added, writing from the stripped region about Orange where his infantry was camped, "I cannot even draw to me the cavalry or artillery of the army, and the season has arrived when I may be attacked any day."

It was a question of subsistence for mounts and men. Scarcely a tree in the district wore its bark below the point to which a horse could lift its mouth, and few of the few animals on hand were fit for rigorous service; "Fully one half of them were incapable of getting up a gallop," a cavalry officer complained, "a trembling trot being their fastest gait." Conditions were nearly as bad for the leaned-down soldiers. Though Davis himself had managed to get hold of 90,000 pounds of meat for shipment to the Rapidan during a critical, near-starvation period that winter, this did not go far with troops whose usual daily ration comprised four ounces of bacon or salt pork, often rancid, and a scant pint of rough-ground corn meal. Sprouting grass was a help to the horses this rainy April, but hunger was still a condition of existence for the men. This pained Lee, who did not like to add to other people's troubles by recounting his own, into making a formal complaint to the President, coupled with the strongest warning he had given at any time in the twenty-two months since he assumed command: "My anxiety on the subject of provisions for the army is so great that I cannot refrain from expressing it to Your Excellency. I cannot see how we can operate with our present supplies. Any derangement in their arrival or disaster to the railroad would render it impossible for me to keep the army together, and might force a retreat into North Carolina."

That too was in mid-April — April 12 — one week after he had alerted the army to prepare for a Union crossing, any day now, of the river to its front. On that same April 5, having pored over information received from scouts, northern papers, and citizens beyond the Rapidan, he gave Davis his estimate of the situation. "The movements and reports of the enemy may be intended to mislead us, and should therefore be carefully observed," he wrote. "But all the information that reaches me goes to strengthen the belief that Genl Grant is preparing to move against Richmond." This was as far as he went at the time; he said nothing of his new opponent's probable route (or routes) or schedule. Three days later, however, he wrote of receiving two more reports from reliable scouts, in which "the general impression was that the great battle would take place on the Rapidan, and that the Federal army would advance as soon as the weather is settled." Continuing to study all the evidence he could gather — including much, of course, that was false or merely worthless — he arrived within another week at a considerably more detailed estimate, and he passed this too along to Davis, saying: "We shall have to glean troops from every quarter to oppose the apparent combination of the enemy."

He expected three attacks, all to be delivered simultaneously from three directions: 1) a main assault across the Rapidan, more or less against his front, 2) a diversionary advance up the Shenandoah Valley, off his western flank, and 3) a rear attack, up the James, to menace Richmond from the east and south. To meet this last, he proposed that General P. G. T. Beauregard be shifted from his present command at Charleston, which Lee believed was no longer on the list of Union objectives, and brought to Petersburg or Weldon to take charge of the defense of southside Richmond. The Valley threat he would leave for the time being to Major General John C. Breckinridge, who had a small command in the Department of Southwest Virginia. As for the main effort, the blue lunge across the Rapidan, he kept that as the continuing exclusive concern of the Army of Northern Virginia. Recent news that Longstreet would soon be coming back with two of his three divisions, after seven months in Georgia and Tennessee, made Lee yearn for a return to the old days and the old method of dealing with such a threat as he faced now. "If Richmond could be held secure against the attack from the east," he told the President on April 15, "I would propose that I draw Longstreet to me and move right against the enemy on the Rappahannock. Should God give us a crowning victory there, all their plans would be dissipated, and their troops now collecting on the waters of the Chesapeake would be recalled to the defense of Washington." Having said as much, however, he returned to such realities as the scarcity of food for his men and horses, then closed on a note of ominous regret: "But to make this move I must have provisions and forage. I am not yet able to call to me the cavalry or artillery. If I am obliged to retire from this line, either by a flank movement of the enemy or the want of supplies, great injury will befall us."

On April 18 he ordered all surplus baggage sent to the rear, a sort of ultimate alert well understood by the troops to mean that fighting might begin at any time. Still Grant did not move. Lee's impatience mounted during the following week — in the course of which Breckinridge was warned to brace

John C. Breckinridge's command was charged with repulsing the Federal advance up the Shenandoah Valley.

★

for action in the Valley and Beauregard, in compliance with orders from Richmond, reached Weldon to assume command of the region between the James and Cape Fear rivers — though he acknowledged that the gain was worth the strain, if only because the half-starved horses thus were allowed more time to graze in peace on the new-sprung grass. "The advance of the Army of the Potomac seems to be delayed for some reason," he wrote Davis on April 25. "It appears to be prepared for movement, but is probably waiting for its coöperative columns." He closed with an invitation for the President to visit the army, "if the enemy remains quiet and the weather favorable," by way of affording himself a diversion from the daily grind in Richmond. Davis declined, under pressure of business; Congress would convene next week, for one thing. But four days later Lee enjoyed a diversion of his own.

Longstreet's two divisions had arrived at last from Tennessee and were in camp around Gordonsville, nine miles south of army headquarters at Orange. Lee did not know whether Meade would cross the Rapidan on his left or right, taking John Pope's intended route down the Orange & Alexandria Railroad or Joe Hooker's through the Wilderness. He rather thought (and certainly hoped) it would be the latter, but since he lacked solid evidence to that effect he kept Longstreet's hard-hitting veterans off to his left rear, in case the bluecoats came that way. On April 29 he rode down to review them for the first time in nearly eight months, which was how long it had been since they left the Old Dominion to supply Bragg's Sunday punch at Chickamauga. They were turned out in their ragged best, leather patched, metal polished, their shot-torn regimental colors newly stitched with the names of unfamiliar western battles, and when Lee drew rein before them, removing his hat in salute, the color bearers shook their flags like mad and the troops responded with an all-out rebel yell that reverberated from all the surrounding hills, causing the gray-haired general's eyes to brim with tears. "The effect was as of a military sacrament," an artillerist later wrote. Lee wept, another veteran explained, because "he felt that we were again to do his bidding." Deep Southerners or Westerners to a man — South Carolinians and Georgians, Alabamians and Mississippians, Arkansans and Texans — there was not a Virginian among them, and yet it was as if they had come home. A First Corps chaplain riding with the staff turned to a colonel as the yell went up and Lee sat there astride his gray horse Traveller, uncovered in salute, and asked: "Does it not make the general proud to see how these men love him?" The colonel shook his head. "Not proud," he said. "It awes him."

Awed or proud — no doubt with something of both, despite the staffer's protest — Lee felt his impatience mount still faster next day, back at Orange, when he got word that a four-division corps under Ambrose Burnside, formerly encamped at Annapolis and thought to be intended for service down the coast, had passed through Centreville two days ago and had by now reached

Hundreds of wagons stand ready to follow Grant's troops across the Rapidan River in the spring offensive against the Army of Northern Virginia.

Rappahannock Station, from which position it could move in direct support of the Army of the Potomac. Perhaps it was for this that Grant had been waiting to put his three-pronged war machine in motion. As for Meade, Lee informed Davis on this final day in April, "Our scouts report that the engineer troops, pontoon trains, and all the cavalry of Meade's army have been advanced south of the Rappahannock. . . . Everything indicates a concentrated attack on this front." His faith was in God and in the "incomparable infantry" of the Army of Northern Virginia, but now as he awaited the onslaught of the blue juggernaut whose numbers were roughly twice his own, he displayed more urgency of manner than those closest to him had ever seen him show on his own ground. Evidence of an early assault continued to accumulate, and still the Federal tents remained unstruck beyond the Rapidan. Lee's aggressive instinct, held in check by hard necessity, broke its bounds at last. "Colonel," he told a member of his staff, "we have got to whip them; we must whip them!" Apparently that was the high point of his impatience, for having said as much he paused, then added with a smile of amused relief: "It has already made me better to think of it."

★

Lee's confidence was based on past performance, against odds as long and sometimes longer, and Davis too drew reassurance from that source, having just completed his third full year of playing Hezekiah to Lincoln's Sennacherib. Whatever frets he had about developments out in Georgia, here in the Old Dominion at least the Confederacy had won for itself the military admiration of the world. Six blue commanders, in all their majesty and might — Irvin McDowell and George McClellan, John Pope and Ambrose Burnside, Joseph Hooker and George Meade — had mounted half a dozen well-sustained offensives, each designed to achieve the reduction of Richmond in short order, and all six had been turned back in various states of disarray. Now there was Grant, who seemed to many only a seventh name to be added to the list of discomfited eastern opponents. "If I mistake not," a young officer on Lee's staff wrote home on hearing of the elevation of this latest transfer from an inferior western school, "[Grant] will shortly come to grief if he attempts to repeat the tactics in Virginia which proved so successful in Mississippi." There were dissenters: Longstreet, for example, who had been Grant's friend at the Academy and a groomsman at his wedding — and who had fought, moreover, in a theater where Grant was in command. "We must make up our minds to get into line of battle and to stay there," Old Peter had told his visitors at Gordonsville the day before, "for that man will fight us every day and every hour till the end of the war." But for the most part there was general agreement that what had been done six times before (four of them, and the last four at that, more or less on this same Rapidan-Rappahannock line) could be done again by Lee, whose army was a rapier in his hand. If Grant was a fighter, as Longstreet said, there would be nothing unusual in that. One of the worst-defeated of the six had been known as "Fighting Joe," and the one who had been given the soundest drubbing of them all — the "miscreant" Pope — had also arrived with western laurels on his brow and a reputation for coming to savage grips with whatever tried to stand in his path of conquest.

Besides, what was called for now was not necessarily the outright defeat or even repulse of the invaders, east or west. What was called for, Davis could remind himself, was a six-month holding action which would allow them no appreciable gain except at a price that would be regarded as prohibitive, in money and blood, by voters who would be making their early-November choice between peace and war. In light of this, a head-down fighter like Grant might serve the South's purpose far better than would an over-all commander who was inclined to count his casualties and take counsel of his fears. Not that Davis abandoned all hope for a repetition of what had happened in the past to opponents who had come in roaring and gone out bleating; he hoped for it profoundly, and not without cause. Don Carlos Buell and William S. Rosecrans were western examples to match the six discomfited in Virginia, and Sherman had shown himself to have many of the qualities that made Grant an ideal opponent at this juncture. In some ways, now that the notion of an offensive against the Union center had been abandoned as a gambit, Joe Johnston seemed an excellent choice as a foil for the red-haired Ohioan, whose impulsiveness might expose him to the kind of damage his government could least afford on the eve of its quadrennial election. By way of further encouragement, Davis had only to consider more recent successes, scored East and West by Kirby Smith, Finegan, Forrest, and Hoke, for proof that the South could still stand up to combinations designed for its destruction, and could also carry the war to the enemy when the opportunity came. Just as Banks and Steele had been driven back across the Atchafalaya and the Saline — not only against the numerical odds, but also, as it were, against the tactics manuals — so might Sherman and Grant be driven back across the Tennessee and the Rappahannock. Like many brave men, before and since, Davis had found that when a difficulty amounted to an impossibility, the best course to pursue was one that did not take the impossibility into account. That was what he had meant all along when he said, "I cultivate hope and patience, and trust to the blunders of our enemy and the gallantry of our troops for ultimate success."

★

For the most part this attitude was shared by the people of Richmond. In fact, among the party-goers and the well-to-do — they had to be that; a dollar in gold was worth more than thirty in Confederate paper, while calico and coffee were $10 a yard and pound, eggs $2 a dozen, and cornfield beans were selling at $60 a bushel — there had never been a social season as lively as the one now drawing to a close. "Starvation parties" were all the rage, along with charades and taffy pulls, although they seemed to one diarist to have a quality of desperation about them, as if the guests were aware that these revels, honoring "Major This, or Colonel That, or Captain T'other," would be the last. In February Lincoln had issued a draft call for 500,000 men — more than the Confederacy could muster in all its camps between the Rappahannock and the Rio Grande — and then in March had upped the ante by calling for "200,000 more." All the South could do, by way of response, was lower and raise the conscription age limits to seventeen and fifty, robbing thus the cradle and the grave, as some complained, or as Davis put it, in regard to the half-grown boys about to be drafted and thrown into the line, "grinding the seed corn of the nation." Meanwhile U. S. Grant, "a bull-headed Suvarov," was poised on the semicircular horizon, about to lurch into motion from three directions, and in Richmond, his known goal, the revelry continued. "There seems to be for the first time," the diarist noted, "a resolute determination to enjoy the brief hour, and never look beyond the day."

Elsewhere about the country it was apparently much the same; a young man just back from Mobile reported that he had attended sixteen weddings and twenty-seven teas within the brief span of his visit. He did not add that he had found the gayety forced in that direction, but to a Richmond belle, looking back a decade later on this fourth and liveliest of the capital's wartime springs, the underlying sense of doom had been altogether inescapable. "In all our parties and pleasurings," she would recall, "there seemed to lurk a foreshadowing, as in the Greek plays where the gloomy end is ever kept in sight."

★　★　★

Shelby Foote

*The 17th Maine poses near
Brandy Station hours before
its march to the Rapidan
River to open the Wilderness
Campaign in May 1864.*

F O U R

Grant Poised; Joe Davis; Lee

1864 ★ ★ ★ ★ ★ Grant was angered throughout April by increasingly glum reports of developments out in the Transmis-sissippi, which in effect snapped off one prong of his spiky offensive before it could even be launched. "Banks, by his failure," he complained to Halleck, "has absorbed 10,000 veteran troops that should now be with Sherman, and 30,000 of his own that should have been moving toward Mobile; and this without accom-plishing any good result." Nor was that the worst of it. Even more exasperating, from a somewhat different point of view, was the knowledge that Johnston now would not only have no worries about his rear and his supply lines to the Gulf, but would also be able to summon to the defense of North Georgia reinforce-ments who otherwise would have been occupied with the defense of South Alabama. Banks and Steele, as co-directors of the Louisiana-Arkansas fiasco, had disarranged the Grand Design at the outset; or as a friend of Grant's, after repeating his complaint that "30,000 men were rendered useless during six of the most important months of the military year," was to put it in a later appraisal of the situation, "The great combination of campaigns was inaugurated with disaster."

By way of insuring against such blunders here in the East, Grant con-tented himself with sending explicit and detailed instructions to Franz Sigel, who had received a military education in his native Germany, regarding the projected movement up the Shenandoah Valley and down the Virginia Central Railroad. But he went in person, soon after his return from Tennessee, to confer with the altogether nonprofessional Ben Butler, whom he had never met and with whom he had had no correspondence as to his share in the three-pronged convergence on Lee and Richmond. Arriving on April 1 at Fortress Monroe, the Massachusetts general's headquarters at the tip of the York-James peninsula, he decided that a good way to size up the former Bay State politician would be to invite his views on the part he thought he ought to play in the campaign scheduled to open within four weeks. Butler promptly gave them, and Grant was pleased, as he said later, to find that "they were very much such as I intended to direct"; that is, an amphibious movement up James River for a landing at City Point, eight miles northeast of Petersburg, the hub of Virginia's life-sustaining rail connections with the Carolinas and Georgia, and a fast northward march of twenty miles for a knock at the back door of the Confederate capital while Meade, so to speak, was climbing the front steps and Sigel was coming in through the side yard. This augured well. Still, gratifying as it was to find his military judgment confirmed in advance by the man who was charged with carrying out this portion of the plan it had produced, Grant did not neglect to give Butler, before he got back aboard the boat next morning for the return up Chesapeake Bay, written instructions as to what would be expected of him when jump-off time came round. "When you are notified to move," he told him, "take City Point with as much force as possible. Fortify, or rather intrench, at once, and concentrate all your troops for the field there as rapidly as you can." He added that, though "from City Point directions cannot be given at this time for your future movements," Butler was to bear in mind "that Richmond is to be your objective point, and that there is to be coöperation between your force and the Army of the Potomac."

The latter, being charged with the main effort, was of course Grant's main concern, and when he returned to Culpeper next day he found it in the throes of an unwelcome top-to-bottom reorganization. Designed to achieve the double purpose of tightening the chain of command and of weeding out certain generals who had proved themselves incompetent or unlucky, the shakeup involved the consolidation of a number of large units. Indeed, there was no unit above the size of a brigade that was unaffected by the change. Two of the five corps were broken up and distributed among the remaining three, while the same was done with four of the fifteen infantry divisions, leaving eleven. The result was painful to men in outfits which thus were abolished or in any case lost their identity in the shuffle. Cast among strangers they felt rejected, disowned, orphaned. They felt resentful at having been cannibalized, stung in their unit pride that theirs had been the organizations selected for such a fate, and they voiced their resentment to all who would listen. "The enemies of our country have, in times past, assailed [this division] in vain," one dispossessed commander

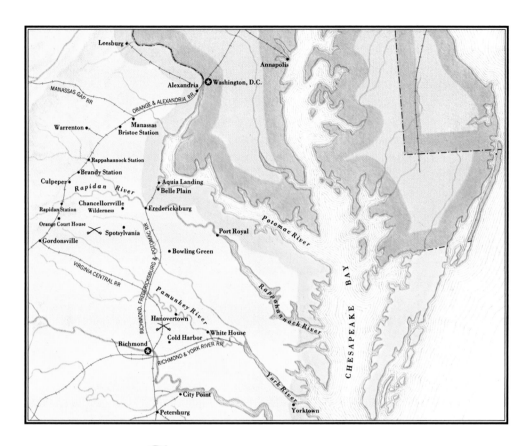

*This map includes the sites of the coming
Wilderness Campaign, where both sides would incur
heavy casualties in the tangled wilds of Virginia.*

protested, "and now it dissolves by action of our own friends." Although the recommendation had been made by Meade before Grant left Tennessee, the soldiers put the blame on the new general-in-chief, since the order of approval came down from Washington just two weeks after his arrival. By way of registering their complaint, at the first large-scale review Grant held after his return from Fortress Monroe in early April the men of one absorbed outfit wore their old corps badge on the crown of their caps, as usual, and — as he could see as soon as they swung past him — pinned the new one to the seat of their trousers.

He took no apparent offense at this, having other, more pressing matters on his mind. One was numbers. However well the chain of command was tightened, however ruthlessly high-ranking incompetents were purged, the army would be able to do little effective fighting, especially of the steam-roller kind Grant favored, unless its ranks were full and reserves were ample. And there was the rub. As spring advanced, the army moved closer to the time when it might lose the very cream of its membership, the men who had come forward on hearing that Sumter had been fired on, back in the pre-draft spring of 1861, and had learned since then, in what Sherman termed "the dearest school on earth," what it meant and what it took to be a soldier. Such veterans, survivors of many a hard-fought field, were scarcely replaceable. They were in fact not only the backbone, they were the body of the army, constituting roughly half the total combat force. Now their three-year enlistments were about to expire, and if they did not reënlist the army was apt to melt away, like the snow on the crest of the Blue Ridge, along with the volunteer organizations whose rolls they filled. Nor was this true only of the Army of the Potomac. Of the 956 volunteer infantry regiments in all the armies of the Union, 455 — nearly half — were scheduled to leave the service before the end of summer, while of the 158 volunteer batteries of artillery, 81 — more than half — would presently be free to head for home: unless, that is, enough of their members reënlisted to justify continuing their existence. By way of encouraging such commitments, the government offered certain inducements designed to make a combined appeal to greed and pride. These included, in the former category, a $400 bounty (to be increased by the amount his home town and county, or rather the civilians who had remained there for whatever reasons, were willing to put up) and a thirty-day furlough. As for pride, a man who reënlisted was to be classified as a "volunteer veteran" and was authorized to wear on his sleeve a special identifying chevron, a certificate of undeniable cold-blood valor. To these was added, as an appeal to *unit* pride, the guarantee that any regiment in which as many as three fourths of the troops "shipped over" would retain its numerical designation and its organizational status.

      This last was perhaps the most effective of the lot: especially when regimental commanders, anxious to hold their outfits together as a prerequisite for holding onto their rank, carried the process down to the company level, where a man's deepest loyalties lay. Any company that attained its quota was encouraged to parade through the regimental camps, fifes shrieking and drums throbbing, while onlookers cheered and tossed their caps. Such enthusiasm was contagious, and the pressure grew heavier on holdouts in ratio to the nearness of the goal, until at last reluctance amounted to disloyalty, not only to comrades already committed, who stood in danger of being scattered among strangers, but also to the regiment, which would die a shameful death without its quota of reënlisted volunteers. "So you see I am sold again," one such wrote home, explaining that he had been swept off his feet by a fervor as strong as the spirit that makes a man be "born again" at a church revival. Not that the bounty and the prospect of a trip home, sporting the just-earned chevron, were not attractive. They were indeed, and especially together; $400, a tempted veteran pointed out, "seemed to be about the right amount for spending-money while on a furlough." Besides, regional supplements often raised the sum to more than a thousand dollars: a respectable nest egg, and enough for the down payment on a farm or a small business, once the fighting ended. Until then, after three years of life in the service, home was likely to be no great fun anyhow, except on a visit — and even that had its limitations, according to some who had been there and found that it fell considerably short of their expectations. "I almost wish myself back in the army," a furloughed soldier, barely a week after his departure, wrote to a comrade still in camp. "Everything seems to be so lonesome here. There is nothing going on that is new." In any case, as a result of these several attractions and persuasions, by mid-April no less than 136,000 veterans had signed on for another three years or the duration of the war.

Most of these were in the West, where the troops expected an early victory and were determined to be in on the kill; "fierce-fighting western men,"

In this Edwin Forbes sketch, a soldier catches up on the news. A new bounty, a liberal furlough, and company loyalty led many Union veterans to reënlist.

one of their generals called them, "in for work and in for the war." In the Army of the Potomac the result was less spectacular; 26,767 veterans reënlisted — about half as many as signed up for another three years under Sherman, and also about half as many as were up for discharge. This meant that about the same number would soon be going home, dropped as emphatically from the army roster as if each man had stopped a rebel bullet. They would have to be replaced, and mainly this would be done by the conscripts and substitutes who now were arriving as a result of Lincoln's February call. Whatever they meant to Grant and Meade, for whom they were merely numbers on a fatted strength report, to the men they joined they were a mixed blessing at best. At worst, they were considerably less. "Such another depraved, vice-hardened and desperate set of human beings never before disgraced an army," an outraged New Englander complained. Partly this was the result of rising wages, which made enlistment a greater sacrifice than ever, and partly it was because the outsized bounties had created a new breed of soldier: the bounty jumper. "Thieves, pickpockets, and vagabonds would enlist," a later observer remarked, "take whatever bounty was paid in cash, desert when opportunity offered, change their names, go to another district or state, reënlist, collect another bounty, desert again, and go on playing the same trick until they were caught." One nimble New Yorker confessed to having made thirty-two such "jumps" before he wound up in the Albany penitentiary, while another New England veteran recorded that no less than half the recruits in his regiment received in one large draft had so quickly forgotten their assumed names, on the trip down to the Rappahannock, that they could not answer roll call when they got there. What was more, the delivery system was far from efficient. Out of a shipment of 625 recruits intended for a distinguished New Hampshire regiment, 137 deserted en route and another 118 managed to do the same within a week of their arrival — 36 to the rear, 82 into the Confederate lines — leaving a residue of 370, who were either the most patriotic or else the least resourceful of the lot. Across the way, on the south bank of the Rapidan, rebel pickets put up a placard: "Headquarters, 5th New Hampshire Volunteers. RECRUITS WANTED." In much the same vein, they sent over a mock-formal message inquiring when they could expect to receive the regimental colors.

Something else this latest influx of draftees brought into the Rappahannock camps that was more disturbing than the rising desertion rate. Though few in numbers, compared to the men already there, the newcomers effected a disproportionate influence on certain aspects of soldier life. "They never tired of relating the mysterious uses to which a 'jimmy' could be put by a man of nerve," a startled veteran would recall, "and how easy it was to crack a bank or filch a purse." Such talents did not go unexercised, so far at least as the limited field allowed; nothing anyone owned was safe that was not nailed down, and there were more ways than one to skin a cat or fleece a sheep. With all that crisp

*With crisp new bounty money injected into the
Union camp economy, gambling increased hugely and
so did the stakes as thousands changed hands daily.*

new bounty money injected into the economy, gambling increased hugely and so did the stakes. According to one awed observer, "Thousands of dollars would change hands in one day's playing, and there were many ugly fights engaged in, caused by their cheating each other at cards." Outraged by what he called "this business of filling up a decent regiment with the outscourings of humanity," another veteran infantryman recorded that "the more we thought of it, the more discontented we became. We longed for a quiet night, and when day came we longed to be away from these ruffians." The result was a necessary tightening of restrictions, in and out of drill hours and applicable to all. That came hard. "No pleasure or privilege for the boys in camp any more," a volunteer lamented, "for the hard lines and severe military discipline apply with a rigidness never before applied." Old-timers yearned for a return to the easy-going life they once had groused about, and they blamed its loss, illogically or not, on Grant, whom they saw as a newcomer like all those unwelcome others, though in fact the change had begun before he had any notion, let alone intention, of coming east to assume command of all the armies.

More logically — quite accurately, in fact — they put the blame on him for another change which was going to have an even more baleful effect on the lives of thousands of men now in his charge. In mid-April, in a further attempt to lengthen his numerical advantage over the forces in rebellion, Grant put an official end to the three-year-old practice of exchanging Federal and Confederate prisoners of war. Whatever its shortcomings from a humanitarian point of view, militarily the decision was a sound one. Not only did a man-for-man exchange favor the side on which a man was a larger fraction of the whole, but in this case there was also the added dividend that, in ending such a disadvantageous arrangement, the Union would be burdening its food-poor adversary with a mounting number of hungry mouths to feed. Just how much prolonged misery this was likely to cause, Grant's own troops knew only too well, either from having been captured in the days when they could be exchanged, or from awareness of what the daily food allowance consisted in the camps across the river. It was hard enough on the rebels, whose stomachs had long since shrunk to fit their rations, but for men accustomed to eating all they could hold ("Our men are generally overloaded, fed, and clad," their chief quartermaster was protesting even now, "which detracts from their marching capacity and induces straggling") such deprivation would amount to downright torture. Moreover, the prospect was further clouded by the knowledge that it had been devised by their own commander, the same man they accused of having foisted the detested reorganization upon them, as well as of having polluted their camps with rowdy gangs of thugs.

Grant ended the three-year-old policy of prisoner exchanges, condemning captured Federals to stays in prisons such as Castle Thunder in Richmond, shown here.

One further thing Grant did, however, that went far toward making up for the unpopularity of those other changes that followed hard on his arrival. This was to reach into the back areas of the war, especially into the fortifications around the capital, and pluck thousands of easy-living soldiers from their cushy jobs for reassignment to duty in the field. Individually and in groups, stripped of their plumes and fire-gilt buttons, they came down to the Rappahannock in a somewhat bewildered condition, if not in a state of downright shock, and the troops already there were glad to welcome them with cheers and jeers. The warmest welcome went to regiments of heavy artillery, prised out of their snug barracks, issued Springfields, and converted overnight into congeries of unblooded rifle companies; "Heavy Infantry," the veterans called them, or just "Heavies." The shocking thing about such regiments, aside from their greenness, was their size. Popular with volunteers in search of easy duty and security from wounds, several of them had as many as 1800 men apiece. "What division is this?" a Mass-achusetts soldier asked when one of them marched in, his own regiment being down to 207 effectives at the time. Other conversions were applauded about as lustily. Parade-ground cavalry units, for example, were suddenly unhorsed, handed muskets in place of carbines, and told that they would henceforth go afoot. "Where are your horses?" a heavy infantryman inquired of a dismounted cavalry outfit that came slogging into camp soon after his own regiment arrived. "Gone to fetch your heavy guns," one of the former troopers snapped. Teamsters too were subject to such abrupt indignity, and many of them were similarly converted and accoutered, as a result of an order reducing transportation to one wagon per brigade. "You needn't laugh at me," a transmuted teamster called to a braying mule in a passing train. "You may be in the ranks yourself before Grant gets through with the army."

In point of fact, now that they had time to look him over and examine the results of some of the changes he introduced, the men had begun to see that, whatever else he might do, in or out of combat, he clearly meant business, and they found they liked the notion of this. Some high-ranking officers, partic-ularly the starch-collared regulars among them, might have doubts about the new general-in-chief (an old-line colonel of artillery, for instance, wrote home that he found him "stumpy, unmilitary, slouchy and western-looking; very ordinary, in fact") but the troops themselves, according to an enlisted diarist, would "look with awe at Grant's silent figure" whenever he rode out on inspec-tion, which was often. They liked his reticence, his disregard of mere trappings, his eye for the essential. He was seldom cheered, except by greenhorn outfits trying to make points, but he seemed not to care or even notice. "Grant wants soldiers, not yawpers," a veteran observed approvingly. What was more, his success in prising the heavies out of the Washington fortifications was good evidence that he had the confidence of the authorities there — something most of his

*G*rant reassigned teamsters, such as this man
sketched by Edwin Forbes, to duty in the field after
reducing transportation to one wagon per brigade.

predecessors had lacked, to their discomfort and the resultant discomfort of the army in their charge. This was seen as an excellent sign, as well as a source of present satisfaction. There was also a solidity about him that was welcome after service under a series of commanders who had shown a tendency, and sometimes more than a tendency, to fly asunder under pressure. A New Englander put it simplest: "We all felt at last that *the boss* had arrived." Grant returned the compliment in kind. "The Army of the Potomac is in splendid condition and evidently feels like whipping somebody," he informed Halleck on April 26, one month after establishing headquarters at Culpeper: adding, "I feel much better with this command than I did before seeing it."

He had good cause to feel so, even though by now he was already one day past the date he had set for the simultaneous jump-off, east and west. Numerically, as a result of those various recruitment stratagems in the army and on the home front, he was in better shape than anyone had dared to hope, particularly on the Rappahannock. After Burnside shifted his corps into position for close-up support of Meade, Grant had 122,146 infantry, cavalry, and artillery effectives on hand for the main-effort crossing of the Rapidan. This figure included only the troops who were "present for duty, equipped"; another 24,602 were on extra duty, sick, or in arrest, bringing the total to just under 147,000. Even at the lower figure, and leaving Butler and Sigel out of account, he had about twice as many effectives as Lee, who had 61,953 of all arms. In Georgia, moreover, the ratio was roughly the same. Sherman had 119,898, including men on reënlistment furloughs, while Johnston had 63,949, including Polk, who would be free to join him once the pressure was on and the Union strategy was disclosed. Just when that would be, East and West, depended in part on the method by which this pressure was to be applied; that is, on the tactical details of the strategy Grant and Sherman had worked out between them, six weeks ago, in the Cincinnati hotel room. Grant was willing to leave the working out of such details to his red-haired friend, as far as they were to be applied in the West. In the East, however, he had made the matter his prime concern ever since he had set up headquarters in the field.

From Culpeper, there in the toppled V of the rivers, and from the peak of nearby Stony Mountain, where an observation post had been established for surveillance of the landscape roundabout, he could give the problem informed attention. South of the V, disposed on a front of nearly twenty miles along the right bank of the river, from Mine Run upstream to Rapidan Station and beyond, Lee and his army lay in wait under cover of intrenchments they had spent the past six months improving. The problem was how to get at him: or, more precisely, how to get around him and then at him, since a frontal assault, across the river and against those earthworks, would amount to downright folly, if not suicide en masse. Once the blue army was on his flank or in his rear, however, with nothing substantial between itself and Richmond, Lee would be obliged to come out of his works for the showdown battle Meade had been told to seek. This being so, the question was reduced to whether to move around his right flank or his left, east or west of that twenty-mile line of intrenchments. Much could be said for the latter course. The country was more open in that direction, affording the attackers plenty of room for bringing all of their superior force to bear, and there was also the prospect of gobbling up what was left of the Orange & Alexandria Railroad, down to Gordonsville, and then moving onto the Virginia Central, converting them into a supply line leading back to the Potomac, while denying their use to the defenders. All this was good, so far as it went, but there were two considerable drawbacks. One was that the rebels would wreck the railroad as they withdrew, requiring the pursuers to rebuild it and then keep it rebuilt despite attempts by regular and irregular grayback cavalry to re-wreck it. To guard against this would require the crippling detachment of fighting men from the front to the rear in ever-increasing numbers, all the way back to the

One line of attack for Grant held the prospect of gobbling up what was left of the Orange & Alexandria Railroad, whose terminus is pictured here.

Rappahannock, since even a temporary break might prove disastrous, dependent as the army would be on that single line for everything it needed, including food for 56,500 horses and mules and better than twice that many soldiers. The other drawback was that a movement around Lee's west flank would uncover the direct approach to Washington. In some ways this was a greater disadvantage than the other; Lincoln was notoriously touchy in regard to the safety of his capital, and every commander who had neglected to remember this had found himself in trouble as a result. So far, since the advent of the new general-in-chief, the President had maintained a hands-off attitude toward all things military, for which Grant was altogether thankful, but that attitude might not extend to the point of seeing Washington endangered, even in theory, especially now that the surrounding fortifications had been stripped of their outsized regiments.

Between them, these two drawbacks — one having to do with supply difficulties, the other having to do with Lincoln — fairly well ruled out a movement around the Confederate left. Grant shifted his attention to the region beyond Lee's right: more specifically, to the country between Mine Run and the confluence of the rivers, fifteen miles east of Stony Mountain and about ten miles this side of Fredericksburg. That way, the march would be shorter, Washington would be covered from dead ahead, and the supply problem would be solved by ready access to navigable streams on the outer flank, affording

★

rapid, all-weather connection with well-stocked depots in the rear and requiring no more than minimal protection.

Here too there was a drawback, however, one that was personally familiar to every soldier who had served for as long as half a year in the eastern theater. The Wilderness, it was called: a forbidding region, some dozen miles wide and eight miles deep, which the army would enter as soon as it crossed that stretch of the Rapidan immediately east of Lee's right flank, a leafy tangle extending from just beyond Mine Run to just beyond Chancellorsville. Joe Hooker, for one, could testify to the pitfalls hidden in that jungle of stunted oak and pine, and so could the present commander of the army that had come to grief in its depths, chief among them being that the force on the defensive had the advantage of silent concealment — an advantage the butternut veterans had used so well, five months ago, that Meade still considered himself lucky to have got back out of there alive. Conversely, the blue army's main advantage, its preponderance in men and guns, would scarcely matter if it was brought to battle there; numbers counted for little in those thickets, except to increase the claustrophobia and the panic that came from being shot at from close quarters by a foe you could not see, and artillery had to fire blind or not at all. As a drawback, this could hardly be overrated; but Grant believed he saw a way to avoid it. The answer was speed. If the troops moved fast enough, and began their march after nightfall screened the crossing from the rebel lookout station on Clark's Mountain across the way, they could get through the Wilderness and gain the open country just beyond it, where there was plenty of room for maneuver, before Lee had time to interfere. Moreover, this belief was founded on experience. Both Meade and Hooker, who had crossed by the same fords Grant intended to use now — Ely's and Germanna — had spent two full days on the far side of the river before they came to grips with anything substantial, and in both cases, what was more, they had done so as part of their plans: Meade by moving directly against the enemy at Mine Run, Hooker by calling a halt at Chancellorsville and inviting the enemy to attack him. Grant had no intention of doing either of these things. He intended to bull right through, covering those eight vine-choked miles in the shortest possible time — certainly less than two full days — and thus be out in the open, where Lee would have nothing better than a choice between attacking or being attacked. Either would suit Grant's purpose admirably, once he had his troops on ground where their superior numbers and equipment could be brought to bear and thus decide the issue in accordance with the odds.

By way of assuring speed on the projected march, or in any case a touch of the hard-driving ruthlessness that would be needed to obtain it, he had already made one important change in the make-up of the arm of the service that would lead the way across the Rapidan and down the roads beyond. In conference with Lincoln and Halleck, soon after his return from Tennessee and before he established headquarters in the field, he had expressed his dissatisfaction with cavalry operations in the eastern theater. What was needed, he said, was "a thorough leader." Various candidates for the post were mentioned and discarded, until Halleck came up with the answer. "How would Sheridan do?" he asked. This was Major General Philip H. Sheridan, then in command of an infantry division under Thomas near Chattanooga. His only experience with cavalry had been a five-week term as colonel of a Michigan regiment after Shiloh, nearly two years ago, and he had not only never served in Virginia, he had never even been over the ground in peacetime, so great was his dislike of all things southern. But Grant thought he would do just fine in command of the eastern army's three divisions of 13,000 troopers. "The very man I want," he said, and Sheridan was sent

Unhappy with the cavalry in the eastern theater, Grant picked General Philip H. Sheridan, shown here in an idealized portrait from Harper's Weekly, to lead his horse soldiers.

for. He arrived in early April, checked into Willard's, and went at once to the White House, much as Grant had done the month before. The interview was marred, however, when the President brought up the familiar jest: "Who ever saw a dead cavalryman?" Sheridan was not amused. If he had his way, there were going to be a great many dead cavalrymen lying around, Union as well as Confederate. Back at Willard's with friends, he said as much, and more. "I'm going to take the cavalry away from the bobtailed brigadier generals," he vowed. "They must do without their escorts. I intend to make the cavalry an arm of the service."

He was different, and he brought something different and hard into the army he now joined. "Smash 'em up, smash 'em up!" he would say as he toured the camps, smacking his palm with his fist for emphasis, and then ride off on his big hard-galloping horse, a bullet-headed little man with close-cropped hair and a black mustache and imperial, bandy-legged, long in the arms, all Irish but with a Mongol look to his face and form, as if something had gone strangely wrong somewhere down the line in Ireland. Just turned thirty-three, he was five feet five inches tall and he weighed 115 pounds with his spurs on; "one of those long-armed fellows with short legs," Lincoln remarked of him, "that can scratch his shins without having to stoop over." Mounted, he looked about as tall and burly as the next man, so that when he got down from his horse his slightness came as a shock. "The officer you brought on from the West is rather a little fellow to handle your cavalry," someone observed at headquarters, soon after Sheridan reported for duty. Grant took a pull at his cigar, perhaps remembering Missionary Ridge. "You'll find him big enough for the purpose before we get through with him," he said. And in point of fact, the undersized, Ohio-raised West Pointer held much the same views on war as his chief, who was Ohio born and had finished West Point ten years earlier, also standing about two thirds of the way down in his class. Those views, complementing Sheridan's even more succinct "Smash 'em up, smash 'em up!" could be stated quite briefly, a staff physician found out about this time. They were sitting around, idle after a hard day's work, and the doctor asked the general-in-chief for a definition of the art of war. Grant turned the matter over in his mind — no doubt preparing to quote Jomini or some other highly regarded authority, his listeners thought — and then replied, as if in confirmation of what his friend Longstreet was telling Lee's staff about now, across the way: "Find out where your enemy is. Get at him as soon as you can, and strike him as hard as you can. And keep moving on."

That was to be the method, and by now he had also arrived at the date on which it would begin to be applied. April 27 — the day after he told Halleck, "I feel much better with this command" — was his forty-second birthday; a year ago today, at Hard Times, Louisiana, he had braced his western army for the crossing of the greatest river of them all, the Mississippi, and the opening of the final stage in the campaign that took Vicksburg. It was therefore a fitting day for fixing the date for what would be the greatest jump-off of them all, east or west, east *and* west. Burnside by now was in motion from Annapolis, charged with replacing Meade's troops on guard along the railroad between Manassas and the Rappahannock, and Meade was free to concentrate his whole force in the V of the two rivers. Today was Wednesday. Allowing a full week for the completion of all this, together with final preparations for crossing the Rapidan at designated fords, Grant set the date for Wednesday next: May 4. Notice of this was sent at once to Meade and Burnside, as well as to Sigel and Butler, at Winchester and Fort Monroe, and to Sherman in North Georgia, who would pass the word to subordinates already poised for the leap at Dalton. This was nine days later than the tentative date Grant had set in early April, but he saw in the delay a double gain. Not only would it afford more time for preparation, which should help to eliminate oversights and confusion; it would also allow the Wilderness roads just that much additional time to dry, an important factor in consideration of the need for speed in getting out of that briery snare in the shortest possible time.

As for getting out of Washington — also a highly desirable thing, from a personal point of view — Grant had done that, for good, the previous Sunday. Except for the chance they gave him to be with his wife, his brief visits there had brought him little pleasure and much strain. The public adulation had increased, and with it the discomfort, including a flood of letters requesting his autograph (he had found a way to cut down on these, however; "I don't get as many as I did when I answered them," he said dryly) and a great deal of staring whenever he ventured out, which he seldom did unless it was unavoidable, as it was for example in getting from the station to Willard's and back. Observing his "peculiar aloofness," a protective garment he wore against the stares, one witness remarked that "he walked through a crowd as though solitary." On his last morning there, having taken breakfast in the hotel dining room before leaving to catch the train for Virginia, he was spotted by a reporter as he came out into the lobby. "He gets over the ground queerly," the journalist informed a friend that night. "He does not march, nor quite walk, but pitches along as if the next step would bring him on his nose. But his face looks firm and hard, and his eye is clear and resolute, and he is certainly natural, and clear of all appearance of self-consciousness." On the theory that this might be his last chance for some time, the reporter presumed to intercept him with a question: "I suppose, General, you don't mean to breakfast again until the war is over?" — "Not here I don't," Grant said, and went on out.

Nothing he had said or written, in conference or in correspondence with Lincoln or Halleck or anyone else, had given any estimate as to how much time the campaign about to open would require before it achieved what he called "the first great object," which was "to get possession of Lee's army." His

★

*The 42-year-old Ulysses S. Grant, who took over
the Army of the Potomac, was considered
aloof but apparently free of any self-consciousness.*

preliminary instructions to Meade, for instance — "Lee's army will be your objective point. Wherever Lee goes, there you will go also" — had been dated
April 9; but whether the result so much desired would be attained within a year,
or more, or considerably less, or not at all, remained to be seen. No one was
more concerned with the specific timing than Lincoln, who would face a fight
for survival in November, a fight he had good cause to believe he would lose

unless the voters' confidence was lifted within the next six months by a substantial military accomplishment, rather than lowered by the lack of one to compensate for the lengthening casualty lists. And yet, despite the anxiety and strain — so well had he learned his lesson in the course of having shared in the planning, and often in the prosecution, of half a dozen failed offensives here in the East in the past three bloody years — he maintained his hands-off attitude, even to the extent of not asking his new general-in-chief for an informal guess at the schedule, east or west. It was as if, having tried interference to the limit of his ability, he now was determined to try abstention to the same extent. He had learned patience, and something more; he had learned submission. "I attempt no compliment to my own sagacity," he recently had told a Kentucky friend in a letter he knew would be published. "I claim not to have controlled events, but confess plainly that events have controlled me."

In line with this, as if to underscore his hands-off intention while at the same time giving assurance of continuing support, he sent Grant a farewell note on the last day of April, four days before the big offensive was to begin.

> *Lieutenant General Grant:*
>
> *Not expecting to see you again before the spring campaign opens, I wish to express in this way my entire satisfaction with what you have done up to this time, so far as I understand it. The particulars of your plan I neither know nor seek to know. You are vigilant and self-reliant; and, pleased with this, I wish not to obtrude any constraints or restraints upon you. While I am very anxious that any great disaster or capture of our men in great numbers shall be avoided, I know these points are less likely to escape your attention than they would be mine. If there is anything wanting which is within my power to give, do not fail to let me know it. And now, with a brave army and a just cause, may God sustain you.*
>
> *Yours very truly,*
>
> *A. Lincoln.*

★

Next day — May Day — Grant "acknowledged with pride" the President's "very kind letter" as soon as it reached him at Culpeper. "It will be my earnest endeavor that you and the country shall not be disappointed," he wrote, and added, by way of returning the compliments paid him: "Since the promotion which placed me in command of all the armies, and in view of the great responsibility and importance of success, I have been astonished at the readiness with which everything asked for has been yielded, without even an explanation being asked. Should my success be less than I desire and expect, the least I can say is, the fault is not with you."

And having said as much he turned his attention back to matters at hand. Two nights from now, in the small hours of Wednesday morning, the army would be moving down to the river for a crossing.

* * * Braced as best he could manage for the blow he knew was coming, though he did not know just when or where it would land, Jefferson Davis had cause to be grateful for the apparent delay beyond the final day of April, which arrived without bringing word to Richmond that the Union drive had opened from any direction, east or west. Not only did this afford him time for additional preparations, such as getting a few more soldiers up to Lee or down to Beauregard; it also seemed to mean that he and his country would emerge unscathed from what had been in the past, for them, the cruelest month. Although he was by no means superstitious, the pattern was too plain to be denied. In April of 1861 the war itself had begun when Lincoln maneuvered him into opening fire on Sumter. Next year it had brought the death of his friend and idol, Albert Sidney Johnston, together with defeat in the half-won Battle of Shiloh. Last year, in that same unlucky month, Grant and Hooker had launched the two offensives that cost the Confederacy the knee-buckling double loss of Vicksburg and Stonewall Jackson. However, this fourth April seemed about to be proved the exception to the rule. Militarily, so far as actual contact was concerned, the news from all three major theaters — from Louisiana and Arkansas, out in the Transmississippi, from Fort Pillow in the West, and from Plymouth, here in the East — had been nothing but good all month. If Davis, on the last morning in April, having walked the four blocks from the White House to his office adjoining Capitol Square and found no unduly woeful dispatch on his desk, paused to congratulate himself and his country on their delivery from the jinx, it would not have been without apparent justification. Yet he would have been wrong, horribly wrong. Before the day was

over he would be struck the heaviest personal blow of the war: just such a blow as his adversary Lincoln had been struck, twenty-six months ago, in that other White House up in Washington.

He worked all morning, partly on administrative matters, which critics saw as consuming a disproportionate share of his time, and partly on intelligence reports — they made for difficult sifting, since different commanders predicted different objectives for the overdue Union offensive, generally in hair-raising proximity to their headquarters — then broke for lunch, which his wife brought on a tray from home to tempt his meager appetite. Before the dishes could be set in front of him, however, a house servant came running with news that Joe, their five-year-old, third of the four children who ranged in age from nine to three, had fallen from a high rear balcony onto the brick-paved courtyard fifteen feet below. They hurried there to find him unconscious. Both legs were broken and his skull was fractured, apparently the result of having climbed a plank some carpenters had left resting against the balustrade when they quit for the noonday meal. He died soon after his mother reached him, and the house was filled with the screams of his Irish nurse, hysterical with sorrow and guilt from having let him out of her sight. His brother Jeff, two years older, had been the one to find him lying crumpled on the bricks. "I have said all the prayers I know how," he told a neighbor who came upon him kneeling there beside his dying brother, "but God will not wake Joe."

Under the first shock of her loss, the emotional impact of which was all the greater because she was seven months pregnant, Varina Davis was nearly as bad off as the nurse. But the most heartbreaking sight of all, Burton Harrison thought, was the father's "terrible self-control," which denied him the relief of tears. Little Joe had been his favorite, the child on whom he had "set his hope," according to his wife. Each night the boy had said his prayers at his father's knee, and often he had come in the early morning to be taken up into the big bed. Davis retired to his White House study, determined to go on with his work as an antidote to thinking of these things, and Mrs Davis joined him there as soon as she recovered from her initial shock. Presently a courier arrived with a dispatch from Lee. Davis took it, stared at it for a long minute, then turned to his wife with a stricken expression on his face. "Did you tell me what was in it?" he asked. Grief had paralyzed his mind, she saw, and her husband realized this too when he tried to compose his answer. "I must have this day with my little son," he cried, and moved blindly out of the room and up the stairs. Visitors heard him up there in the bedroom, pacing back and forth and saying over and over as he did so: "Not mine, O Lord, but thine." Meantime the boy was laid out in a casket, also in one of the upper rooms. His nurse lay flat on the floor alongside him, keening, while across the hall the father paced and paced the night away. "Not mine, O Lord, but thine," he kept saying, distracted by his grief.

All night the mourners came and went, cabinet members, high-ranking army and navy officers, dignitaries in town for the convening of Congress two days later, and yet the tall gray stucco house had an aspect of desolation, at once eerie and garish. Every room was brightly lighted, gas jets flaring, and the windows stood open on all three stories, their curtains moving in and out as the night breeze rose and fell. Next afternoon — May Day: Sunday — the funeral procession wound its way up the steep flank of Oregon Hill to Hollywood Cemetery, where many illustrious Confederates lay buried. Although Joe had been too young for school, having just turned five in April, more than a thousand schoolchildren followed the hearse, each bearing a sprig of evergreen or a spray of early flowers which they let fall on the hillside plot as they filed past. Standing by the open grave, Davis and his wife were a study in contrast. Heavy with the child she would bear in June, she wore black, including a veil, and her tall figure drooped beneath the burden of her grief, while her husband, twenty years her senior at fifty-five, yet

The tall gray stucco house had an aspect of desolation, at once eerie and garish. Every room was brightly lighted, gas jets flaring, and the windows stood open . . .

lithe of form and erect as one of the monuments stark against the sky behind him, wore his accustomed suit of homespun gray. Down below, the swollen James purled and foamed around its rocks and islands, and now for the first time, as they watched him stand uncovered in the sunlight beside the grave of the son on whom he had set his hope, people saw that Davis, acquainted increasingly with sorrow in his private as in his public life, had begun to look his age and more. The words "vibrant" and "boyish," so often used by journalists and others to describe their impression of him, no longer applied. Streaks of gray were in his hair, unnoticed until now, and the blind left eye looked blinder in this light.

There was no evidence of this, however, in his message of greeting to the newly elected Second Congress when it convened the following day on Capitol Hill. Though the words were read by the clerk, in accordance with custom, their tone of quiet reliance and not-so-quiet defiance was altogether characteristic of their author. "When our independence, by the valor and fortitude of our people, shall have been won against all the hostile influences combined against us, and can no longer be ignored by open foes or professed neutrals, this war will have left with its proud memories a record of many wrongs which it may not misbecome us to forgive, [as well as] some for which we may not properly forbear from demanding redress. In the meantime, it is enough for us to know that every avenue of negotiation is closed against us, that our enemy is making renewed and strenuous efforts for our destruction, and that the sole resource for us, as a people secure in the justice of our cause and holding our liberties to be more precious than all other earthly possessions, is to combine and apply every available element of power for their defense and preservation." By way of proof that such a course of action could be effective against the odds, he was pleased to review the triumphs scored in all three major theaters since the previous Congress adjourned: after which he passed at once to the expected peroration, assuring his hearers that, just as they were on God's side, so was God on theirs. "Let us then, while resolute in devoting all our energies to securing the realization of the bright auspices which encourage us, not forget that our humble and most grateful thanks are due to Him without whose guidance and protecting care all human efforts are of no avail, and to whose interposition are due the manifold successes with which we have been cheered."

★ ★ ★ *J*ust over sixty air-line miles northwest of the chamber in which the clerk droned through the presidential message, Lee was meeting with his chief infantry lieutenants atop Clark's Mountain, immediately northeast of the point where the railroad crossed the Rapidan north of Orange. He had called them together, his three corps and eight division commanders, to make certain that each had a good inclusive look at the terrain for which they would be fighting as soon as Grant made the move that Lee by now was convinced he had in mind. Not that most of them had not fought there before; they had, except for Longstreet and his two subordinates, who had missed both Chancellorsville and Mine Run; but the panoramic view from here, some six or seven hundred feet above the low-lying country roundabout, presented all the advantages of a living map unrolled at their feet for their inspection and instruction, and as such — lovely, even breath-taking in its sweep and grandeur, a never-ending carpet with all the vivid greens of advancing spring commingled in its texture — would serve, as nothing else could do, to fix the over-all character of the landscape in their minds.

For the most part — though their youth was disguised, in all but two heavily mustached cases, by beards in a variety of styles, from full-shovel to Vandyke — they were men in their prime, early-middle-aged at worst. Longstreet was forty-three, and the other two corps commanders, Lieutenant Generals Richard S. Ewell and A. P. Hill, were respectively four years older and five years younger, while the division commanders averaged barely forty, including one who was forty-eight; "Old Allegheny," he was called, as if he vied in ancientness with the mountains beyond the Blue Ridge. Aside from him, Lee at fifty-seven was ten years older than any other general on the hilltop, and like

Davis, despite the vigor of his movements, the quick brown eyes in his high-colored face, and the stalwart resolution of his bearing, he had begun to show his age. His hair, which had gone from brown to iron gray in the first year of the war, was now quite white along his temples, and the same was true of his beard, which he wore clipped somewhat closer now than formerly, as if in preparation for long-term fighting. The past winter had been a hard one for him, racking his body with frequent attacks that were diagnosed as lumbago, and though his health improved with warming weather, the opening months of spring had been even harder to endure, not only because they brought much rain, which tended to oppress him, but also because it galled his aggressive nature to be obliged to wait, as he fretfully complained, "on the time and place of the enemy's choosing" for battle. Just over twenty months ago, after less than three months in command of the newly-assembled army with which he had whipped McClellan back from the outskirts of Richmond, he had stood on this same mountaintop and

Lee at fifty-seven was ten years older than any other general on the hilltop, and like Davis, despite the vigor of his movements, the quick brown eyes in his high-colored face, and the stalwart resolution of his bearing, he had begun to show his age.

watched Pope's blue host file northward out of the trap he had laid for it there in the V of the rivers, and he had said to Longstreet then: "General, we little thought that the enemy would turn his back upon us thus early in the campaign." It was different now. Grant he knew would move, not north across the Rappahannock, but south across the Rapidan, and all Lee could do was prepare to meet him with whatever skill and savagery were required to drive him back: which, in part, was why he had brought his ranking subordinates up here for a detailed look at the terrain on which he planned to do just that. Believing as he did that an outnumbered army should be light on its feet and supple in the hands of its commander, his custom was to give his lieutenants a great deal of latitude in combat, and he wanted to make certain that they were equipped, geographically at least, to exercise with judgment the initiative he encouraged them to seize whenever they were on their own — as, in fact, every unit commander, gray or blue, was likely to be in that tangled country down below, especially in the thickets that lay like pale green smoke over that portion called the Wilderness, stretching eastward beyond Mine Run.

The Rapidan flowed to their right, practically at their feet as they stood looking north toward Culpeper, the hilltop town ten miles away, where A. P. Hill had been born and raised and where Grant now had his headquarters. Another ten miles farther on, hazy in the distance, the dark green line of the Rappahannock crooked southeast to its junction with the nearer river, twenty miles due east of the domed crest of Clark's Mountain, and then on out of sight toward Fredericksburg, still another ten miles beyond the roll of the horizon. All this lay before and below the assembled Confederates, who could also see the conical tents and white-topped wagons clustered and scattered in and about the camps Meade's army had pitched in the arms of the stream-bound V whose open end was crossed by the twin threads of the railroad glinting silver in the

sunlight. There was a good deal of activity in those camps today, as indeed there had been the day before, a Sunday, but the generals on the mountain gave their closest attention to the gray-green expanse of the Wilderness, particularly its northern rim, as defined by the meandering Rapidan; Hooker and Meade had both crossed there in launching the two most recent Union offensives, and Lee believed that Grant would do the same, even to the extent of using the same fords, Ely's and Germanna, four and ten miles respectively from the junction of the rivers. He not only believed it, he said it. Apparently that was another reason he had brought his lieutenants up here: to say it and to show them as he spoke. Suddenly, without preamble or explanation, he raised one gauntleted hand and pointed specifically at the six-mile stretch of the Rapidan that flowed between the two points where the Federals twice had thrown their pontoon bridges in preparation for all-out assaults on the Army of Northern Virginia. "Grant will cross by one of these fords," he said.

Deliberately spoken, the words had the sound of a divination, now and even more so in the future, when they were fulfilled and his hearers passed them down as an instance of Lee's ability to read an opponent's mind. However, though this faculty was real enough on the face of it, having been demonstrated repeatedly in most of his campaigns, it was based on nothing occult or extrasensory, as many of his admirers liked to claim, but rather on a careful analysis of such information as came to hand in the normal course of events — from ene-

From Pony Mountain near Culpeper, Union Signal Corps officers keep an eye on enemy encampments south of the Rapidan River in this sketch by Edwin Forbes.

my newspapers closely scanned, from scouts and spies and friendly civilians who made it through the Yankee lines, from loquacious deserters and tight-mouthed prisoners tripped by skillful interrogation — plus a highly developed intelligence procedure, by which he was able not only to put himself in the other man's position, but also to *become* that man, so to speak, in making a choice among the opportunities the situation seemed to afford him for accomplishing the destruction of the Army of Northern Virginia. Like other artists in other lines of endeavor, Lee produced by hard labor, midnight oil, and infinite pains what seemed possible only by uncluttered inspiration. Quite the opposite of uncanny, his method was in fact so canny that it frequently produced results which only an apparent wizard could achieve. The Clark's Mountain prediction was a case in point. Lee had spent a major part of his time for the past two months — ever since Grant's arrival and elevation, in early March — at work on the problem of just what his new adversary was go-

Like other artists in other lines of endeavor, Lee produced by hard labor, midnight oil, and infinite pains what seemed possible only by uncluttered inspiration.

ing to do, and for the past two weeks — ever since April 18, when he ordered all surplus baggage sent to the rear — he had given the matter his practically undivided attention: with the result that, after a process of selection and rejection much like Grant's across the way, he had come up with what he believed was the answer. Grant would cross the Rapidan by Ely's Ford or Germanna Ford, and having done so he either would turn west for an attack on the Confederate right flank, as Meade had done in November, or else he would do as Hooker had intended to do, a year ago this week, and maneuver for a battle in the open, where he could bring his superior numbers to bear. Which of these two courses the Federal commander meant to adopt once he was across the river did not really matter to Lee, since he did not intend to give him a chance to do either. Lee's plan was to let him cross, then hit him there in the Wilderness with everything he had, taking advantage of every equalizing impediment the terrain afforded, in order to whip him as thoroughly as possible in the shortest possible time, and thus drive him, badly cut up, back across the Rapidan. He did not say all this today, however. He merely said that Grant would cross by one of those fords on the rim of the Wilderness, and then he mounted Traveller and led the way back down the mountain.

Nor did he act, just yet, on the contingent decision he had reached.

★

Only today, in fact, he had instructed Longstreet to shift one of his two divisions northwest of Gordonsville, in order to have it in a better position to meet the challenge Grant would pose if he attempted a move around the Confederate left, in the opposite direction from the one predicted. Lacking definite confirmation of what was after all no more than a theoretical opinion, an educated guess, Lee could not commit his army to a large-scale counteraction of a movement which there was even an outside chance the enemy might not make; he had to leave a sizeable margin for error, including total error. That night, however, the signal station on Clark's Mountain reported observing moving lights in the Federal camps, and next morning — May 3: Tuesday — there were reports of heavy clouds of dust, stirred up by columns marching here and there, and smoke in unusual volume, as if the bluecoats were engaged in the last-minute destruction of camp equipment and personal belongings for which they would have no use when they moved out.

All day this heightened activity continued, past sundown and into the night. Presently the signalmen blinked a message to army headquarters that long columns of troops were passing in front of campfires down there on the far bank of the Rapidan. Headquarters responded with a question: Was the movement west or east, upstream in Hill's direction on the left or downstream in Ewell's direction on the right? The signal station was in visual communication with both corps commanders, as well as with Lee, but it could find no answer to the question. All that could be seen across the way was the winking of campfires as files of men passed in front of them. There was no way of telling, from this, whether the troops were moving upstream or down, to the left or to the right. By now it was close to midnight; May 4 would be dawning within five hours. Lee decided to act at last on yesterday's prediction, and sent word accordingly for the signalmen to flash a message to the corps on the right, down toward Mine Run: "General Ewell, have your command ready to move at daylight."

★ ★ ★

In this Julian Scott painting, skirmishers from the Federal VI Corps probe the Wilderness's thick underbrush as a brigade draws up in line for battle behind them.

Grant Crosses, the Wilderness

1864 ★ ★ ★ ★ ★

Grant came as Lee had said he **would,** only more so, crossing the Rapidan not merely by "one of those fords," Ely's or Germanna, but by both — and, presently, by still another for good measure. Sheridan's new-shod cavalry led the way, splashing across the shallows in the darkness soon after midnight, May 4, and while the engineers got to work in the waist-deep water, throwing a pair of wood and canvas pontoon bridges at each of the two fords, the troopers established bridgeheads on the enemy side of the river at both points and sent out patrols to explore the narrow, jungle-flanked, moonless roads tunneling southward through the Wilderness. Near the head of one column the horsemen got to talking as they felt their way toward Chancellorsville, a name depressing to the spirits of any Federal who had been there with Joe Hooker just a year ago this week. One of the group, anticipating a quick pink-yellow stab of flame and a humming, bone-thwacking bullet from every shadow up ahead, remarked uneasily that he had never supposed "the army went hunting around in the night for Johnnies in this way."

"We're stealing a march on old man Lee," a veteran explained.

They thought this over, remembering the loom of Clark's Mountain and the rebel lookout station on its peak, and before long someone put the thought into words. "Lee will miss us in the morning."

★

"Yes, and then watch out," another veteran declared. "He'll come tearing down this way ready for a fight."

Though all agreed that this would certainly be in character, Lee did no such thing: at least not yet. Morning came and the crossing progressed smoothly in their rear, including the installation of still a fifth bridge at Culpeper Mine Ford, two miles above Ely's, to speed the passage of the army train, the laggard, highly vulnerable element to which all the others, mounted or afoot, had to conform for its protection on the march. Slow-creaking and heavily loaded with ten days' subsistence for nearly 150,000 men and ten days' grain for better than 56,000 mules and horses (strung out along a single road, if any such had been available, this monster train would have covered the sixty-odd miles from the Rapidan to Richmond without a break from head to tail) the wagons passed over the two lower fords in the wake of Major General Winfield S. Hancock's II Corps, the largest of Meade's three, which crossed at Ely's in the darkness and began to make camp at Chancellorsville, five miles from the river, before noon. The brevity of the march was necessary if the combat units were to provide continuous protection for the road-jammed train, but the men, slogging along under packs about as heavy-laden as the wagons in their rear, were thankful for the early halt; they carried, as directed in the carefully worded order, "50 rounds of ammunition upon the person, three days'

full rations in their haversacks, [and] three days' bread and short rations in their knapsacks." At Germanna, meantime, Major General Gouverneur K. Warren's V Corps crossed and marched six miles southeast to Wilderness Tavern, near the intersection of the Germanna Plank Road and the Orange-Fredericksburg Turnpike, where it made camp in the early afternoon, five miles west of Hancock, leaving room behind for Major General John Sedgwick's VI Corps to bed down beside the road, between the tavern and the river, well before sundown. Grant was pleased, when he reached the upper ford about midday and clattered over with his staff, to note that the passage of the Rapidan was being accomplished in excellent order, strictly according to schedule, and without a suggestion of enemy interference. "This I regarded as a great success," he later reported, because "it removed from my mind the most serious apprehensions I had entertained, that of crossing the river in the face of an active, large, well-appointed, and ably-commanded army."

Gratified by the evidence that he had indeed stolen a march on old man Lee, he got off a wire at 1.15 to Burnside at Rappahannock Station, instructing him to bring his IX Corps down to Germanna without delay. Another went to Halleck, back in Washington: "The crossing of the Rapidan effected. Forty-eight hours now will demonstrate whether the enemy intends giving battle this side of Richmond. Telegraph Butler that we have crossed." This done, he

On May 4, John Sedgwick's VI Corps, trailed by a long supply train and heading toward the Wilderness, troops across the Rapidan River on a pontoon bridge.

rode on a short distance and established headquarters beside the road, near a deserted house whose front porch afforded him and his military family a shaded, airy position from which to observe his soldiers on the march. He was dressed uncharacteristically in full regimentals, including his sword and sash and even a pair of brown cotton-thread gloves, three stars glinting impressively on each shoulder of his best frock coat. What was more, his manner was as expansive as his trappings — a reaction, apparently, to his sudden release from concern that he might be attacked with his army astride the river. As he sat there smoking and swapping remarks with his associates, a newspaper correspondent approached and asked the question not even Lincoln had put to him in the past two months. How long was it going to take him to reach Richmond?

Grant not only expressed no resentment at the reporter's inquisitive presumption; he even answered him. "I will agree to be there in about four days," he said, to the astonishment of the newsman and his staff. Then he added: "That is, if General Lee becomes a party to the agreement. But if he objects, the trip will undoubtedly be prolonged."

Laughter increased the pervasive feeling of well-being and relief, and orders soon were distributed for tomorrow's march, which had been prepared beforehand for release if all went well: as, indeed, all had. One change there was, however, occasioned by a report that Sheridan received that afternoon. Chagrined at encountering none of Major General J. E. B. Stuart's highly touted butternut troopers in the course of his probe of the Wilderness south of the two fords, he learned that this was because they were assembled near Fredericksburg for a grand review next day at Hamilton's Crossing, a dozen miles to the east, and he asked permission to take two of his three divisions in that direction at first light in order to get among them, smash them up, and thus abolish at the outset of the campaign one of the problems that would have to be solved before its finish. Grant was willing, and so was Meade, though more reluctantly, being hidebound in his notion as to the primary duty of cavalry on a march through enemy country. In any case, the army would still have one of its mounted divisions for such work, and that seemed ample, especially if tomorrow's advance required no more of the blue outriders than today's had done. For one thing, since the train would not complete its crossing of the Rapidan before late tomorrow afternoon, and would thus require that the three infantry corps hold back and keep well closed up for its protection, the marches were to be about as brief. Hancock would move south and west, first to Todd's Tavern and then to Shady Grove Church, down on the Catharpin Road, extending his right toward Parker's Store on the Orange Plank Road, which was to be Warren's stopping point. Warren in turn would extend his right toward Wilderness Tavern, his present position astride the Orange Turnpike, which Sedgwick would occupy tomorrow, leaving one division on guard at Germanna Ford until Burnside's lead division

In the Wilderness's haunted woodlands, where men's bones from earlier battles abounded, soldiers avoided the singing and small talk typical around campfires.

arrived. Despite their brevity (Hancock had nine miles to cover, Warren and Sedgwick barely half that) all marches were to begin at 5 o'clock promptly, which was sunup. Upon reaching their designated objectives, Wilderness Tavern, Parker's Store, and Shady Grove Church — each commanding a major road coming in from the west, where Lee presumably still was unless he had already taken alarm and fallen back southward — all units were to prepare at once for getting under way as promptly the following day, Friday the 6th, which would take them out of the Wilderness and into the open country beyond, in position for coming to grips with the Confederates on terrain that would favor the army superior in numbers.

Forty-eight hours would tell the story, Grant had informed Halleck early that afternoon, and all the indications were that the story would have an ending that was happy from the Federal point of view. Careful planning seemed to have paid off handsomely. Not only were his "most serious apprehensions" — that he would be jumped while astride the Rapidan — behind him, but his second greatest worry — that he would have to fight in the blind tangle of the Wilderness — was all but behind him, too. "Enemy moving infantry and trains toward Verdiersville," the signal station on Stony Mountain informed him at 3 p.m. "Two brigades gone from this front. Camps on Clark's Mountain breaking up. Battery still in position behind Dr Morton's house, and infantry pickets on the river." That had far more the sound of preparations for a withdrawal than for an attack, and there seemed to be little of urgency in the Confederate reaction, such as it was. Grant could turn in for a good night's sleep in a much less fretful state of mind than the one in which he had lain down the night before, while poised for the crossing which now was complete except for a couple of thousand more wagons and Burnside's corps, whose arrival would give him a combat strength of 122,000 effectives on the rebel side of the river: an army which, arrayed for battle, two ranks deep, with one third of its units held rearward in reserve, would extend for twenty-five miles from flank to flank. That was roughly twice as many troops as Lee could muster of all arms. Grant was not only willing, he was altogether anxious to take him on at the earliest possible moment, preferably out in the open, where he could bring his superior ordnance to bear, or if not there then here in this green maze of vines and briers and stunted oaks and pines, if the opportunity offered and that was what it came to. He turned in early and apparently slept well.

Such was not the case with a good many of the men who were bivouacked in this haunted woodland by his orders. Unlike him, they had been here before, and the memory was painful. In the fields around Wilderness Tavern, it was afterwards recalled — including the one just east of the deserted, ramshackle tavern itself, where Stonewall Jackson's maimed left arm was buried — there was little or no singing round the campfires, the usual pastime after a not-too-hard day's march, and there was even a tendency to avoid the accustomed small talk. This was due, one soldier declared, to "a sense of ominous dread which many of us found it almost impossible to shake off." There was, in fact, much about the present situation that was remindful of the one a year ago, when all ranks had engaged in a carnival of self-congratulation on the results of careful planning and stout marching; "The rebel army is now the legitimate property of the Army of the Potomac," Hooker had announced on that other May Day, just before he came to grief, suffering better than 17,000 casualties before he managed to scurry out of this scrub oak jungle and back across the Rappahannock, beyond the reach of a gray army barely one third the size of his own. Grant, they knew, was no such spouter, but they remembered Fighting Joe and other even more unpleasant things, such as brush fires set by bursting shells, in which men with broken backs and bullet-shattered legs had been roasted alive before the stretcher bearers could get at them. Even recruits could see the danger. "These woods will surely be burned if we fight here," one said when they first called a halt that afternoon.

Over near Chancellorsville, where the whippoorwills began calling plaintively soon after sunset, now as then, the mood was much the same. The fighting had been heaviest around here last year, and there still were many signs of it, including skeletons in rotted blue, washed partly out of their shallow graves by the rains of the past winter. No one but the devil himself would choose such ground for a field of battle, veterans said; the devil and old man Lee. In an artillery park near the ruin of the Chancellor mansion, which had burned to its brick foundations on the second day of conflict, a visiting infantry-man looked glumly at a weathered skull that stared back with empty sockets, grinning a lipless grin. He prodded it with his boot, then turned to his comrades — saying "you" and "you," not "we" and "us," for every soldier is superstitious about foretelling his own death, having seen such words come true too many times — and delivered himself of a prediction. "This is what you are all coming to," he told them, "and some of you will start toward it tomorrow."

*M*ost of Union General Winfield Scott Hancock's
troops ended their long May 4 march here around
the burned-out remains of the Chancellor house.

★

*T*n point of fact, the conversion of the blue invaders into
★ ★ ★ skeletons was just the kind of grisly work Lee had in mind,
and he was moving toward it, even now, with everything he
had. Grant had taken care, in his assignment of objectives for the following day,
to see that each of the three main roads coming in from the west would be
covered by a corps of infantry; for though logic and the evidence, such as it was,
tended to indicate that his adversary was in the process of falling back to a
strong defensive position athwart his path — probably on the banks of the
North Anna, twenty miles to the south — there was a chance that the old fox
might mass his troops for an attack, down one or another of those roads, in an
attempt to strike while the Union army was strung out in the Wilderness. The
truth was, Lee was coming by all three, a corps on each.

Ewell, alerted the night before, would march eastward on the Orange
Turnpike, nearest the river, while Hill took the Orange Plank Road, which
paralleled the turnpike at a distance that varied from one to three miles until the
two converged, just short of Chancellorsville, twenty-five miles away;
Longstreet, down around Gordonsville, had a greater distance to travel and
would make a later start, having to call in his troops from the far-left positions
they had been obliged to hold until Grant was committed to the upstream
movement with all his force. Ewell, with three divisions, began his march at 9
o'clock. Hill reached Orange before noon, left one division there to guard the
nearby Rapidan crossings, and had his other two in motion on the plank road
shortly afterwards, the army commander riding with him near the head of the
column. Since the troops on the turnpike had a three-hour head start and a
straighter route, Ewell was told to regulate his speed by that of Hill. Longstreet
then was notified by courier to set out with his two divisions, crossing the
North Anna by Brock's Bridge, due east of Gordonsville, then turning north to
strike the Catharpin Road at Richard's Shop, from which point his march would
parallel those of the other two corps, on his left between him and the Rapidan.
Lee's plan, though he announced no details yet, was to get within reach of the
Federals as soon as possible, bring them to a Wilderness-hampered halt with Hill
and Ewell, then launch an all-out hip-and-thigh assault with all three corps, as
soon as Longstreet came up on the right.

Ewell stopped for the night at Locust Grove, a couple of miles into
the Wilderness beyond Mine Run. Clustered about their skillet wagons for supper,
the men of his three divisions had no such reaction to their surroundings as the
men of Warren's four divisions were experiencing around Wilderness Tavern, five
miles up the pike, or those of Hancock's four at Chancellorsville, another five
miles east. Outnumbered as usual on the eve of contact, and having fought here
against odds as long and longer, the butternut veterans understood that the
cramped, leaf-screened terrain would work to their advantage, now as before, and

their bivouacs hummed with banter and small talk as they bedded down, after ravening their rations, to rest for the shock they knew was likely to come tomorrow. Five miles southwest on the plank road, and still five miles short of the western limits of the Wilderness, it was much the same with the men of Hill's two divisions, rolled in their blankets and sleeping under the stars. At sundown he had called a halt at Verdiersville, eleven miles beyond Orange and nine from Parker's Store; "My Dearsville," Hill's troops dubbed the hamlet. Here Lee had had his head-quarters during the Mine Run confrontation last November, and his tent was pitched, tonight as then, in a field beside the road. Soon there began to come to its flap a series of couriers bearing dispatches from all quarters of Virginia — dispatches which in turn bore out, to the letter, predictions he had been making for the past month as to the nature of the offensive the Federals now had launched.

Of these, the most alarming came from the President himself. A blue force, estimated at 30,000 of all arms and said to be commanded by Ben Butler, was unloading from transports at City Point and Bermuda Hundred, on the south bank of the James less than twenty miles from Richmond, in position to break its vital rail connections with Petersburg and points south, if not indeed to come swarming across its bridges and into its streets in a matter of hours, since the capital had scarcely one tenth that many troops for its defense. "With these facts and your previous knowledge," Davis wired, demonstrating his accustomed calmness under pressure, as well as his abiding trust in Lee, "you can estimate the condition of things here, and decide how far your own movements should be in-fluenced thereby." Lee's decision was not to allow his movements to be influenced at all by this development. He would continue to concentrate on meeting the threat to his immediate front, he informed Davis, and leave Butler to Beauregard, who had been ordered to proceed at once from Weldon to confront the southside invaders with such troops as he could muster in his newly formed department. Lee's reaction to a second grievous danger, reported from out in the Shenandoah Valley, was much the same. Warned that a force of undetermined strength under Sigel had begun an advance up the Valley in conjunction with another movement west of the Alleghenies, he replied with a wire instructing Breckinridge to assume "general direction of affairs" beyond the Blue Ridge. "I trust you will drive the enemy back," he told him. This done, he put both dangers — one to his rear, the other to his flank, and both to his lines of supply and communication — out of his mind, at least for the present, in order to give his undivided attention to the prob-lem at hand: specifically, how best to deal with Meade's blue host, which had crossed the Rapidan bent on his destruction, but which was camped for the present across his front in the green toils of the Wilderness.

That the Federals had called at least a temporary halt, instead of pressing ahead on a night march to escape those toils and oblige him to race southward for a meeting in the open, was welcome news indeed, received in a series of messages Jeb Stuart kept sending to Verdiersville from shortly after dark until near midnight, when he apparently decided that the time had come to give his short-winded animals some rest. Abandoning his plans for the Hamilton's Crossing review next day, the cavalry leader was bringing his spruced-up troopers westward along the southern fringes of the Wilderness in order to get in position by morning on the right front of the army, there to protect its open flank and reconnoiter the enemy advance when it resumed. That too was welcome news, ensuring a continuous stream of intelligence, such as only cavalry could gather, and providing a resilient cushion against shock. Welcome, too, was a late-evening dispatch from Longstreet informing head-quarters that he had crossed Brock's Bridge and would camp there tonight, on the near bank of the North Anna; he expected to reach Richard's Shop by noon tomorrow, nine miles from Shady Grove Church and twelve from Todd's

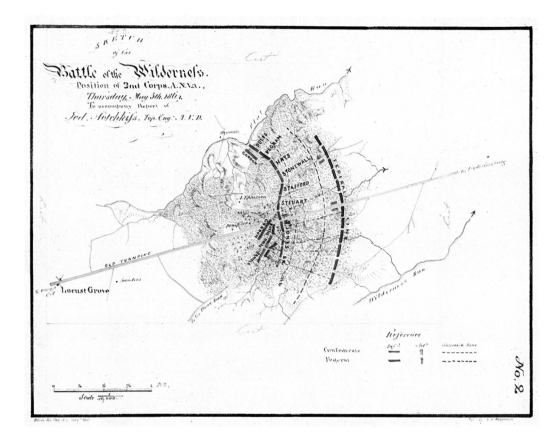

This map by Confederate topographer Jedediah Hotchkiss illustrates the positions held by Ewell's Second Corps on the opening day of the Wilderness.

★

Tavern. This meant that he most likely would be able to move into his assigned position, up the Catharpin Road, by nightfall, in plenty of time for launching the all-hands attack at first light Friday, after Ewell and Hill made contact tomorrow and set the bluecoats up for the assault designed to drive them back across the river they had crossed today. Accordingly, Lee had his adjutant notify Ewell that he was to move out early in the morning, continuing his march up the turnpike in order to menace the Union flank if Grant kept heading south. If he veered east, toward Fredericksburg, Ewell was to pursue him and fall upon his rear; or if he turned this way, Ewell was to take up a strong defensive position and hold him there in the tangled brush until Hill and Longstreet came up on the right, at which point they would all three go over to the offensive in accordance with Lee's plan. In any case, the adjutant added, "the General's desire is to bring him to battle as soon now as possible."

At breakfast next morning between dawn and sunup Lee was in excellent spirits, refreshed by four or five hours of sleep and encouraged by a follow-up message, just in from Stuart, that the three Federal corps had in fact spent the whole night in their Wilderness camps. He expressed his satisfaction at this evidence that all was working as he hoped, as well as at information that a brigade of Ewell's, detached for guard duty at Hanover Junction, would be rejoining no later than tomorrow. Together with last-minute piecemeal reinforcements sent from Richmond during the past week, this would give him an over-all strength of nearly 65,000 men in his eight divisions of infantry and three of cavalry. Four brigades were still detached (Hoke's, in North Carolina, and three with Major General George E. Pickett, comprising Longstreet's third division, still convalescing in southside Virginia from its brief, horrific experience on the third day at Gettysburg, ten months back) but Lee regretted this less than he might have done except for a miscalculation that contributed to the boldness of his plan for the annihilation or quick repulse of the enemy in the thickets up ahead. He estimated the combined strength of Meade and Burnside at not more than 75,000 men, and therefore assumed — quite erroneously, since the Federals, with considerably better than half again that many troops, had in fact almost twice the number Lee could muster — that he was about to fight against the shortest odds he had faced at any time since he assumed command of the Army of Northern Virginia, two victory-crowded years ago next month. Rising from breakfast he mounted Traveller and gave A. P. Hill the word to resume his march up the plank road, first across the "Poison Fields," as the leached-out mining region west of the Wilderness was called, and then into the briery hug of the jungle where he intended to come to grips with the invaders who, Stuart reported, seemed unaware of his presence on their flank.

Beyond the moldering six-months-old intrenchments around the headwaters of Mine Run, a couple of miles out of Verdiersville, this unawareness ended with a spatter of fire from a detachment of Union cavalry armed with seven-shot carbines. They were few in number, apparently, and easily driven back (Stuart had arrived by now, resplendent in his red-lined cape, to attend to this by fanning his horsemen out on the right and front) but word was certainly on the way to Grant that graybacks were approaching Parker's Store in strength. Moreover, a staff officer arrived from Ewell about this time to report that he had sighted heavy columns of bluecoats crossing the Wilderness Tavern intersection, two miles ahead on the Germanna Plank Road, perpendicular to the turnpike. It stood to reason that if Ewell could see the enemy, so could the enemy see him; Grant would be forewarned in that direction, too. Lee repeated his instructions that the Second Corps, continuing to regulate its march by that of the Third, was to move on and make contact, but added that he preferred not to "bring on a general engagement" until Longstreet came up. Hill was deep in the Wilderness by then, out of touch with Ewell as a result of a widening divergence, beyond Verdiersville, of the plank road from the turnpike, which was almost three miles away by the time he reached Parker's Store at noon. At this point, still riding near the head of Hill's two-division column, Lee heard a rising clatter of rifle fire from the left front. Obviously there was fighting on the turnpike, and from the sound of it, filtered through three miles of brush and branches, the engagement was indeed "general," mounting to a quick crescendo like the rapid tearing of canvas, though it lacked the deeper, rumbling tones artillery gave a battle at that distance.

Mindful of Lee's admonition not to "bring on a general engagement," Ewell had deployed his lead division when he got within a couple of miles of the Union-held crossroad, then brought up the second for close support on both sides of the pike, warning the two commanders — Major Generals Edward Johnson and Robert Rodes, who at forty-eight and thirty-five were the oldest and youngest infantry division commanders in the army — "not to allow themselves to become involved, but to fall back slowly if pressed." So he later reported, but the words had little application when the time came, as it did all too soon: especially for the men of Johnson's lead brigade, Virginians under Brigadier General John M. Jones, who caught the initial and overwhelming impact of a whole blue division that came hurtling at them, as if out of nowhere, through brush and vines that limited vision to less than sixty feet in any direction. Caught thus, they found it as impossible to "fall back slowly" as they had to avoid becoming "involved." Losing Jones, who was killed by an early volley from the dense wave of attackers, they broke and fled, spreading panic through the ranks of an Alabama brigade Rodes had posted in their rear. Ewell, so close to the front that the attack exploded practically in his face, whirled his horse and raced back to bring help from his third division, Major General Jubal Early's, which had kept to the road in order to come up fast in an emergency such as the

Brigadier General John M. Jones was killed by an early volley from the dense wave of a Union charge that overwhelmed his brigade of Virginians.

one that was now at hand. In the lead was Brigadier General John B. Gordon's brigade, Georgians who had a reputation for aggressiveness on short notice.

"General Gordon!" Ewell cried, his dragoon mustache bristling and his prominent eyes bulging as he checked his mount with a hard pull on the reins, "the day depends on you!"

"These men will save it, sir," Gordon replied, partly for the benefit of the troops themselves, who had come crowding up, as was their custom at such times, to hear what the brass had to say.

Going at once from march to attack formation, he advanced one regiment unsupported in a countercharge straight up the pike, while the rest deployed to go in on the right. On the left, two of Johnson's three intact brigades reacted by clawing their way through the brush toward the sound of firing, and Rodes's four did likewise, including the Alabamians who had been rattled by the flight of the Virginians through their ranks. As suddenly as it had risen, the tide of battle turned, and for the former attackers, overlapped on both flanks and savagely assailed from dead ahead by the screaming Georgians, the outcome was even more disastrous. Now it was their turn to backtrack, losing heavily in the process — though not as heavily as two other blue divisions, coming up in sequence on the left and groping blindly for the flank they had been told to support but could not find. Struck before they could form for attack or defense, they were driven eastward in confusion, suffering grievously in killed and wounded and losing several hundred prisoners, many of whom fled unknowingly into the rebel lines, bereft of all sense of direction in that maze of vines and brambles. It was, as one veteran said, a conflict "no man saw or could see"; "A battle of invisibles with invisibles," another called it. "As for fighting," a third declared, "it was simply bushwhacking on a grand scale, in brush where all formation beyond that of regiments or companies was soon lost and where such a thing as a consistent line of battle on either side was impossible."

The pattern of Wilderness fighting had been set, and one of its principal elements was panic, which came easily and spread rapidly on terrain that had all the claustral qualities of a landscape in a nightmare, with a variety of background sounds that ranged from a foreboding silence, so dense that a man was likely to jump six feet at the snap of a twig, to a veritable cataract of noise, referred to by a participant as "the most terrific musketry firing ever heard on the American continent."

Ewell, still mindful of Lee's admonition, did not pursue beyond the point at which the fight had opened, just under two miles west of the crossroad. It was 3 o'clock by now, and he could tell himself, quite truthfully, that he had done all that was asked of him and more, inflicting much heavier casualties than he suffered and fixing the enemy there in the tangled depths of the Wilderness. He put his men to work intrenching a line that extended about a mile to the left and a mile to the right of the turnpike, and after hauling off two guns he had captured in the course of his counterattack, he settled down to wait for tomorrow, when Longstreet would be up and the army would go over to the offensive. Fighting continued on a lesser scale all afternoon and into the evening, and though he lost two more brigade commanders — Brigadier Generals Leroy Stafford of Louisiana and John Pegram of Virginia, the former mortally wounded and the latter shot in the leg — Ewell had no doubt that he would be able to hold his newly-fortified position, no matter what the Yankees sent against him.

On May 5, General John Pegram was shot in the leg while leading a counterattack on the Union VI Corps.

There was no such assurance down on the plank road, three miles south, where a separate battle swelled to a sudden and furious climax at about the time the disjointed contest on the pike began to wane. For Hill, whose two divisions were struck by a much heavier and far better coördinated attack than the one that had been launched against Ewell's three, there was no waning; there was hard, stand-up fighting from the moment of earnest contact, around 4 o'clock, until darkness and exhaustion persuaded the troops of both sides to rest on their arms, where they then were, for a resumption at first light tomorrow of a struggle that had been touch-and-go for the past four hours. His two divisions, commanded by Major Generals Henry Heth and Cadmus Wilcox, had continued their march beyond Parker's Store to within a mile of the Brock Road, on which the Union infantry was known to be moving south, when stiffened resistance brought the head of the gray column to a halt. Heth formed for battle astride the road, and Lee — taking over for Hill, who was sick today, as he had been at Gettysburg — set up headquarters in a roadside clearing near the farmhouse of a widow named Tapp. He had no sooner dismounted to confer with Stuart and Hill, who had stayed with his men despite his disability, than a platoon of blue-clad skirmishers walked into the clearing from behind a stand of pines in its northeast corner, rifles at the ready. Apparently as startled as the high-ranking Confederates were by the sudden confrontation, the Federals faded back into the pines instead of opening fire or advancing to make the capture that would have changed the course of the war. However thankful Lee was for this deliverance from the hands of the bluecoats, their presence served to emphasize the dangerous possibility of an enemy plunge, whether on purpose or by accident, into the heavily wooded gap which the divergence of the two routes had created between Hill, down here on the plank road, and Ewell, whose battle was still in full swing on the turnpike. Accordingly, Lee sent word for Wilcox to extend Hill's left by moving his division northward into the brush beyond the clearing, thus to forestall a penetration of the gap, while Heth resumed his eastward advance to develop the strength of the blue force in his front. Though he still intended to withhold delivery of his main effort until Longstreet was on hand, the southern commander's hope was that Heth would be able to carry the Brock Road intersection, less than a mile away, as an effective means of bringing the Union army to a severed, panicky halt in the very depths of the Wilderness, half a dozen miles from open ground in any direction.

It was now past 3 o'clock. A note went at once to Heth asking whether, in his judgment, he could seize the intersection without bringing on a "general engagement." Heth replied that the enemy seemed to be there in strength; he could not tell how much an attack would spread the action, but he was willing to give the thing a try if that was what was wanted. While Lee was turning this over in his mind, back at the Widow Tapp's, a sudden uproar from the immediate front — louder, even, than the one that had exploded in Ewell's face, four hours ago — informed him that the decision had been taken out of his hands. Unsupported by Wilcox, who had moved off to the left, Heth was under heavy, all-out assault from dead ahead.

★ ★ ★ *B*oth attacks — the one against Ewell, up on the turnpike, and the present one down the plank road against Hill — were the result of a deliberate decision by Grant, whose self-confidence and natural combativeness had not been lessened by the enlargement of his responsibilities and who was determined, moreover, not to yield the tactical initiative to an opponent with a reputation for making the most of it on all occasions. If this meant the abandonment of his original intention to get into, through, and out of the Wilderness in the shortest possible time, then that just had to be. His primary talent had always been instinctive, highly improvisatorial at its best, and though there was little about him that could be described as Napoleonic, he trusted, like Napoleon, in his star. The overriding fact, as Grant saw it, was that the rebels were there in the tangled brush, somewhere off to the west, and he was determined to hit them. He was determined, in Sheridan's phrase, to smash them up at every opportunity.

Meade began it, quite on his own. Shortly after 7 o'clock that morning, by which time the leading elements of all three corps had been two hours on the march, he was notified by Warren that the commander of his rear division, preparing to head south from Wilderness Tavern, had sighted a heavy butternut column moving toward him on the turnpike, two or three miles west of the Germanna Plank Road intersection. Reacting fast, Meade ordered Warren to bring his other three divisions back to their starting point and advance his whole corps down the pike, in order to confront and, if possible, destroy the rebel force. He believed that it amounted to no more than a division, "left here to fool us," he told Warren, "while they concentrate and prepare a position toward the North Anna," and he saw in the situation an opportunity to effect a considerable subtraction from Lee's army before coming to earnest grips with the rest of it in the open country to the south. With time to spare and the train still grinding slowly down the crowded roads to the east, he could afford a brief delay, especially one that held the promise of so rich a prize. In any case, with his exterior flank so threatened by a force of undetermined strength, he believed the decision was tactically sound; for, as he told Grant in a note informing him of the order for Warren to countermarch and attack, "until this movement of the enemy is developed, the march of the corps must be suspended."

Arriving shortly afterward for a meeting near the tavern, in whose yard Meade was conferring with Warren, Grant not only indorsed his chief lieutenant's aggressive reaction to the news that there were rebels on his flank;

Warren's V Corps marched this stretch of the Orange Turnpike past the ruins of Wilderness Tavern on May 5. Ewell's rebels awaited them behind the distant treeline.

he also enlarged upon it, in a characteristic manner, with words that applied not only here but elsewhere. "If any opportunity presents itself for pitching into a part of Lee's army," he told him, "do so without giving time for disposition." In accordance with this policy — which might be described as: "Hit now. Worry later" — when word was brought that another gray force had been spotted marching eastward on the plank road, down around Parker's Store, Hancock too was given orders to backtrack. Instead of continuing down the Catharpin Road to Shady Grove Church, his previous objective, he would turn left when he reached Todd's Tavern and take the Brock Road north to its intersection with the road on which this second rebel column was advancing. Similarly, now that the plot had thickened, Sedgwick was told to send one division to join Warren's turnpike attack and another down the Brock Road to the intersection Hancock had been assigned to cover. His third division would remain on guard at Germanna Ford until Burnside's arrival, expected by midday, when it too would come down and get in on the action — whichever, if either, fight was still in progress by that time — leaving Burnside's four divisions as an available reserve, to be on call if they were needed. Thus Grant, though he still had no specific information as to the size or composition of either rebel column approaching his open flank, was determined to strike them both with everything he had.

While couriers went pounding off to deliver these several messages, Grant and Meade rode a short way down the pike, a bit under half a mile beyond a boggy little stream called Wilderness Run, and turned off into the southwest quadrant of the Germanna Plank Road intersection, where there was a meadow adjoined by a farmhouse belonging to a family named Lacy. Headquarters tents were being pitched there, in accordance with the change in plans, and the two generals dismounted and climbed a knoll on the far side of the field. Grant took a seat on a convenient stump, lighted another of the twenty cigars he distributed among the various pockets of his uniform at the start of every day, and sat calmly, an imperturbable figure wreathed in tobacco smoke, waiting for the attack to be launched beyond the heavy screen of brush at the rim of the clearing. Time dragged, the sun edging slowly toward meridian, and presently he took a penknife out of his trouser pocket, picked up a stick, and started to whittle. Snagged by the blade, the fingertips of his thread gloves began to fray, until at last they were ruined. He took them off, unbuttoned his coat because of the increasing heat, and resumed his whittling. At noon, or a little after, a sudden clatter of stepped-up rifle fire announced that the action had finally opened about one mile down the turnpike.

At first it was difficult to tell how the thing was going. The clatter moved westward, diminished briefly, as if it had paused for breath, then swelled louder than ever and rolled back east for another pause: after which a similar uproar came from the left front, subsided, and then was repeated. Along the limited horizon, west and southwest, the trees began leaking smoke along a line that seemed to conform in general to the one from which the initial attack had been launched an hour ago. All that was clear, so far, was that little or nothing had been gained, although it was fairly certain by now that there were a good many more graybacks out there in the brush than Meade had supposed at the outset. Grant kept whittling.

Presently details filtered rearward, brought to the Lacy meadow by dispatch bearers on lathered horses. Complying with Grant's instructions, relayed by Meade, that he was to give no "time for disposition," Warren had told Brigadier General Charles Griffin, the commander of what had been his rear but now was his lead division, not to wait for word from the heads of the three divisions assigned to support him on the flanks — Brigadier General Horatio G. Wright

Grant Crosses the Wilderness

On May 5, Union General Governeur K. Warren, given no "time for disposition," sent his troops into a murderous game of Blindman's Buff against the rebels.

of Sedgwick's corps, on the march down from Germanna to go in on his right, and Brigadier Generals James S. Wadsworth and Samuel W. Crawford of his own corps, who were countermarching to come up on his left — but to pitch right into the Confederates, hard and fast, as soon as he got his troops in line astride the pike, trusting that the others would be there in time to furnish whatever assistance he might need. That was what he did; but he did so, as it turned out, unsupported in the crisis that resulted. Wright did not arrive for a full two hours, having gotten lost in the woods about as soon as he left the road, and Wadsworth and Crawford only came up in time to get badly mauled themselves, floundering around in the brush as if they were involved in a gigantic and altogether murderous game of Blindman's Buff: as indeed they were — particularly Wadsworth, a Hudson River grandee who, at fifty-six, was nine years older than any other division commander in the army. Just now he was feeling the weight of all those years. Trying to navigate by compass in that leafy sea of green, he got badly turned around and drifted northward so that his naked left was exposed to a sudden descent by Gordon's screaming Georgians, who tore into it so savagely that the whole division fell back in disorder, the men crying "Flanked! We're flanked!" as they ran. Crawford caught it even worse from the rallied Alabamians when he came up, groping blind after he lost touch with the navigating Wadsworth. A former army surgeon who had been on duty at Fort Sumter when it fell, he was thirty-four, the next-to-youngest of Meade's division commanders, but he looked considerably older after three years of combat, including

225

a bad wound taken at Antietam. "A tall, chesty, glowering man, with heavy eyes, a big nose, and bushy whiskers," he habitually wore what one of his soldiers described as "a turn-out-the-guard expression." His expression just now, however, was one of outrage. His division had once been Meade's own, made up entirely of Pennsylvanians, and Crawford was outraged at the heavy and useless losses he had suffered, including one veteran regiment captured practically intact when it fled in the wrong direction and found itself surrounded by grinning rebel scarecrows when it stumbled to a halt.

Unquestionably though, to judge by individual reaction, the most outraged man on the field today was Griffin. A hard-case West Pointer and a veteran of the Mexican War at thirty-eight, he was much admired by his men, including a brigade of regulars who had followed him through a lot of fighting over the past two years. An old line artilleryman, he was especially furious at the loss of a section of guns which had to be abandoned down the turnpike when his flanks were overlapped and his troops fell back to avoid being swamped by no less than seven Confederate brigades. The blame, as he saw it, lay with the commanders who had failed to come up on his left and right, and as soon as he managed to stabilize the line his three brigades had fallen back to, he got on his horse and galloped off to protest to Meade in person. Crossing the headquarters meadow, he dismounted and stalked up the knoll at the far side, fuming and cursing as he came. Meade heard him out and did what he could to soothe him, although with small success. The air was full of God-damns. Finally, relieved by at least having vented his spleen, Griffin went back down the knoll, remounted his horse, and rode off to rejoin his division on the firing line. Grant, who had stopped whittling for the first time while the tirade was in progress, got up from his stump and walked over to Meade. He had not quite caught Griffin's name, but he had never been one to put up with out-of-channels insubordination, even in the easier-going West. "Who is this General Gregg?" he asked. "You ought to put him under arrest." Meade, whose extreme irascibility was masked today by an unaccustomed calm, turned to Grant with the same

John B. Gordon flanked and badly mauled the Union troops sent against his savage Georgians on May 5.

gentleness he had shown the angry brigadier. "His name's Griffin, not Gregg," he said, "and that's only his way of talking." In grizzled contrast to his younger chief, and towering a full head above him, Meade leaned forward as he spoke and buttoned up Grant's coat for him, as if in concern that he might catch cold after being overheated. Grant went back to his stump and his whittling.

By then it was close to 3 o'clock. Off to the south, although the sound of it did not get through until Warren's had died down, the second battle had been shaping up for the past hour. All that was there at the start was Brigadier General George W. Getty's division of Sedgwick's corps, which had come down from Germanna before midday to take over from a hard-pressed regiment of cavalry the task of delaying the progress of the second Confederate force, in position astride the plank road about half a mile from the Brock Road intersection, while Hancock came up from Todd's Tavern on a march that was much impeded by V Corps artillery, which had halted to await developments. Hancock arrived at 2 o'clock, riding at the head of his four-division column, and when Getty informed him that the graybacks to his front were commanded by the ever-aggressive A. P. Hill and that he might have to fall back at any moment under increasing pressure from such a savage fighter, thus uncovering the crossroad whose loss would cut the army in two and expose its train to capture or destruction, Hancock ignored Grant's instructions to forgo time-consuming preparations and instead put his troops to work improvising crude log breastworks along the road in rear of the position, north and south of the plank road intersection, thus to provide them with something on which to rally in case they were repulsed. Peremptory orders for an immediate advance put an end to this at about 3.30. Leaving Brigadier Generals Francis Barlow's and John Gibbon's divisions posted well down the Brock Road to guard against an attack from the southwest — he had been warned that Longstreet's corps was on the march, somewhere off in that direction, though it was not expected to arrive until tomorrow — Hancock put Major General David Birney's and Brigadier General Gershom Mott's divisions in line on the right and left of Getty's and sent them forward with orders to drive the enemy back on Parker's Store, three miles from the vital crossroad in their rear, and thus abolish, for once and for all, this threat to the safe passage of the army through the Wilderness, together with its train. It was just past 4 o'clock by then, and on second thought, by way of giving more weight to the blow, he had Gibbon send two of his three brigades to stiffen the center of the attack which had now begun to roll.

It did not roll far, even though at this stage all that blocked the path of these 25,000 attackers was a single gray division with fewer than 7500 in its ranks. Advancing through the tangled brush, the Federals delivered blind volleys of musketry that lopped the saplings at breast height, all across their front, and made it nearly impossible, so heavy and continuous was the fire, for any standing defender to survive. The trouble was that scarcely a Confederate was standing. While waiting for a reply to his offer to go forward, if that was what Lee wanted, Heth — like Hancock, who was similarly engaged at the same time, half a mile away on the Brock Road — had had his men dig in and lie low along the slight, densely wooded ridge on which they had halted when the blue resistance stiffened. Prone beneath solid-seeming sheets of lead that slashed the leaves and clipped the breast-high branches, the troops along the ridge replied with volleys of their own. Not only were these as heavy as the ones the front-rank Federals were throwing; they were also a good deal more deadly. Caught thus, erect and unprotected by anything more substantial than smoke and foliage, the attackers suffered cruelly from a foe they could not see. Mott's division, bogged shoetop-deep in a swamp on the left, directly in front of the ridge, broke and ran from that first decimating fire, as did other outfits all along the line. Whole companies, whole regiments fell back in shock and panic, some of them all the way to the log defenses they had built an hour ago. There they were met, individually and collectively, with a curt demand from provost guards with leveled bayonets: "Show blood!" Those who could not show it were hoicked back into line alongside the troops who had not bolted, who were still in position, up there in the bullet-whipped brush, firing blind — "by earsight," it was called — in the general direction of the rebels lying prone in comparative safety on their ridge, pumping volley after horrendous volley into the blue mass down in the boggy swale to their immediate front.

Hancock, a hard hitter, never hit harder than he did here in the Wilderness today, despite confounding difficulties of terrain far better suited for defense (once the shock of surprise had been dispelled) than for attack. A second assault was mounted and delivered, then a third and a fourth, all with the disadvantage of trying to maintain alignment, as well as a precarious sense of direction, while attacking veterans who had only to lie low and fire as rapidly as they could load their overheated rifles. Up at army headquarters, where there was full awareness of the importance of keeping the Brock Road clear for travel, Meade had Warren send Wadsworth's division south, across the mile-wide gap between him and Hancock, with instructions to strike the left flank of the rebels, fixed in position by headlong pressure from the front. Hancock meantime was doing all he could to increase that pressure, having added two of Barlow's four brigades to the struggle. This gave him close to 30,000 men in his attack force, even after the deduction of casualties, which were heavy and getting heavier by the minute, including Brigadier General Alexander Hays, a lifelong friend of Grant's and one of the heroes of Gettysburg, killed at the head of his brigade in Birney's division. However, Lee by then had recalled Wilcox from his attempt to link up with Ewell and close the gap across the center. He came back fast and went in hard, supporting Heth just as his flank was about to crumble. This doubled the

*In this Alfred Waud sketch, Mott's Federal division
breaks for the rear as Jenkins' regiments gain
the Yankee breastworks at the Brock Road.*

number of defenders and reduced the odds from three- to two-to-one. Even so, the issue could not have remained much longer in doubt, except that gathering darkness finally ended the contest. It dwindled by common consent, then flared up momentarily as Wadsworth finally arrived in the twilight after thrashing around in the brush on a three-hour search for the battle raging furiously one mile to the south. When he came up, in position at last to wreck the interior rebel flank, Lee had no reserves to throw in his path except a single Alabama battalion of 125 men, detailed to guard the host of prisoners who had been streaming rearward ever since the fight began. The Alabamians formed a widespread skirmish line, leaving the prisoners to the care of a handful of wounded, and went in yelling for all they were worth, quite as if they had an army at their backs. Wadsworth stumbled to a halt, apparently convinced that his jungle-foundered soldiers were about to be swamped by superior numbers, and hastily took up a stout defensive position on Hancock's right as night came down.

★

While both sides turned to attend to such of their wounded as they could reach — lucky ones, these, compared to others caught between the lines, calling for help that could not come because the slightest movement drew instant volleys from troops made panicky by fear of a night attack at such close quarters, or trapped by fires that sprang up and spread rapidly when the night breeze rose and fanned the sparks in the dry leaves to flames — Grant went to his headquarters tent in the Lacy meadow to study reports of what had happened today and to make plans for what he wanted to happen tomorrow. He would, of course, continue the offensive on both fronts, though his best chance for a breakthrough seemed to lie with Hancock, who reported that he would have made one today if darkness had not ended the battle an hour too soon. Sedgwick, joined late in the day by his third division under Brigadier General James B. Ricketts, would remain in position on the right of the northern sector, with Warren, minus Wadsworth, on the left. These five divisions had attacked again near sunset, but with no greater success than before; Ewell, buttoned up tight in his intrenchments, would not budge. Tomorrow's attack in this sector would be made primarily to prevent him from sending reinforcements down to Hill, who was to be hit with everything Hancock could lay hands on: his own four divisions, plus one from each of the other three corps, including Burnside's, which had

*L*ate on May 5, Richard S. Ewell was buttoned up tight in these hastily thrown together rebel breastworks, the first to be erected during the Wilderness Campaign.

been arriving all afternoon, too late for today's fight but in plenty of time for tomorrow's. In addition to sending one division to Hancock, Burnside would leave another on guard at Germanna Ford and march the other two down the Germanna Plank Road tonight, turning off, south of the turnpike intersection, to move west through the woods for a plunge into the gap between Warren's left and Hancock's right and a drive against Hill's interior flank, which he would assail by turning south again, as soon as he was well into the gap between the two Confederate corps. Such was Grant's victory formula, compounded tonight for application tomorrow.

Jump-off time, he said, would be at first light, 4 o'clock. Sedgwick and Warren, with five divisions, would attack and pin down Ewell, while Hancock and Burnside, with nine divisions, were overrunning Hill — and Longstreet too, if he arrived by then and was put into that portion of the line. All that was known just now was that he was on the march, somewhere off to the south and west; Hancock was warned to be on the lookout for him on the far left, in case Lee tried something foxy in that direction, though Grant was as usual a good deal more intent on what he had in mind to do to the enemy than he was on what the enemy might or might not do to him. Meade was in full agreement with these orders, as indeed he had been with all orders from the start, except that he suggested that the jump-off be advanced an hour to sunrise, 5 o'clock, so that the troop commanders would have a little daylight time in which to get their men in line for the assault. Grant considered this briefly, then agreed, and the two turned in, along with their staffs, to get some sleep for the hard day coming up.

★ ★ ★   *L*ee too was planning an offensive for tomorrow, and he intended, moreover, to launch it in the same region Grant had chosen as the scene of his main effort: in the vicinity of the plank road intersection. This involved a revision, not of purpose — the Virginian had counted, all along, on going over to the offensive as soon as his whole army was at hand — but of method. Formerly Longstreet had been told to proceed up the Catharpin Road to Todd's Tavern, a position from which he could turn the Union left, but the daylong need for closing the tactically dangerous gap between Hill and Ewell now provoked a change of plans, whereby Old Peter would shift from the Catharpin to the Plank Road and come up, not on Hill's right, but in his rear; Little Powell then could sidle northward to connect with Ewell, thus abolishing the gap, while Longstreet took over his position and prepared to launch, with his own two divisions and Hill's third, a dawn attack designed to crumple Grant's left flank, roll it up, and in conjunction with Hill and Ewell, who would advance in turn against the Federals to their front, fling the blue invaders back across the Rapidan. Accordingly, around 7 o'clock, while Hill's battle was still raging and the outcome was in doubt, Lee sent Longstreet

★

word of the change in objectives, together with a guide to insure against going astray on the cross-country night march he would have to make in order to get from one road to the other. A message went at the same time to Major General Richard Anderson, commander of Hill's third division, which had moved from Orange to Verdiersville today, instructing him to continue his march up the plank road beyond Parker's Store tonight, in order to be with Longstreet in plenty of time for the attack at first light tomorrow.

Heth and Wilcox — who could testify to the all-too-probable truth of Hancock's claim, across the way, that another hour of daylight would have given him the breakthrough he had been seeking — were pleased to learn from Hill that Longstreet and Anderson would be up tonight to relieve

Worried rebel General Henry Heth asked three times if he could change the battle line assigned to him.

their fought-out men. Whether Lee had revised his previous estimate of the enemy strength or not, Little Powell was convinced that his 15,000 veterans had taken on upwards of 40,000 bluecoats in the Wilderness today, and he had little patience with the concern of his two division commanders about the tangled condition of their lines, which had come so close to buckling under repeated assaults that, in the words of one witness, "they were like a worm fence, at every angle." Heth went to Hill and told him flatly: "A skirmish line could drive my division and Wilcox's, situated as we now are." He proposed that a new line be drawn, just in rear of their present disordered position, for them to fall back on before morning, when, as he predicted, "we shall certainly be attacked." Little Powell would not hear of this, partly because such a move would have meant abandoning many of the wounded and also because it would rob his soldiers of their hard-earned rest. "Longstreet will be up in a few hours," he said. "He will form in your front. . . . The men have been marching and fighting all day and are tired. I don't wish them disturbed." Heth went back to his troops, but soon returned with Wilcox, who joined him in the proposal that both divisions be withdrawn to a new line. Hill repeated that he wanted the men to get their sleep between now and midnight, when Longstreet was expected. They went away, but Heth, whose heart was heavy with foreboding, came back for still a third time to renew the argument. This vexed Hill, whose own sleep was being interrupted now. "Damn it, Heth," he said angrily, "I don't want to hear any more about it. The men shall not be disturbed." Heth retired for good this time, though it was already after midnight and Longstreet was obviously behind schedule. 1 o'clock, 2 o'clock, 3 o'clock passed, and still there was no news that Old Peter was approaching. Not long before dawn, the two division commanders sent for a battalion of corps engineers to come forward with picks and shovels in a belated attempt to complete the neglected intrenchments before they were overrun by the blue attackers Heth was convinced would come with the sun, if not sooner.

Back at the Tapp farm, Lee had known since 10 o'clock that the First Corps would not be up till daylight at the earliest. The young cavalry officer who had ridden down to the Catharpin Road with instructions for the change in routes, Major Henry McClellan of Stuart's staff, had also been charged with giving Longstreet's lead division verbal orders to press on without delay, thereby assuring an early arrival in Hill's rear. He left about 7 and returned three hours later, highly indignant, to report to Lee that the commander of that division, Major General Charles W. Field, a West Pointer and a stickler for regulations — he had lately been promoted and appointed to his post, having served in Richmond as superintendent of the Bureau of Conscription since the loss of a leg at Second Manassas, twenty months ago — flatly declined to accept from a stray cavalryman possibly garbled verbal orders that were in contradiction to the ones he had received from his corps commander, which were that he was to rest his men at Richard's Shop until 1 o'clock in the morning. Then and not until then, he said stiffly, would the march be resumed. This meant that Old Peter's leading elements could scarcely arrive before sunup, since the distance from Richard's Shop was about a dozen miles, two or three of them over rugged terrain, across fields, through woods, and by roundabout lanes connecting the two main roads; but Lee seemed oddly unperturbed. When McClellan offered to ride back with written orders which Field would have no choice except to obey, the Virginian declined with a shake of his gray head. "No, Major," he said calmly. "It is now past 10 o'clock, and by the time you could return to General Field and he could put his division in motion, it would be 1 o'clock. At that hour he will move."

Lee returned to his tent for more paper work, including an 11 o'clock dispatch informing the Secretary of War of what had occurred since Grant's crossing of the Rapidan the day before — "By the blessing of God," he wrote of today's hard fight, "we maintained our position against every effort until night, when the contest closed" — then turned in for another four or five hours of sleep before rising to face what might well be disaster.

He did not mention the possibility of disaster or its cause, either to Seddon in Richmond or to Hill, whose troops were sleeping helter-skelter in the brush, in whatever random positions they had occupied when darkness ended the fighting and they fell asleep on their arms, many of them too weary to eat the scant rations sent up later in the evening. Perhaps, like Little Powell, Lee reasoned that rest would do more for them than would fretting about a situation they could do but little to repair in the few hours of darkness that remained. In any case, he left them and their commander undisturbed until dawn began to filter through the thickets and a popping of rifles, like individual handclaps, warned that another day of battle had begun: May 6. Exposed by daylight to this picket fire, the engineers dropped their picks and shovels, which they had had small chance to use, and scuttled rearward. Within an hour, sharply at 5 o'clock as the sun was rising, this intermittent racket merged and grew in abrupt intensity to a steady clatter, described by one observer as "the noise of a boy running with a stick pressed against a paling fence, faster and faster until it swelled into a continuous rattling roar." The Federals were attacking in greater strength than yesterday, along and down both sides of the plank road, and after a brief resistance

> *"We are driving them, sir! Tell General Meade we are driving them most beautifully."*
>
> — Winfield Scott Hancock

the two Confederate divisions did just what Heth had said they would do. They broke. Though they did not scatter in panic or drop their rifles, still they made for the rear, more or less in a body, some among them firing as they went. "The men seemed to fall back upon a deliberate conviction that it was impossible to hold the ground and, of course, foolish to attempt it," one among them later wrote by way of explanation, adding rather philosophically: "It was mortifying, but it was only what every veteran has experienced."

Up on Ewell's front the dug-in troops held firm under assault, but Sedgwick and Warren were accomplishing all that was asked of them by keeping him from sending reinforcements down to the far end of the line. Such flaw as there was in the execution of Grant's plan was in the center. Burnside, ordered to penetrate the rebel gap and descend on Hill's interior flank, had gotten himself and his two divisions lost as soon as he left the road last night and struck out through the brush; he was somewhere rearward now, behind the space between Warren and Hancock, disoriented and wandering in circles while the conflict raged, first to his right, then his left, sometimes front and sometimes rear. Hancock was furious at this dereliction. Shouting to be heard above the din on the plank road, he told one of Meade's staff officers that if those missing 10,000 men could be added to the pressure being exerted, "we could smash A. P. Hill all to pieces!" In point of fact, he seemed well on the way to doing it anyhow. Except for the troops with Barlow, whose division had been reunited down the Brock Road to guard against a possible flank attack, he had all the men assigned to the main effort massed and in motion, flushing graybacks as they went. Forty years old, "a tall, soldierly man with light brown hair and a military jaw," he had what the staffer described as "the massive features and the heavy folds round the eye that often mark a man of ability." Elated by the propitious opening of that portion of the battle in his charge, he made a handsome figure on horseback, and his elation grew as the attack continued. Just ahead was the Tapp clearing, and beyond it the white tops of wagons parked in the Confederate rear. "We are driving them, sir!" Hancock called proudly to the staff man. "Tell General Meade we are driving them most beautifully."

Lee was there in the clearing, doing all he could to stiffen what little was left of Hill's resistance, and so had Longstreet himself been there, momentarily at least, when the blue assault was launched. He came riding up just before sunrise, a mile or two in advance of his column, the head of which had reached Parker's Store by then, and Hill's chief of staff crossed the Tapp farmyard to welcome him as he turned off the road. "Ah, General, we have been looking for you since 12 o'clock last night. We expect to be attacked at any moment, and are not in any shape to resist." Unaccustomed to being reproached by unstrung colonels, however valid their anxiety, Old Peter looked sternly down at him. "My troops are not up," he said. "I've ridden ahead —" At this point the sudden clatter of Hancock's attack erupted out in the brush, and Longstreet, without waiting to learn more of what had happened, whirled his horse and galloped back to hurry his

This slouch hat, bearing the clover-leaf of the Federal II Corps, was shot off a surprised but unharmed soldier by a bullet piercing its crown on May 6.

two divisions forward. So Lee at least knew that the First Corps would soon be up. His problem, after sending his adjutant to order the wagon train prepared for withdrawal, was to hang on till these reinforcements got there, probably within the hour, to shore up Hill's fast-crumbling line. Presently, though, this began to look like more than he could manage; Wilcox and Heth, overlapped on both flanks, gave ground rapidly before a solid mass of attackers, and skulkers began to drift rearward across the clearing, singly and in groups, some of them turning to fire from time to time at their pursuers, while others seemed only intent on escape. Their number increased, until finally Lee saw a whole brigade in full retreat. Moreover, this was not just any brigade; it was Brigadier General Samuel McGowan's brigade of South Carolinians, Wilcox's best and one of the finest in the army.

"My God, General McGowan!" Lee exclaimed from horseback, breasting the flood of fugitives. "Is this splendid brigade of yours running like a flock of geese?"

"General, these men are not whipped," McGowan answered, stung in his pride by this public rebuke. "They only want a place to form and they will fight as well as they ever did."

But there was the rub. All that was left by now for them to form on was a battalion of Third Corps artillery, four batteries under twenty-eight-year-old Lieutenant Colonel William Poague, lined up along the west side of the clearing which afforded one of the Wilderness's few real fields of fire. The cannoneers stood to their loaded pieces, waiting for Hill's infantry to fall back far enough to give them a chance to shoot at the bluecoats in pursuit. However, there was no time for this; Poague, with Lee's approval, had his guns open at what was already point-blank range, shaving the heads of the Confederate retreaters in order to throw their anti-personnel rounds into the enemy ranks. This took quick effect, particularly near the road, where the Federals tended to bunch up. Flailed by double-shotted grape and canister, they paused and began to look for cover: seeing which, the cannoneers stepped up their rate of fire. Lee remained mounted alongside Poague, who kept his men at their work — "getting the starch out of our shirts," they called it — without infantry support. This could not continue long before they would be overrun, but meantime they were making the most of it. Smoke from the guns drifted back, sparkling in the early-morning sunlight, and presently Lee saw through its rearward swirls a cluster of men running toward him, carrying their rifles at the ready and shouldering Hill's fugitives aside.

"Who are you, my boys?" he cried as they came up in rear of the line of bucking guns.

"Texas boys!" they yelled, gathering now in larger numbers, and Lee knew them: Hood's Texans, his old-time shock troops, now under Brigadier General John Gregg — the lead brigade of Field's division. Longstreet was up at last.

In support of A.P. Hill's infantry, twenty-eight-year-old William T. Poague (left), one of Lee's best artillerists, deployed his guns at the Widow Tapp's farm.

"Hurrah for Texas!" Lee shouted. He took off his wide-brimmed hat and waved it. "Hurrah for Texas!"

No one had ever seen him act this way before, either on or off the field of battle. And presently, when the guns ceased their fuming and the Texans started forward, they saw something else they had never seen: something that froze the cheers in their throats and brought them to a halt. When Gregg gave the order, "Attention, Texas Brigade! The eyes of General Lee are upon you. Forward . . . march!" Lee rose in his stirrups and lifted his hat. "Texans always move them," he declared. They cheered as they stepped out between the guns. "I would charge hell itself for that old man," a veteran said fervently. Then they saw the one thing that could stop them. Lee had spurred Traveller forward on their heels; he intended to go in with them, across the field and after the bluecoats in the brush. They slacked their pace and left off cheering. "Lee to the rear!" began to be heard along the line, and some of them addressed him directly: "Go back, General Lee, go back. We won't go unless you go back." He was among them now, flushed with excitement, his eyes fixed on the woods ahead. They stopped, and when an attempt by Gregg to head him off had no effect, a sergeant reached out and took hold of Traveller's rein, bringing the animal to a halt. "Lee to the rear! Lee to the rear!" the men were shouting. But his blood was up; he did not seem to hear them, or even to know that he and they were no longer in motion. At this point a staff colonel intervened. "General, you've been looking for General Longstreet. There he is, over yonder." Lee looked and saw, at the far end of the field, the man he called his war horse. For the first time since he cleared the line of guns he seemed to become aware that he was involved in something larger than a charge. Responding to the colonel's suggestion, he

This battle flag was carried by the 5th Texas Infantry during the Wilderness Campaign, where some 60 percent of the unit fell to Federal fire.

turned Traveller's head and rode in that direction. On the way he passed in rear of Brigadier General Evander Law's Alabama brigade, about to move out on the left. "What troops are these?" he asked, and on being told he called to them: "God bless the Alabamians!" They went forward with a whoop, alongside the Texans, who were whooping too. "I thought him at that moment the grandest specimen of manhood I ever beheld," one among them later wrote. "He looked as though he ought to have been, and was, the monarch of the world."

Longstreet yielded to no man in his admiration for Lee, yet his admiration never amounted to idolatry, especially if idolatry included a willingness to put up with tactical interference. Seeing him thus "off his balance," he later wrote, he informed him with jocular bluntness, as soon as he came up, "that his line would be recovered in an hour if he would permit me to handle the troops, but if my services were not needed I would like to ride to some place of safety, as it was not quite comfortable where we were." Lee complied by retiring westward a short distance with his staff officers, who no doubt were glad to get him out of there, and Old Peter kept his word, here and on the opposite side of the plank road as well.

There his other division had been put in line by its commander, Brigadier General Joseph Kershaw, whose Georgians, South Carolinians, and Mississippians hooted cruelly when Heth's badly shaken troops fell back through their ranks. "Do you belong to Lee's army?" they jeered, seeing their old comrades thus for the first time in eight months. "You don't look like the men we left here. You're worse than Bragg's men!" Taking over, they stalled Hancock's advance on this side of the road, while Field was doing the same across the way. Then the two divisions went forward together against the Federals, who were wearier and a good deal more disorganized than they had known until they were brought to a halt, first by Poague's four rapid-firing batteries and then by 10,000 newly committed rebels whose appearance was as sudden as if they had dropped out of the sky. Still, the going was rough for the First Corps, most of whose members had never fought in the region west of Fredericksburg before. Some brigades lost heavily, including the Texans, who went in boasting that they had "put General Lee under arrest and sent him to the rear." A captured private from the brigade expressed its collective opinion when his captors asked him what he thought of this Battle of the Wilderness. "Battle be damned," he said hotly. "It aint no battle, it's a worse riot than Chickamauga! At Chickamauga there was at least a rear, but here there aint neither front nor rear. It's all a damned mess! And our two armies aint nothing but howling mobs."

Longstreet yielded to no man in his admiration for Lee, yet his admiration never amounted to idolatry, especially if idolatry included a willingness to put up with tactical interference.

Before 10 o'clock, despite the various impediments of terrain and the refusal by most of Hancock's men to panic under pressure, Longstreet fulfilled his promise to recover the line that had begun to be lost at sunrise. Halting there, within half a mile of the Brock Road, he proceeded to consolidate the position, reinforced presently by Anderson, whose division arrived while the First Corps was advancing and moved up in its support. Hill meantime had rallied his other two divisions and swung them northward, in accordance with Lee's orders, to plug the gap that had yawned since yesterday between him and Ewell. Finding it unexploited by the Federals, whose own gap had been enlarged by Longstreet — Law's whooping Alabamians had struck and scattered Wadsworth's ill-starred division on Hancock's right, driving the remnant west and north, all the way to the Lacy meadow, and Burnside was still on his circuitous tour of the brush — Hill's men, willingly and hurriedly, did what they had failed to do the night before. They intrenched. Lee's line was now a continuous one, reasonably compact, and he had all his troops on hand at last, including Ewell's detached brigade, which arrived at midmorning from Hanover. The time had come for him to go over to the all-out offensive he had planned to launch as soon as he managed to bring Grant to a standstill in the thickets — as he now had done.

"There was a lull all along the line," a regimental commander later said of this period during which reconnaissance parties went out and came back and last-minute instructions were delivered: adding, "It was the ominous silence that precedes the tornado."

★ ★ ★ actically, **Grant was in far worse shape** than he or anyone else in the Lacy meadow seemed to know. In addition to the unmanned gap across his center, he had both flanks in the air. No blue army had ever remained long in any such attitude, here in Virginia, without suffering grievously at the hands of Lee for having been so neglectful or inept; Hooker, for example, had left only one flank open, but his discomfiture had been complete. Now the same treatment might well be in store for Grant, on practically that same ground just one year later.

Headquarters had been more or less in a turmoil for the past two hours, ever since Hancock's attack went into reverse. First, there was the matter of Burnside's nonarrival, which not only reduced the intended strength of the main effort but also left it unsupported on the right, exposing Wadsworth to the catastrophe that ensued. In point of fact, after all that had happened yesterday, the aging New Yorker — a brigadier since shortly after First Bull Run, military governor of the District of Columbia during the tenure of McClellan, whom he had helped to frustrate, and an unsuccessful candidate for governor of his home state on the Republican ticket in '62, the year of the Democratic sweep — had seemed to suspect from the start that today would be no better. He was feeling his years, and he told an aide he thought perhaps he ought to turn the command of his division over to someone else and go to the rear. As it was, however, he stayed and managed, today as yesterday, to lose his sense of direction in the course of the attack and came crowding down on the units to his left, creating a jam on the near side of the plank road and thereby adding to the effectiveness of Poague's fire from the Tapp farmyard, as well as to the confusion that prevailed when Law assailed his unprotected right. One of his three brigades disintegrated without more ado, and Wadsworth, in an attempt to keep the other two from doing likewise, appealed to them from horseback to stand firm; whereupon he was hit in the back of the head and fell to the ground with a bullet in his brain. His troops ran off and left him, pursued by the rebels, who gathered him up and took him back to one of their aid stations. He died there two days later, having been stared at by a great many of his enemies, who came for a look at a man reputed to possess "more wealth than the treasury of the Confederate government." Rich men were not unusual in the armies of the South, where the West Point tradition was strong in leading families and no $300 commutation fee could secure exemption from conscription, but were rarely encountered on the other side, particularly on the firing line. Meantime the fallen general's troops continued their flight all the way to the Lacy meadow, as if they expected to find sanctuary there with Grant, who sat on his accustomed stump atop the knoll, still whittling, still wreathed in cigar smoke. Headquarters was alarmed by their sudden appearance, even though they did not seem to be pursued, and presently, when long-range shots began to fall in the vicinity, an anxious staffer, fearful that the meadow was about to be overrun, suggested that it would be prudent to shift the command post rearward. Grant stopped whittling. "It strikes me it would be better to order up some artillery and defend the present location," he said quietly. This was done, although there was nothing the gunners could see in the way of targets, and Hancock bolstered what remained of Wadsworth's division by sending reinforcements over from the left.

On the right, Sedgwick and Warren had suffered heavy losses in carrying out their instructions to keep attacking Ewell's intrenchments and thus prevent his sending reinforcements down to Hill. This they had done, and in doing it they had kept him on the defensive. But if they assumed from this that he would remain so, or that Sedgwick's outer flank was secure because it was covered by Flat Creek, they would be disabused before nightfall; Gordon, whose brigade was on the left, was trying even now to get permission from his superiors to turn the Federal flank, which he insisted was wide open to such a maneuver, having scouted it himself. So far, Ewell and Early had declined to let him try it, being convinced that Burnside's corps was posted rearward in support. Obviously, Sedgwick's immunity from attack, based as it was on this misconception by Gordon's superiors, was going to last no longer than Burnside remained unaccounted for in the Union order of battle. Once he found his way up to the firing line and was identified, Ewell and Early would have to abandon their objection to Gordon's proposal and unleash him, with results that were likely to be spectacular if Sedgwick's dispositions were as faulty as the Georgian claimed to have seen with his own eyes.

Just now, however — for Burnside, having spent the past five hours out of pocket, was to spend an-

Aged 56, Brigadier General James Wadsworth was shot from his horse by a rebel bullet to his brain on May 6.

*Federal troops from Wadsworth's division,
formed in line of battle, fight their way through the
woods north of the Orange Plank Road on May 6.*

other three in the same fashion, lost to friend and foe alike, before he managed to get where he belonged — the gravest danger was on the opposite flank, which was also exposed to being turned or struck end-on. This was due to a combination of misconceptions, based on erroneous information from headquarters. Hancock had kept Barlow in position down the Brock Road all this time, yesterday and today, in expectation that Longstreet would arrive from that direction. Instead he had come up the plank road, converting Hill's near rout into a counteroffensive; but Hancock still held Barlow where he was, outside the action, because only two of Old Peter's divisions, Field's and Kershaw's, had so far been identified. The third, Pickett's — reported to have been with Longstreet at Gordonsville, though in fact it was south of Richmond — might be maneuvering for an attack up the Brock Road, perhaps in conjunction with Anderson's division of Hill's corps, which had also not yet been accounted for. So Barlow was kept where he was, a mile and a half from the plank road intersection, to guard against a tangential strike by these 10,000 missing rebels. Meantime, evidence had accumulated to support the belief that they were already at hand, including one frantic eyewitness report that they were advancing in mass up the Brock Road. This was a case of mistaken identity; the advancing mass turned out

★

to be a herd of Federal convalescents, marching from Chancellorsville to rejoin the army by Hancock's roundabout route. No sooner was this mistake discovered, however, than heavy firing was heard from down around Todd's Tavern, where the Brock and Catharpin roads intersected, less than three miles from Barlow's outpost on the Union left. The assumption was that the cavalry must have encountered Pickett's column, coming up from the Catharpin Road, and was doing what it could to hold him off while Barlow got ready to receive him. This was partly correct and partly wrong. It was cavalry, right enough, but that was all it was. The blue troopers were shooting, not at Pickett (who was perhaps of greater service to his country here today, though he was not within sixty miles of the battle, than he had been ten months ago at Gettysburg, leading the charge that would be known forever after by his name) but at Stuart. Sheridan had served Grant poorly yesterday by plunging eastward, with two thirds of the army's cavalry, into the vacuum Stuart had left around Fredericksburg when he moved westward to take position on Lee's right. Still intent on closing with the graybacks, more for the purpose of destroying them than of finding out what was happening in their rear, Sheridan's horsemen made such a racket with their rapid-firing carbines that Barlow thought a large-scale action was in progress, though in fact it was nothing more than an unprofitable skirmish, which did not result in the slightest penetration of the cavalry screen Stuart kept tightly drawn to prevent his adversary from catching even a glimpse of the preparations now being made for attack, four miles northwest. As it was, Barlow was so impressed by the uproar down around Todd's Tavern that he called urgently for reinforcements to help him meet what he was convinced was coming, and Hancock obliged by sending him two brigades from the main body, which by then was back on the line it had left at sunrise.

Hancock had his hands full where he was, holding Longstreet west of the Brock Road, immediately north and south of the plank road intersection. For better than five hours now, advancing and retreating, the fighting had been as heavy as any he had ever seen, and so too had his casualties and the expenditure of ammunition. Drummer boys were pressed into unfamiliar service as stretcher bearers, and when they got to the rear with their anguished burdens, the stretchers were loaded with boxes of cartridges for the return to the firing line, so that, as one reporter wrote, "the struggle shall not cease for want of ball and powder." Involved as he was in the direction of all this, blinded by thickets and appealed to simultaneously from the left and right — Barlow was convinced that he was about to be hit by Pickett, and Wadsworth's division, adjacent to the unmanned gap across the army's center, had just come apart at the seams — Hancock was apparently too busy to notice that the contraction of his front in the vicinity of the crossroad, resulting from his losses and the withdrawal of four brigades to meet the reported dangers on the far left and the right, had widened to about a mile the brush-choked interval between the main body and Barlow's outpost position down the road. Consequently, though he was reasonably well protected against a flank attack by Pickett, who wasn't there, he was not protected at all from one by Longstreet, who was. His immediate left — as Gordon was saying of Sedgwick's right, four miles away — was wide open to either a turning movement or an end-on strike.

Then came the lull, a half-hour breathing space. Hancock spent it shoring up his line against an expected renewal of Longstreet's frontal effort to drive him back from the vital crossroad. Atop the knoll in the Lacy meadow, Grant, with a hole in his center and both flanks in the air, continued to whittle. Then, around 11 o'clock, the storm broke. Within minutes of the opening shots, according to Meade's chief of staff, the uproar of the rebel attack "approached the sublime."

★ ★ ★ *L*ongstreet, always grand in battle, never shone as he did here," a First Corps artillerist said of the general in his conduct of this morning's fighting on the right. Within three hours of his arrival he introduced tactics into a battle which, up to then, had been little more than a twenty-hour slugging match, with first one side then the other surging forward through the brush, only to fall back when momentum was lost and the enemy took his turn at going over to the offensive. All attacks had been frontal except for chance encounters, when some confused unit — a regiment or a brigade or, as in Wadsworth's case, a division — got turned around, usually in the course of an advance through blinding thickets, and exposed a naked flank to being torn. Now Old Peter, who was always at his calmest when the conflict roared its loudest, undertook to serve a Federal corps, reinforced to a strength of seven divisions, in that same tearing fashion.

Lee had ordered the army's chief engineer, Major General Martin L. Smith, to report to Longstreet at about the time the Federals began to yield the ground they had won from Hill. Sent out to reconnoiter the Union left, Smith — a forty-four-year-old New-York-born West Pointer whose most distinguished service to his adopted country up to now had been at Vicksburg, where he not only laid out and supervised the construction of its hilly defenses, but also commanded one of the divisions that manned them under siege — returned at 10 o'clock to report that he had found Hancock's flank wide open to attack from within the mile-wide gap that yawned between his main body and Barlow's outpost. Moreover, an unfinished and unmapped railroad, work on which had been abandoned when the war began, afforded an ideal covered approach to that vulnerable point; troops could be massed in the brush-screened cut, just where the roadbed made a turn southeast, perpendicular to the unguarded flank a briery quarter mile away. Old Peter's eyes lighted up at the news, but he was no more inclined to be precipitate here than he had been at Second Manassas when a similar opportunity arose. He summoned his young chief of staff, Lieutenant Colonel G. Moxley Sorrel, instructed him to take charge of a force made up of three brigades, one from each of the three divisions at hand, and conduct them to the designated point for the attack. Knowing how likely such maneuvers were to become disorganized under the influence of exuberance, he stressed the need for careful preparation. "Form a good line," he told him, "and then move, your right pushed forward and turning as much as possible to the left." Characteristically, before sending him on his way, he added in true First Corps style: "Hit hard when you start, but don't start until you have everything ready."

Sorrel assembled the three brigades, headed by Brigadier Generals William Wofford, G. T. Anderson, and William Mahone, respectively from Kershaw's, Field's, and Richard Anderson's divisions, and just as he was about to move out, Colonel John M. Stone of Heth's division, in position on Longstreet's left, requested permission to add the weight of his Mississippi brigade to the blow about to be struck. Hill and Heth were willing, and that made four brigades from as many divisions, a pair each from two corps, not one of them under a professional soldier and all in charge of a young staff officer who never before had commanded troops in action. Sorrel was a former bank clerk, twenty-six years old, intensely ambitious and strikingly handsome, a Georgian like his chief, though of French not Dutch extraction. As he set out, leading this force of about 5000 into the railway cut, then eastward through its leafy tunnel to the bend where they would mass for the attack, he knew that his great hour had come and he was determined to make the most of it, for his own and his country's sake. Old Peter, who had a great affection for him dating back to First Manassas, watched him disappear in the woods, then settled back to wait for the uproar that would signal the launching of the flank assault. He kept his remaining eleven brigades in position astride the plank road, maintaining frontal contact and preparing to increase the pressure

Confederate Lieutenant Colonel G. Moxley Sorrel (above) led the daring attack on Hancock's flank.

when the time came. Already he was planning a larger turning movement to follow the one about to start. Once Hancock's line had been rolled up, the fronts of
the other two Confederate corps would be uncovered in rapid sequence; Hill's
two divisions would join the grand left wheel, and Ewell's three would drive
straight ahead, cutting the Federals off from the fords by which they had crossed
the Rapidan. Obliged to fall back on Fredericksburg, Grant's army would be cut
to pieces, train and all, as it jammed the narrow Wilderness trails and scattered in
the brush. Anticipation made the wait seem long, though in fact it was quite
brief. At 11 o'clock, within half an hour of his setting out, Sorrel's attack exploded
on the Union left and began to roll northward, clattering across the right front of
the Confederate position. Longstreet ordered his main body forward simultaneously to exploit and enlarge the panic already evident in the enemy ranks.

The end-on blow was as successful as even Sorrel had dared to hope
it would be. Struck without preamble by a horde of rapid-firing rebels who
came screaming through what up to then had been a curtain of peaceful green,

> *Struck without preamble by a horde of rapid-firing rebels who came screaming through what up to then had been a curtain of peaceful green, the first blue unit . . . disintegrated on contact . . .*

the first blue unit — a brigade that had just been withdrawn from the line to
catch its breath while the lull was on — disintegrated on contact, its members
taking off in all directions to escape the sudden onslaught, and though others
reacted differently, having at least had a semblance of warning that something
horrendous was headed in their direction from the left, the result was much the
same in the end, as unit after unit, finding itself under simultaneous fire from
the front and flank, sought to achieve a similar deliverance from fury.
Consternation in such cases was followed by a strangely deliberate acceptance of
the military facts of life, the difference being that they reacted, not as individuals,
but as a group seeking safety in numbers. A man from one of Gibbon's brigades
reported that the first he knew of a flank attack was when he saw troops from
Mott's division, on his left, trudging rearward in a body. At first, so deliberate
was their step, so oddly sullen their expression, he could not make out what was
happening. "[They] did not seem to me demoralized in manner," he declared,
"nor did they present the appearance of soldiers moving under orders, but
rather of a throng of armed men returning dissatisfied from a muster." The best

explanation another observer could give was that "a large number of troops were about to leave the service," and apparently they were doing all they could to leave it alive. One thing at least was clear to a staff officer who watched them slogging rearward, oblivious to pleas and threats alike. "They had fought all they meant to fight for the present," he said, "and there was an end to it." Hancock himself put it simplest, in a statement years later to Longstreet: "You rolled me up like a wet blanket."

Elation on the Confederate side was correspondingly great, and it too was a sort of mass reaction. Here, the cheering troops perceived as soon as the flank attack began to roll, was another Chancellorsville in the making. Moreover, they were aware of the highly encouraging difference that, instead of launching their turning movement with a scant two hours of daylight left for its exploitation, as Jackson's men had done, they now had a substantial eight or nine such hours: enough, surely, to complete the destruction already under way. Not that they wasted time, simply because so much of it was available; Sorrel had carried out his orders with speed and precision. Wofford and Mahone were abreast in front, respectively on the left and right, supported by G. T. Anderson and Stone, whose added pressure shattered what little resistance was encountered or by-passed in the course of the advance. Within less than an hour they had driven northward all the way to the plank road; some of Wofford's Georgians, in fact, plunged eagerly across it, intent on the chase, though Mahone's Virginians called a halt at that point, in accordance with instructions. When Sorrel rode up he found the plank road unobstructed all the way to its intersection with the Brock Road, where the displaced and rattled Federals were taking shelter behind the breastworks Hancock had had them build the day before. From the opposite direction he saw Longstreet and his staff riding toward him on the plank road, accompanied by several unit commanders to whom the burly lieutenant general was apparently giving directions for the follow-up assault. They made up a sizeable cavalcade, and Sorrel could see from their manner, their gestures and expressions as they rode, that they shared the exuberance he was feeling at the success of his first experience as a leader of men in battle.

Their high spirits were voiced by Brigadier General Micah Jenkins, the twenty-eight-year-old commander of a brigade in Field's division, who had just been informed that his troops would play a major role in the follow-up attack. "I am happy," the young South Carolina aristocrat told Longstreet, excited by the prospect of enlarging the gains already made. "I have felt despair for the cause for some months, but now I am relieved, and feel assured that we will put the enemy back across the Rapidan before night." When Sorrel came up Jenkins embraced and congratulated him warmly. "We will smash them now," he said.

Old Peter thought so, too. Engineer Smith had returned from a second reconnaissance of the Union left to report that a second turning movement,

*A very ill
Brigadier General
Micah Jenkins,
leading his troops at
Brock Road, fell
victim to the fatal
Confederate volley
that damaged his
sword and
scabbard below.*

designed to flank the rallying bluecoats out of their breastworks along the Brock Road, was altogether as feasible as the first. Just then, however, as the cavalcade continued its ride east to within musket range of the Brock Road intersection, there was a sudden spatter of fire from the woods to the right front; some of Mahone's men were shooting at some of Wofford's, having mistaken them for Federals when they came hurrying back across the plank road to take their proper place in line. Aggressive as always, Longstreet whirled his horse in that direction, apparently intending to stop the undisciplined firing. Others followed his example — including Joe Kershaw, who had ridden forward to confer with Wofford on the condition of his detached brigade — and were met by a heavier volley from the Virginians in the woods. Four men were hit: a courier and a staff captain, both of whom were killed instantly, Micah Jenkins, who died a few

★

hours later with a bullet in his brain, and Longstreet. "Friends! They are *friends!*" Kershaw shouted in a voice that rang above the clatter and the groans, and almost at once Mahone's veterans ceased firing and hurried out of the woods to express their regret for what had happened.

By then solicitous hands were helping the wounded lieutenant general to dismount. Hit solidly by a bullet that passed through the base of his neck and lodged in his right shoulder, he had been lifted straight up by the impact and had come down hard, his right arm hanging useless, though he managed to stay in the saddle, bleeding heavily, until his companions were there to ease him to the ground, the upper part of his body propped against the trunk of a roadside tree. Exultation turned to dismay as word spread rapidly through the Wilderness that Old Peter had been hit. All down the line, men's thoughts were more than ever of Chancellorsville, but with the bitter irony of remembering that Jackson too had been shot by his own soldiers, less than four miles up the road through these same woods, at the climax of a successful flank attack. As for Longstreet, his thoughts were neither on the past nor on the present, despite his pain. His concern was for the immediate future, the follow-up assault that would complete his victory. Field being the ranking division commander present in the corps, Longstreet blew the bloody foam from his mouth to say to Sorrel: "Tell General Field to take command, and move forward with the whole force and gain the Brock Road." Soon his staff physician was there to tend his wounds, and when Lee arrived he told him, in such detail as his shaken vocal cords allowed, of his plan for turning the Federals out of their new position. By now a stretcher had been brought. He was lifted onto it, his hat placed over his face to shield his eyes, and carried back down the plank road to a waiting ambulance. On the way, when he heard troops by the roadside saying, "He is dead. They are only telling us he is wounded," he raised his hat from his face with his usable hand. The answering cheers, he declared long afterward, served to ease his pain somewhat on the jolting rearward journey.

A wandering artillery major, on a fruitless search for a decent gun position, came up just as the ambulance moved off. Later he wrote of what he saw and felt. Members of the general's staff, "literally bowed down with grief," were all around the vehicle; "One, I remember, stood upon the rear step of the ambulance, seeming to desire to be as near him as possible. All of them were in tears." The doctor had said that Longstreet's wounds were not necessarily fatal, but they recalled that the prognosis had been even more favorable in Jackson's case right up to the day he died, a year ago next week. Though he had never really liked Old Peter, the artillerist wanted to see for himself what his condition was. For one thing, the procession's resemblance to a funeral cortege lent credence to a rumor that the general was dead. "I rode up to the ambulance and looked in. They had taken off Longstreet's hat and coat and boots. The blood had paled out of his face and its somewhat gross aspect was gone. I noticed how white and dome-like his great forehead looked and, with scarcely less reverent admiration, how spotless white his socks and his fine gauze undervest, save where the black red gore from his breast and shoulder had stained it. While I gazed at his massive frame, lying so still except when it rocked inertly with the lurch of the vehicle, his eyelids frayed apart till I could see a delicate line of blue between them, and then he very quietly moved his unwounded arm and, with his thumb and two fingers, carefully lifted the saturated undershirt from his chest, holding it up a moment, and heaved a deep sigh. He is not dead, I said to myself, and he is calm and entirely master of the situation. He is both greater and more attractive than I have heretofore thought him."

Back up the road, at the scene of the wounding, Field was doing what he could to carry out his orders to "take command, and move forward." But this was by no means as easy a task as Longstreet seemed to think. Other disruptive accidents, like the one that had just cost the corps its chief, were apt to follow if the main body, still in line astride the plank road, and Sorrel's flankers, drawn up facing it, were left to fight with their fronts at right angles. Lee ordered a postponement of the follow-up assault until the lines were readjusted. This was done, although the process was a slow one. Not only was

Shot through the neck and shoulder, rebel General James Longstreet (center) keeps his composure as Micah Jenkins (left) reels from a mortal head wound.

★

the confusion greater than had been thought, it had also been increased by the loss of Jenkins and Old Peter. Four mortal hours, from noon to 4 o'clock, were required to get the troops untangled and into satisfactory positions for attack, and when they went forward at 4.15 they found that Hancock, too, had made good use of the time afforded for adjustments. He had strengthened his breast-works, brought up reinforcements, and posted a secondary line in support of the first. Worst of all (or best, depending on the point of view) he had shored up and realigned his outer flank, which the attackers found no longer dangling in the air. At a couple of points the Confederates achieved a penetration — one, where the log breastworks caught fire, forcing the defenders to abandon them, and Jenkins's Carolinians came leaping through the flames, intent on avenging the fall of their young brigadier — but in both cases supporting troops came up and restored the line by driving them out again: proof, if any such was needed, that seven divisions, snug behind breastworks and with both flanks secure (Burnside had come up at last, midway through the four-hour lull, and gone into position on Hancock's right) were not to be driven, or even budged, by three divisions attacking head-on through bullet-flailed brush. An hour of such fighting was quite enough to show that nothing more was going to be accom-plished here. It was time — indeed, almost past time — to look elsewhere: meaning in Ewell's direction, up on the opposite flank.

All day, though he had had no chance to go in person, Lee had been sending messages to the Second Corps, urging an offensive in that quarter to relieve the pressure on the First or, if that was impracticable, the detachment of reinforcements to strengthen the offensive on the right. Invariably Ewell had replied that he could do neither. There was no fit opening for an attack; he needed all his troops to maintain his position astride the turnpike. When Lee arrived at 5.30 asking, "Cannot something be done on this flank?" Ewell said again that he believed it would be unwise to assault the Federals in their intrench-ments, and he was supported in this by Early, who was at corps headquarters when Lee rode up. Gordon was also there, intending to renew his daylong plea that he be unleashed, and when his two superiors finished protesting that there was nothing to be done, he presumed to appeal to the army commander himself for permission to strike at the enemy flank, which he insisted had been wide open to attack for more than eight hours now. Ewell and Early repeated their objections, based on the conviction that Burnside was posted in Sedgwick's rear to forestall such a move. Lee, who knew that Burnside was in front of Hill, wasted no more time on reproaches, although, as Gordon later wrote, "his silence and grim looks . . . revealed his thoughts almost as plainly as words could have done." He simply ordered the attack to be made at once.

It was launched at straight-up 6 o'clock, and within the limitations of the little daylight time remaining — sunset came at 6.50 and darkness followed quickly in the thickets of the Wilderness — it was altogether as successful as Gordon, for the past nine hours, had been telling Ewell and Early it would be. With the support of the brigade that had arrived that morning from Hanover, North Carolinians under twenty-seven-year-old Brigadier General Robert D. Johnston, the Georgians struck and scattered Ricketts's unwary flank brigade and captured its commander, Brigadier General Truman Seymour. Seymour had led a division in the ill-starred Florida campaign, and after being whipped at Olustee had returned to Virginia to head a brigade whose members were known in both armies as "Milroy's weary boys," a description applied two years ago, after Stonewall Jackson gave them the runaround in the Shenandoah Valley, and confirmed last year when Ewell encountered them near Winchester on his way to Gettysburg. Weary or not, they broke badly again today and spread panic through the rest of the division, as well as through part of Wright's division, which was next in line and which also had a brigade commander scooped up by the rebels in the confusion. This was Brigadier General Alexander Shaler, a Connecticut-born New Yorker whose capture was especially welcome because he had recently been in charge of the prison for Confederate officers on Johnson's Island in Sandusky Bay, where winters were cold and blankets few; now he would get a taste of prison life from the inside, looking out, instead of from the outside, looking in. Seymour and Shaler, for all their lofty rank, were only two among some 600 Federals taken captive in the attack, while about as many more were killed or wounded, bringing Sedgwick's total loss to well over a thousand in one hour. Gordon himself lost only about fifty in the course of what his men referred to, ever afterwards, as their "finest frolic." The blue right flank was "rolled up" for more than a mile before dusk put an end to the advance and obliged the Georgians and Carolinians, who by then had plunged all the way to the Germanna Plank Road, to pull back with their prisoners, their booty from the overrun camps, and their conviction that an earlier attack, in Gordon's words, "would have resulted in a decided disaster to the whole right wing of General Grant's army, if not in its entire disorganization."

General Truman Seymour was captured when his troops' formation disintegrated before a rebel assault.

Lee was inclined to think so, too, especially if the attack on this flank, against Sedgwick, had been delivered at the same time as Longstreet's against Hancock, on the other; in which case the indications were that Grant would have been overwhelmed and routed, not merely discomfited and bled down another one percent. An earlier visit to the left by the army commander would no doubt have resulted in an earlier attack, but Lee had come as soon as he felt he could leave the critical right, where the contest had been touch-and-go since sunrise. The trouble was that he could not be everywhere at once, despite the need for him to do just that. Although this impossible need had grown more pressing ever since the death of Stonewall Jackson, today it had become downright acute. Longstreet's departure left his corps in the hands of a newly promoted major general who had been with it less than three months, none of the time in combat, and whose deskbound year in Richmond seemed to have made him utterly inflexible at a time when flexibility was among the highest virtues. Hill's failing health, worse today than yesterday, and likely to be still worse tomorrow, obviously required him to take a sick leave that would deprive the army, however briefly, of the most aggressive of its corps commanders. It was harder, even, to think of Lee without A. P. Hill than it was to think of him without Longstreet, for Hill had never been detached. As for Ewell, although by ordinary

The rebels welcomed the capture of Alexander Shaler, former head of a Federal prison.

standards he had done well today and yesterday, holding his own against the odds, he seemed incapable of doing one whit more than was required by specific orders; Ewell in the Wilderness, unable to bring himself to unleash Gordon despite repeated pleas from headquarters that *some*thing be attempted in that direction, was disturbingly like Ewell at Gettysburg, where his indecisiveness had cost the army its one best chance for a quick victory in what, instead, turned out to be a bloody three-day battle that ended in retreat.

All this might well have been heavy on Lee's mind as he rode southward, three miles through the twilight, to the Tapp farm. He was faced, at this most critical juncture, with a crisis of command: a crisis that would have to be resolved if the Army of Northern Virginia — at the close of only the second day of fighting, in what promised to be the longest and grimmest of its campaigns — was to survive the continuing confrontation, here in the depths of the Wilderness, with an enemy force roughly twice its size, superbly equipped, and still in possession of the main artery leading southeast, through the thickets and beyond into open country, where the tactical odds would lengthen and the capital itself would be in danger of being taken, either by sudden assault or inexorable maneuver.

All around him, as he dismounted in front of his tent in the Tapp farmyard, was confusion. East and north, out in the jungle where the battle had raged for two incredibly savage days, the moans of the wounded, blue and gray, were heightened to screams of terror when a brisk wind sprang up, shortly after dark, and fanned random smouldering embers into flames that spread faster through the underbrush than an injured man could crawl. Dead pines, their sap long dried to rosin, burned like twenty-foot torches, and the low clouds took on an eerie yellow cast, as if they reflected the glow from molten sulphur on the floor of hell. The roar of wind-whipped flames through crackling brush was

In an Alfred Waud sketch, Federal soldiers – using muskets and blankets as a makeshift litter – rescue a stricken comrade from the burning woods of the Wilderness.

★

punctuated from time to time by a clatter resembling the sudden clash of pickets, as groups of disabled men from both sides, huddled together against a common danger, were engulfed by the inferno and the paper-wrapped charges in their pockets or cartridge boxes caught fire and exploded. While stretcher bearers and volunteers did what they could to rescue all the wounded they could reach, others along the Confederate line of battle — including those Third Corps veterans who had thought they were too tired for such exertion the night before — worked hard to strengthen their defenses for a renewal of the contest at first light tomorrow. They expected it, and so did their commander. Less soundly beaten, tactically, and with no greater losses, Hooker had pulled back across the river. But neither Lee nor his soldiers thought it likely that Grant would do what Fighting Joe had done; at least not yet. Judging their new opponent by his western reputation, as well as by his aggressive performance over the past two days, they believed he would stay and fight.

Next to a retreat, which he did not expect, Lee preferred a Federal attack, and that was what he had his men prepare for. If Grant was to be beaten further, to and beyond the point at which he would have no choice except to pull back across the river, it would have to come as the result of a bloody, morale-shattering repulse. In any case, the next move was up to the invader. Today's abortive follow-up assault by the First Corps, launched after the long delay occasioned in part by the fall of its commander, had shown only too clearly that the Confederates, whatever their successes when they caught the enemy off balance, lacked the strength to drive an opponent who was not only twice their size but was also braced for the shock in well-prepared intrenchments — and there could be no doubt that the Federals were as hard at work on their defenses, left and right and center, as the graybacks were on their side of the line. Obliged as he was, now that all chances for surprise had been exhausted, to rule out a resumption of the offensive by his badly outnumbered army, Lee's decision not to attack amounted to a surrender of the initiative. This was a dangerous procedure against an adversary as nimble as Grant had shown himself to be in the campaign that brought Vicksburg under siege, but Lee had no choice. His hope, as he turned in for the night, was that Grant, despite his freedom to maneuver, would continue to forget his Vicksburg method and hold instead to the pattern of headlong assault he had followed so far in Virginia. That might lead to his repulse, and another repulse, if decisive enough, might lead to his destruction. The alternative for Lee, who had no such freedom to maneuver, was stalemate and defeat.

★ ★ ★   **T**his second day of battle in the Wilderness had been Grant's hardest since the opening day at Shiloh, where his army and his reputation had also been threatened with destruction. Here as there, however — so long, at least, as the fighting was in progress —

he bore the strain unruffled and "gave his orders calmly and coherently," one witness noted, "without any external sign of undue tension or agitation." Internally, a brief sequel was to show, he was a good deal more upset than he appeared, but outwardly, as he continued to sit on his stump atop the knoll in the Lacy meadow, smoking and whittling the critical hours away, he seemed altogether imperturbable. When word came, shortly before noon, that Hancock's flank had been turned and the left half of his army was in imminent danger of being routed, his reaction was to send more troops in that direction, together with additional supplies of ammunition, followed at 3 o'clock by orders for a counterattack to be launched at 6 to recover the lost ground and assure the holding of the Brock Road leading south. As it turned out, Hancock was himself assaulted a second time, nearly two hours before that, and had to use up so much of the ammunition in repelling the attack that not enough was left for compliance with the order. Besides, Grant by then was faced with an even graver crisis on his right. Sedgwick too had been flanked and was being routed, he was told, by a rebel force that had penetrated all the way to the Germanna Plank Road, cutting the army off from its nearest escape hatch back across the Rapidan.

Meade was a steadying influence, in this case as in others. "Nonsense," he snorted when a pair of flustered staffers came riding in from the crumpled flank after sundown to report that all was lost in that direction, including all hope of deliverance from the trap the rebels had sprung on Sedgwick and were about to enlarge in order to snap up everything in blue. "Nonsense! If they have broken our lines they can do nothing more tonight." He had confidence in John Sedgwick, the least excitable of his corps commanders, and he showed it by sending reinforcements from the center to help shore up the tottered right. Grant approved, of course, and had an even stronger reaction to an officer of higher rank who came crying that this second flank assault meant the end of the northern army unless it found some way to get out from under the blow about to fall. "This is a crisis that cannot be looked upon too seriously," he declared. "I know Lee's methods well by past experience. He will throw his whole army between us and the Rapidan, and cut us off completely from our communications." Grant was not a curser, but his patience had run out. He got up from the stump, took the cigar out of his mouth, and turned on this latest in the series of prophets of doom and idolators of his opponent. "Oh, I am heartily tired of hearing about what *Lee* is going to do," he said testily. "Some of you always seem to think he is suddenly going to turn a double somersault and land in our rear and on both our flanks at the same time. Go back to your command and try to think what we are going to do ourselves, instead of what *Lee* is going to do."

Further reports of havoc on the right were received with the same firmness, the same quick rejection of all notions of defeat, although — as Rawlins told a friend who rode over to headquarters to see him later that evening — "the coming of officer after officer with additional details soon made it apparent that the general was confronted by the greatest crisis in his life." By nightfall, however, Meade's assessment was confirmed; Sedgwick established a new and stronger line, half a mile south and east of the one he had lost to Gordon's flankers, who withdrew in the twilight from their position astride the road leading back to Germanna Ford. Then, and not until then, did the general-in-chief show the full effect of the strain he had been under, all this day and most of the day before. He broke. Yet even this was done with a degree of circumspection and detachment highly characteristic of the man. Not only was his personal collapse resisted until after the damage to both flanks had been repaired and the tactical danger had passed; it also occurred in the privacy of his quarters, rather than in the presence of his staff or gossip-hungry visitors. "When all proper measures had been taken," Rawlins confided, "Grant went into his tent, threw himself face downward on his cot, and gave way to the greatest emotion." He wept, and though the chief of staff, who followed him into the tent, declared that he had "never before seen him so deeply moved" and that "nothing could be more certain than that he was stirred to the very depths of his soul," he also observed that Grant gave way to the strain "without uttering any word of doubt or discouragement." Another witness, a captain attached to Meade's headquarters — Charles F. Adams, Jr, son and namesake of the ambassador — put it stronger. "I never saw a man so agitated in my life," he said.

However violent the breakdown, the giving way to hysteria at this point, it appeared that Grant wept more from the relief of tension (after all, both flanks were well shored up by then) than out of continuing desperation. In any case it was soon over. When Rawlins's friend, Brigadier General James H. Wilson — a friend of Grant's as well, formerly a member of his military family and recently appointed by him to command one of Sheridan's cavalry divisions — reached headquarters about 9 o'clock, less than an hour after the collapse Rawlins presently described, he found the general "surrounded by his staff in a state of perfect composure," as if nothing at all had happened. And in fact nothing had: nothing that mattered, anyhow. Unlike Hooker, who broke inside as a result of similar frustrations, Grant broke outside, and then only in the privacy of his tent. He cracked, but the crack healed so quickly that it had no effect whatever on the military situation, then or later. Whereas Hooker had reacted by falling back across the river, such a course was no more in Grant's mind now than it had been that morning, before sunup, when he was accosted by a journalist who was about to leave for Washington to file a story on the first day's fighting. Asked if he had any message for the authorities there, Grant, whose usual procedure was to hold off sending word of his progress in battle until the news was good, thought it over briefly, then replied: "If you see the President, tell him,

from me, that, whatever happens, there will be no turning back."

Late that evening another journalist, New York *Herald* correspondent Sylvanus Cadwallader, was reassured to find that Grant still felt that way about the matter, despite the tactical disappointments of the day just past. Seated on opposite sides of a smouldering headquarters campfire, these two — the reporter because he was too depressed for sleep, and the general, he presumed, for the same reason — were the last to turn in for the night. Formerly of the Chicago *Times*, Cadwallader had been with Grant for nearly two years now, through the greatest of his triumphs, as well as through a two-day drunk up the Yazoo last summer, and for the first time, here in the Wilderness tonight, he began, as he said afterward, "to question the grounds of my faith in him. . . . We had waged two days of murderous battle, and had but little to show for it. Judged by comparative losses, it had been disastrous to the Union cause. We had been compelled by General Lee to fight him on a field of his own choosing, with the certainty of losing at least two men to his one, until he could be dislodged and driven from his vantage ground. [Yet] we had gained scarcely a rod of the battlefield at the close of the two days' contest." He wondered, as a result of this disconsolate review of the situation, whether he had followed Grant all this long way, through the conquest of Vicksburg and the deliverance of Chattanooga, only "to record his defeat and overthrow" when he came up against Lee in the Virginia thickets. Musing thus beside the dying embers of the campfire, he looked across its low

Mounted VI
Corps officers sur-
vey their Union
lines north of the
Orange Turnpike
while smoke billows
in the distance from
the guns of a Mass-
achusetts battery.

glow at the lieutenant general, who seemed to be musing too. "His hat was drawn down over his face, the high collar of an old blue army overcoat turned up above his ears, one leg crossed over the other knee, eyes on the ashes in front." Only the fitful crossing and recrossing of his legs indicated that he was not asleep, and Cadwallader supposed that the general's thoughts were as gloomy as his own — until at last Grant spoke and disabused him of the notion. He began what the reporter termed "a pleasant chatty conversation upon indifferent subjects," none of which had anything to do with the fighting today or yesterday. As he got up from his chair to go to bed, however, he spoke briefly of "the sharp work General Lee had been giving us for a couple of days," then turned and went into his tent to get some sleep. That was all. But now that Cadwallader realized that the general had not been sharing them, he found that all his gloomy thoughts were gone. Grant opposed by Lee in Virginia, he perceived, was the same Grant he had known in Mississippi and Tennessee, where Pemberton and Bragg had been defeated. "It was the grandest mental sunburst of my life," he declared years later, looking back on the effect this abrupt realization had had on his state of mind from that time forward. "I had suddenly emerged from the slough of despond, to the solid bedrock of unwavering faith."

In the course of the next twenty hours or so — May 7 now, a Saturday — the whole army experienced a like sequence of reactions, from utter doubt to mental sunburst. Reconnaissance parties, working their way along and across the charred, smoky corridors last night's fires had left, found the rebels "fidgety and quick to shoot" but content, it seemed, to stay tightly buttoned up in the breastworks they had built or improved since yesterday. Lee preferred receiving to delivering an attack, and Grant apparently felt the same, since he issued no orders directing that one be made. For this the troops were duly thankful, especially those who had had a close-up look at the enemy lines, but they were also puzzled. The Federal choice seemed limited to attack or retreat, and they had not thought that Grant, despite the drubbing he had received these past two days, would give up quite this early. Still, word soon came that the pontoon bridges had been taken up at Germanna and relaid at Ely's Ford to hasten the passage of the ambulance train with the wounded, who were to be sent by rail to Washington. This meant that a withdrawal of the army, whether by that route or through Fredericksburg, would have to proceed by way of Chancellorsville, the hub where roads from the south and west converged to continue north and east. Swiftly now the conviction grew that everything blue would be headed in that direction after sundown. Sure enough, such guns as had found positions for direct support of the infantry — including those on the knoll in the Lacy meadow — were limbered and started rearward that afternoon, obviously to avoid jamming the roads that night, and in this the men saw confirmation of their worst judgments and suspicions. Grant, for all his western bulldog reputation, was merely another Pope, another Hooker, at best another Meade. They had been through this before; they recognized the signs. "Most of us thought it was another Chancellorsville," a Massachusetts infantryman would remember, while a Pennsylvania cavalryman recorded that his comrades used a homelier term to describe the predicted movement. They called it "another skedaddle."

If the Chancellorsville parallel was obvious — both battles had been waged in the same thicket, so to speak, between the same two armies, at the same time of year, and against the same Confederate commander — it was also, at this stage, disturbingly apt. By every tactical standard, although the earlier contest was often held up as a model of Federal ineptitude, the second was even worse-fought than the first. Hooker had had one flank turned; Grant had both. Hooker had achieved at least a measure of surprise in the opening stage of his campaign; Grant achieved none. Indeed, the latter had been surprised himself, while on a march designed to avoid battle on the very ground where this one raged for two horrendous days, not only without profit to the invaders, but also at a cost so disproportionate that it emphasized the wisdom of his original intention to avoid a confrontation on this terrain. Moreover, it was in the three-way assessment of casualties, Hooker's and Lee's, along with his own, that the comparison became least flattering. Grant lost 17,666 killed and wounded, captured and missing — about four hundred more than Hooker — while Lee, whose victory a year ago had cost him nearly 13,000 casualties, was losing a scant 7800, considerably fewer than half the number he inflicted. Here the comparison tended to break down, however, because for anything like comparable losses, North and South, it was necessary to go back to Fredericksburg, the most one-sided of all the large-scale Confederate triumphs. In plain fact, up to the point of obliging Grant to throw in the sponge and pull back across the river, Lee had never beaten an adversary so soundly as he had beaten this one in the course of the past two days.

What it all boiled down to was that Grant was whipped, and soundly whipped, if he would only admit it by retreating: which in turn was only a way of saying that he had not been whipped at all. "Whatever happens, there will be no turning back," he had said, and he would hold to that. The midafternoon displacement of the guns deployed along the Union line of battle was in preparation for a march, just as the troops assumed, but not in the direction they supposed. No more willing to accept a stalemate than he was to accept defeat, he would shift his ground, and in doing so he would hold to the offensive; he would move, not north toward Washington, but south toward Richmond, obliging Lee to conform if he was to protect the capital in his rear. Grant thus clung to the initiative Lee surrendered when he had exhausted all his chances for surprise. Now it was Grant's turn to try again for a surprise, and he planned accordingly.

The objective was Spotsylvania Court House, less than a dozen miles down the Brock Road from the turnpike intersection. With an early start, to be made as soon as darkness screened the movement from the rebels in their works across the way, it was not too much to expect that the leading elements would be in position there by dawn, plying shovels and swinging axes in the construction of fortifications which Lee, when he caught up at last, would be obliged to storm, even if the storming meant the destruction of his army, because they would stand between him and the capital whose protection was his prime concern. Warren would have the lead and would go all the way tonight, marching down the Brock Road across the rear of Hancock, who would fall in behind, once Warren had passed, and stop at Todd's Tavern, where he would guard the rear and slow the progress of the rebels if they attempted to follow by this route. Sedgwick would move east on the turnpike to Chancellorsville, then south by the road past Piney Branch Church to its junction with the Brock Road at Alsop, between Todd's Tavern and Spotsylvania, close in Warren's rear and also within supporting distance of Hancock. Burnside would follow Sedgwick after taking the plank road to Chancellorsville, but would call a halt at Piney Branch Church to protect the trains and the reserve artillery, which were to assemble at that point. Sheridan's troopers would probe the darkness in advance of both columns, and he was directed to patrol the western flank in strength, in order "to keep the corps commanders advised in time of the approach of the enemy." Warren and Sedgwick would move out at 8.30, Hancock and Burnside as soon

*Ignoring orders to keep quiet lest rebels hear them,
Federal troops cheer General Grant (mounted,
center) for his decision to press on to Richmond.*

thereafter as the roads were clear. The emphasis was on silence and speed, both highly desirable factors in a maneuver designed to outfox old man Lee.

Meade issued the march order at 3 o'clock, in compliance with earlier instructions from Grant, and when the guns pulled out soon afterward, taking a five-hour lead to clear the roads for the infantry that night, the troops along the line of battle drew their conclusions and went on exchanging occasional long-range shots with the graybacks while awaiting their turn to join what they were convinced was a retreat. Soon after dark the expected orders came; Warren's and Sedgwick's veterans slung their packs, fell in quietly on the Brock Road and the turnpike, and set out. To the surprise of the V Corps men, the march was south, in rear of Hancock's portion of the line. At first they thought that this was done to get them onto the plank road, leading east to Chancellorsville, but when they slogged past the intersection they knew that what they were headed for was not the Rapidan or the Rappahannock, but another battle somewhere south, beyond the unsuspecting rebel flank. Formerly glum, the column now began to buzz with talk. Packs were lighter; the step quickened; spirits rose with the growing realization that they were stealing another march on old man Lee.

★

Then came cheers, as a group on horseback — "Give way, give way to the right," one of the riders kept calling to the soldiers on the road — doubled the column at a fast walk, equipment jingling. In the lead was Grant, a vague, stoop-shouldered figure, undersized-looking on Cincinnati, the largest of his mounts; the other horsemen were his staff. Cincinnati pranced and sidled, tossing his head at the sudden cheering, and the general, who had his hands full getting the big animal quieted down, told his companions to pass the word for the cheers to stop, lest they give the movement away to the Confederates sleeping behind their breastworks in the woods half a mile to the west. The cheering stopped, but not the buzz of excitement, the elation men felt at seeing their commander take the lead in an advance they had supposed was a retreat. They stepped out smartly; Todd's Tavern was just ahead, a little beyond the midway point on the march to Spotsylvania.

Up on the turnpike, where Sedgwick's troops were marching, the glad reaction was delayed until the head of the column had covered the gloomy half dozen miles to Chancellorsville. "The men seemed aged," a cannoneer noted as he watched them slog past a roadside artillery park. Weary from two days of savage fighting and two nights of practically no sleep, dejected by the notion that they were adding still another to the long list of retreats the army had made in the past three years, they plodded heavy-footed and heavy-hearted, scuffing their shoes in the dust on the pike leading eastward. Beyond Chancellorsville, just ahead, the road forked. A turn to the left, which they expected, meant recrossing the river at Ely's Ford, probably to undergo another reorganization under another new commander who would lead them, in the fullness of time, into another battle that would end in another retreat; that was the all-too-familiar pattern, so endless in repetition that at times it seemed a full account of the army's activities in the Old Dominion could be spanned in four short words, "Bull Run: da capo." But now a murmur, swelling rapidly to a chatter, began to move back down the column from its head, and presently each man could see for himself that the turn, beyond the ruins of the Chancellor mansion, had been to the right. They were headed south, not north; they were advancing, not retreating; Grant was giving them another go at Lee. And though on sober second thought a man might be of at least two minds about this, as a welcome or a dread thing to be facing, the immediate reaction was elation. There were cheers and even a few tossed caps, and long afterwards men were to say that, for them, this had been the high point of the war.

"Our spirits rose," one among them would recall. "We marched free. The men begin to sing. . . . That night we were happy."

★ ★ ★

★

*During the Wilderness Campaign,
some of the bloodiest fighting occurred
in trenches, some reinforced with
log and earth breastworks like these
at the Mule Shoe salient.*

SIX

Spotsylvania;
"All Summer"

1864 ★ ★ ★ ★ ★

Lee was marching too, by then, having divined once more his adversary's intention. That morning, after riding the length of his Wilderness line and finding it strangely quiet — in contrast, that is, to the fury of the past two days, when better than 25,000 men had been shot or captured, blue and gray, along that four-mile stretch of tangled woodland — he drew rein on the far left to talk with Gordon, who supposed from Grant's lack of aggressiveness that he was about to retreat. "Grant is not going to retreat," Lee told him. "He will move his army to Spotsylvania." Surprised, the Georgian asked if there was any evidence that the Federals were moving in that direction. "Not at all, not at all," Lee said as he turned Traveller's head to ride back down the line. "But that is the next point at which the armies will meet. Spotsylvania is now General Grant's best strategic point."

There was, as he said, no indication that Grant was moving, but there was at least negative evidence that when he did move — as obviously he would have to do, in lieu of assaulting the Wilderness intrenchments, before he used up the supplies in his train — it would not be back across the Rapidan; Ewell had sent word, shortly after sunup, that the Federals were dismantling their pontoon bridges at Germanna, and though Ely's Ford was still available it seemed unlikely that they would give up either if they intended to retire to the north bank. That

★

left Fredericksburg as a possible escape route, and in fact there were reports from cavalry scouts that wagon traffic was heavy in that direction. But there was also a report from Stuart, waiting for Lee when he got back to the Widow Tapp's, that the Union cavalry had returned to Todd's Tavern this morning, in strength enough to drive the Confederate horsemen out and hold the place against all efforts to retake it. Todd's Tavern was down the Brock Road, midway between Grant's present position and Spotsylvania, which lay in the angle between the Richmond, Fredericksburg & Potomac and the Virginia Central railroads and offered an excellent approach to Hanover Junction, where the two lines crossed en route to Richmond from the north and west, both of them vital to the subsistence of Lee's army. Spotsylvania then, as Lee told Gordon, was his adversary's "best strategic point," if what he wanted was either to steal the lead in a race for Richmond or to take up a stout defensive position which Lee would be obliged to attack, whatever the tactical disadvantages, not only because it would sever his lines of supply, but also because it lay between him and the capital whose protection was his primary concern.

As evidence, this was far from conclusive, but it was persuasive enough to cause him to summon Brigadier General William N. Pendleton, the fifty-four-year-old former Episcopal rector who served as his chief of artillery, and instruct him to begin at once the cutting of a road through the woods, due south from the army's right flank on the Orange Plank Road, down to Shady Grove Church on the Catharpin Road — the midpoint for Lee, as Todd's Tavern, which was also on the Catharpin Road, was for Grant — to be used as soon as the first hard evidence reached headquarters that his opponent had taken, or was about to take, the first step in the race for Spotsylvania. The new road, if it was finished in time, would shorten the march by doing away with the need to back-track down the plank road to Parker's Store before turning south; but this was small comfort alongside the knowledge that Grant even then would have a shorter route, a better road to travel all the way, and the advantage of deciding when the race would begin or whether, indeed, it would be run at all.

Another, and possibly greater, disadvantage lay in the fact that the lead corps on the march would be the First, since its position was on the right and therefore closest to the objective. Normally — as in the case of the movement into the Wilderness earlier this week — one or both of the other two corps, composed for the most part of Jackson's famed "foot cavalry," sought out the foe or rounded his flank to set him up for the Sunday punch methodical Old Peter would deliver when he came up in turn. Moreover, the corps was now to be commanded by a general, forty-two-year-old Richard Anderson, whose reputation had never been one for dash or fire and whose performance over the past year under Hill had been undistinguished at best, while at worst it had been a good deal less than that. At Gettysburg, for example, the kindest thing that could be said of the easy-going South Carolinian's lack of aggressiveness was that it had been due to sloth. His earlier record, made in the days when he commanded first a brigade and then a division under Longstreet, had been better, and this was Lee's main reason, together with the consideration that he was the senior major general with the army, for giving the post to him instead of Early, whom Lee otherwise preferred. A former member of the corps, which Early was not — Field was of recent appointment and Kershaw was still a brigadier — Anderson would be welcomed back by the officers and men of the two divisions he would command, while his Third Corps division would pass into the capable hands of Mahone, the army's senior brigadier. Yet this was

Confederate Major General Richard H. Anderson did not have a reputation for dash and fire.

perhaps the greatest of all gambles, the appointment of genial, uninspired Dick Anderson to replace his most dependable lieutenant at a time when dash and fire, both of which were conspicuous by their absence from his record, seemed likely to be the decisive factors in a contest that would begin at any moment and had Richmond for the prize. The fact that Lee was more or less obliged to take that gamble was one measure of the extent to which attrition was wearing down the army in his charge.

That afternoon he saw that still another such change was in the offing. Riding his line for the second time that day, he stopped off at Third Corps headquarters, which had been set up in a deserted house about midway between the plank road and the turnpike, and found A. P. Hill looking paler and sicker than ever. Though red-bearded Little Powell was unwilling to relinquish command at this critical juncture, it was evident that he soon would be obliged to do so. This meant that, once more — with Anderson transferred and Heth and Wilcox insufficiently seasoned — a temporary successor would have to be found outside a corps whose regular chief was incapacitated. In this case, however, the problem was simplified by having been faced beforehand, although in another connection; Jubal Early, runner-up as a candidate for command of the First Corps, would be brought in from the Second to lead the Third, at least until Hill recovered from the ailment he would not yet admit was grave enough to require him to step down. One dividend of this arrangement, similar to the one that had given

Anderson's division to Mahone, was that Early's division could pass to Gordon, for whom Lee felt a growing admiration because of his performance yesterday. Lee's conversation with Little Powell was interrupted about 4 o'clock by a staff colonel who came down from the attic of the house, where he had established an observation post by ripping some shingles from the roof, to report on something he had seen with the aid of a powerful marine glass trained on what he believed was Grant's headquarters, a bit under two miles across the way. A number of heavy guns, held in reserve there all through the fighting, had just pulled out and headed south down the Brock Road, toward the Confederate right.

Though Grant's dead were still thickly strewn in the woods in front of his line, along with a few surviving wounded, and though none of the blue infantry had yet shown any sign of preparing for a shift, Lee took this limited artillery displacement as the first step in the race for Spotsylvania, which lay in the direction the guns had gone. Accordingly, he returned at once to the Tapp farm and issued orders for Anderson to march that night, taking Pendleton's just-cut southward trace through the woods to Shady Grove Church, then eastward across the Po River to Spotsylvania, which he was to hold against all comers: provided, of course, that he got there first. The new corps commander's instructions were for him to withdraw his two divisions from their present lines as soon as darkness masked the movement from the enemy, then give the troops a few hours' rest and sleep before setting out, at 3 o'clock in the morning, on the race for the objective a dozen miles away. Ewell and Hill were told to follow, in that order, as soon as they judged that the situation in their front would justify withdrawal.

Confederate engineer Jedediah Hotchkiss made this map showing the Mule Shoe and other earthworks held by the rebels around Spotsylvania Court House beginning May 9.

★

In accordance with these instructions, Anderson pulled back about 9 o'clock, but finding no suitable rest area in the immediate rear — fires had sprung up again in the smouldering brush, fanned alive, as on the past two nights, by the early evening breeze — he set out at once, down Pendleton's trace, with the intention of making a bivouac farther south, outside the smoky battle zone, in which the men could get some rest between then and 3 a.m., the

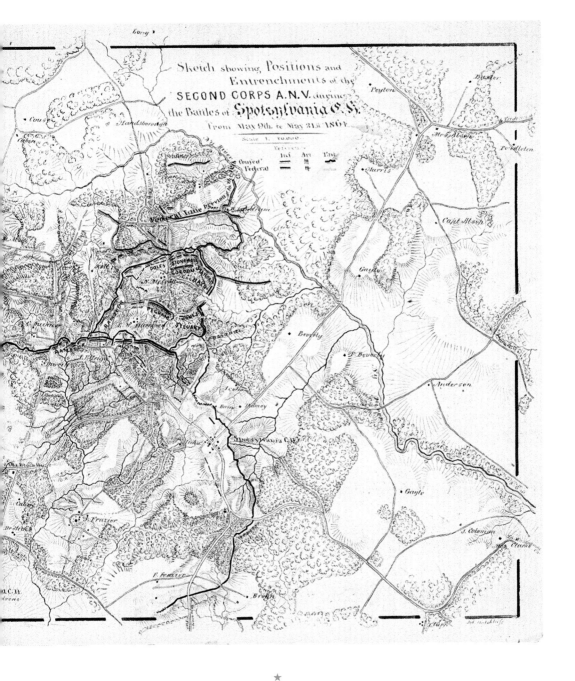

designated hour for the start of the march. He had not gone far, however, before he abandoned the notion of making any considerable halt at all. For one thing, there simply was no usable stopping place this side of Shady Grove, down along the fringes of the Wilderness, and for another the condition of the newly built "road," stump-pocked and cluttered with fallen trunks and limbs, was so miserable that the rate of march along it in the dark could scarcely be much better than a mile-an-hour crawl. He perceived that if he was to win the race for Spotsylvania he would need every minute of the four or five hours he would gain by keeping moving instead of halting in accordance with Lee's order; so he kept moving. Eager to do well on his first assignment as a corps commander, Anderson here rendered Lee and the Confederacy the greatest service of his career.

Jeb Stuart too had one of his great days, perhaps his finest, although the action promised little of the glory he had chased in former times. His three cavalry divisions, under Major Generals Wade Hampton, Fitzhugh Lee, and W. H. F. Lee — the first was a wealthy South Carolina planter-sportsman, fifteen years older at forty-six than his cinnamon-bearded chief, while the second and third, Virginians both, were respectively the commanding general's twenty-eight-year-old nephew and twenty-seven-year-old son — were scattered about the landscape to undertake the double task of protecting the Confederate march and impeding that of the Federals. There were six brigades, two in each division. Stuart assigned half of these to accompany the gray column, shielding its flank and clearing its front, while the other three moved out ahead to block and bedevil the bluecoats who were slogging southeast on a parallel route, a couple of densely wooded miles away. Brigadier General Thomas Rosser, detached from Hampton, led his brigade directly to Spotsylvania, under instructions to hold the place, if possible, until Anderson arrived. Fitz Lee meantime turned northwest, up the Brock Road, to give his full attention to the Federals moving down it: two brigades of mounted men opposing a four-division corps of infantry preceded by a cavalry division half again larger than his own. Near Todd's Tavern he put his troopers to work in the darkness, felling trees to obstruct the road as they withdrew. This gave the blue marchers almost as hard a time as their opponents were having on the crude trace across the way, and presently they had an added problem the Confederates did not have. When daylight began to filter through the thickets, the graybacks began to take potshots at the head and flanks of the Federal column, bringing it to a stumbling halt from time to time while details moved cautiously forward to flush the rebel marksmen out of their ambuscades. This continued, down past Alsop, to within two miles of Spotsylvania. There at last, beyond the fringes of the Wilderness and on comparatively open ground where he could bring his horse artillery into play, Fitz Lee had his dismounted men pile fence rails for a barricade and get down behind it, there in the dust of the road and the grass of the adjoining fields, for

★

a last-ditch fight while couriers set out to bring Anderson cross-country to join in the defense. So far it had been cavalry against cavalry, and Fitz had managed to hold his own, despite the Union advantage of numbers and rapid-fire weapons. Sooner or later, however, the blue troopers would be replaced by infantry, brought forward Grant-style in a solid mass to overlap and overrun his flimsy breastwork. Unless Anderson came up fast and first, there would be nothing substantial between the Federals and Spotsylvania; Grant would have won the race whose prize was Richmond.

The sun by then was an hour high, and Anderson's two divisions, having covered nine miles on their all-night march out of the Wilderness, were ending an hour-long breakfast halt in the open fields, half a mile short of the Po and within about three miles of their objective. Sustained and heartened by the meal, such as it was — a frizzled chunk of fatty bacon, a piece of hardtack warmed and softened in the grease, and a cup of "coffee" boiled from roasted

When daylight began to filter through the thickets, the graybacks began to take potshots at the head and flanks of the Federal column . . .

peanuts: poor fare, by any ordinary standards, but quite as much as they were accustomed to (and considerably more, in any case, than Warren's road-worn men received across the way) — the troops resumed their eastward march across the Po. Kershaw's division had the lead. About halfway to Spotsylvania, as he drew near a peculiar roadside dwelling built of squared logs and referred to locally as the Block House, he was met by a cavalry courier urging speed in the final heat of the race; Fitz Lee needed help, and he needed it quick. Fortified by the meager Sunday breakfast, the two front brigades quickened their step and hurried a mile northward, across the fields, to where the dismounted troopers were making their last-ditch stand on the Brock Road. "Run for our rail piles!" a cavalryman shouted as the men of the leading regiment came up. "The Federal infantry will reach them first if you don't run!"

They did run, and barely made it. Crouching behind the hastily improvised works, they opened fire on the advancing bluecoats at a range of sixty yards and blasted them back, at least for the moment. Thanks to Lee and Anderson, as well as to Stuart and Fitzhugh Lee — not to mention their own stout legs — they had won the race, although by a margin of less than a minute.

Whether it would stay won was another matter. Apparently not; for while the Federal infantry, recovering from the shock of having encountered more than cavalry in defense of the stacked rails, was massing for a heavier assault, Stuart sent word that Rosser's brigade had been driven out of Spotsylvania by a division of blue troopers who came surging down the road from Fredericksburg. Calm despite this evidence that the race had been lost after all, Anderson rerouted Kershaw's other two brigades, instructing them to proceed at once to the courthouse and fling the Federals out before they had time to intrench or bring in reinforcements. Field's division was coming up by now, and Anderson got the men into line on Kershaw's left, just in time to repulse a second and much heavier attack, which otherwise would have turned his western flank. No sooner had this been done than word came from the south that the blue horsemen had withdrawn from Spotsylvania of their own accord, apparently in the belief that they were escaping from a trap. Anderson at once summoned Kershaw's two detached brigades to rejoin him, leaving the defense of the town to Stuart, who by now had brought Fitz Lee down to help Rosser prevent a return by the rapid-firing Federals, in case they got their nerve back. Kershaw's men came hurrying up the Brock Road in time to extend his right and share in the repulse of a still heavier third assault by the Union infantry. This time, though they were punished even more cruelly in the course of their advance across the open fields and down the road, the bluecoats did not scatter or fall back as far as they had done before; they took up a semicircular position, just beyond easy rifle range of the defenders, and began to intrench.

This last was something the Confederates had been doing all along. Familiar enough with Grant's method by now to expect that at least one more all-out attack would be made on their line before the Union commander would be satisfied that it could not be shattered, they worked with picks and shovels and axes, bayonets and frying pans, tin cups and anything else that came to hand, improving and extending the fence-rail "works" they had inherited from Fitz Lee. By the time the sun swung past the overhead and the third assault had been repulsed, the artillery-studded defenses, extending about one mile west and half a mile east of the Brock Road, roughly a mile and a half from Spotsylvania, had grown as formidable as if they had been occupied for days. Across the way, however, in the woods and fields beyond the line the Federals were at work on, more blue troops were coming up and massing south of Alsop, obviously in preparation for a fourth assault, to be launched with greater numbers and on a broader front. Anderson's two divisions had fought Warren's four to a standstill, but now that Sedgwick's three were being added to the weight that Grant could bring to bear, the odds seemed overwhelming. About 2.30 the commanding general arrived, having ridden across the Po ahead of Ewell, whose corps by now was passing Shady Grove Church, a good two hours from the field of fight. Informed of the situation, Lee sent word for Ewell to hasten his march. This was no easy thing to ask of men who were trudging wearily through heat that

*In this sketch, Grant and his staff (11) watch Union troops
march down the Brock Road (4) past the Alsop house (3)
toward enemy lines (1) and Spotsylvania Court House (7).*

was more like June than May, but fortunately the weather seemed to be having
an even more lethargic effect on the Federals, who, unlike Ewell, had been
marching all the previous night. It was 5 o'clock before they completed their
leaden-legged dispositions and started forward. By then, Ewell's lead division
had arrived and gone into position on Anderson's right, in time to block the
attack on that flank and assist in driving the bluecoats back upon their works. It
was smartly done, and that ended the fighting for the day.

Lee turned in early, rounding out a busy, fateful Sunday. Rising at
3 o'clock next morning — May 9; just one week ago today, although it seemed
a great deal longer, he had stood on Clark's Mountain, extended a gauntleted
hand, and told his assembled generals: "Grant will cross by one of those fords"
— he wired the President of his success in frustrating the designs of the Army of
the Potomac by winning the race for Spotsylvania: "We have succeeded so far in

keeping on the front flank of that army, and impeding its progress, without a general engagement, which I will not bring on unless a favorable opportunity offers, or as a last resort. Every attack made upon us has been repelled and considerable damage done to the enemy." He expected the attacks to be renewed today, but he had little doubt of being able to withstand them, so long as the Federals held to the headlong methods they had favored on three of the past four days. A. P. Hill's corps, under Early — Hill had broken down at last, too sick to mount a horse, though he insisted on riding along in an ambulance in order to be with his men — was on the march even now, under instructions to come up on Ewell's right. With his army united and intrenched, dispositions complete and both flanks snug, Lee feared nothing the blue force could do, at least on this front, and he said as much in the telegram this morning. "With the blessing of God," he told Davis, "I trust we shall be able to prevent General Grant from reaching Richmond."

★ ★ ★   On the Union side, the trouble the leading elements had encountered in losing the race for Spotsylvania was compounded, in about equal parts, of weariness and Sheridan. Or perhaps it just came down to a prevalent loss of temper; weariness made tempers short, and Sheridan's was short enough already. In any case, after the elation that came with finding they were advancing, not retreating, the troops settled down to an ill-regulated march — stop and go, but mostly stop — that soon became what one of Sedgwick's men described as "a medley of phantasmagoria." Down on the Brock Road, tunneling southeast through the blackness, Warren's dust-choked marchers had it worse, for though the total distance was less, their progress was jerkier, mainly because of the cavalry up front, which seemed not only to have no definite notion of where it was going, but also to be in no hurry whatever to get there. One delay of about an hour, for example, was occasioned by an all-out fistfight between two cavalry regiments, one composed of veterans who effected a forcible exchange of their run-down horses for the well-groomed mounts of the other, made up of recruits who were not so green as to take such treatment without protest, even though the protest accomplished nothing except a prolongation of the delay. All this was short of Todd's Tavern, the midpoint of the march, where the real jam-up began.

Sheridan, like Stuart except that he began the campaign with 13,000 sabers, as compared to the Confederate 8500, had three divisions in his charge. One of these, James Wilson's, he ordered to move roundabout by the Fredericksburg road to Spotsylvania, while the other two, under Brigadier Generals Alfred Torbert and David Gregg, moved out in front of Warren's infantry to block the crossings of the Po before the rebels got there. So he intended. As all too often happened, however, someone failed to get the word — in this case, two someones:

Gregg and Torbert. Reaching Todd's Tavern around midnight, Meade and his escort found the infantry column stalled and the crossroad jammed with Gregg's troopers, held up in turn by Torbert's, who were waiting for orders on the road beyond. Neither had been told what to do, and neither was doing anything at all. Meade got them moving by telling Gregg to proceed down the Catharpin Road toward Corbin's Bridge, where he would cover the wooded approaches from Parker's Store, and Torbert (or rather his senior brigadier, Wesley Merritt; Torbert was sick tonight) to remain on the Brock Road, clearing the way to Spotsylvania for the infantry and sending one brigade to the Block House, where it would stand in the path of any rebels on the march from Shady Grove. After issuing these instructions Meade sent word of them to Sheridan, wherever he might be, and rode back to get Warren on the move again. By now it was past 1 a.m. and the going was even slower than before. Up ahead, in the woods beyond the tavern, Merritt's troopers found the narrow road obstructed and enemy horsemen taking shots at them, out of the darkness, when they dismounted by lantern light to drag the just-felled timber from their path. This got worse as the march continued, especially for the infantry, with sudden starts and stops, races to close the resultant gaps, and long waits for the column to lurch into motion, segment by jangled segment. The first glimmers of daylight, so fervently hoped for in the gloom, only made things worse by improving the marksmanship of the snipers in the brush. Just before sunup Sheridan himself came pounding onto the scene on his big black horse. Fuming at Meade's highhanded "interference," which seemed to him to have exposed the cavalry to piecemeal destruction by

Around midnight on the evening of May 8, Union General Meade and his escort reached Todd's Tavern, shown here, at the intersection of the Brock and Catharpin roads.

scattering it about the countryside, he sent word for Wilson to withdraw at once from Spotsylvania, lest he be trapped there without adequate support when the rebel infantry arrived. Meantime the dismounted graybacks continued to snipe at the head of the column, toppling riders from their saddles. Beyond Alsop, within two miles of the courthouse — where, for all he knew, Wilson was being cut to pieces by superior numbers before he could pull out — Sheridan was galled even more by having to call on Warren's infantry to come forward with their bayonets and pry Fitz Lee's stubborn troopers out of their fence-rail barricade, which had proved too formidable for Merritt's frazzled cavalry to storm.

Chafed by the delays and aggravations, Warren was determined, now that Sheridan had his horsemen out of the way, to settle the issue before the defenders had time to strengthen their position on the low ridge just ahead, barely a mile and a half from the objective of his disjointed nightlong march. He told

---

Chafed by delays and aggravations, Warren was determined, now that Sheridan had his horsemen out of the way, to settle the issue before the defenders had time to strengthen their position on the low ridge just ahead . . .

Brigadier General John C. Robinson, whose division had the lead, to attack as fast as his men could make it down the road. Weary, outdone, and unfed as they were, wobbly on their legs for lack of sleep, this wasn't very fast; but it was fast enough, as the thing developed, to accomplish their destruction in short order.

Robinson, a large, hairy New Yorker with an outsized beard and shaggy brows, a crusty manner, and a solid reputation earned in practically all of the major eastern battles, was at forty-seven Wadsworth's successor as the oldest division commander in the army. He studied the terrain, peering briefly out across a shallow valley, scarped along its bottom and lightly timbered, then up the gentle slope on its far side to where the graybacks crouched behind the fence rails they had stacked along the thickly wooded crest, about a quarter mile away. The scene had a certain bucolic charm, particularly by contrast with the smothering hug of the Wilderness, but Robinson found the situation tactically unpromising and he said as much to Warren, asking for time to bring up his three strung-out brigades and mass them before launching the assault. Warren said no, there was nothing across the way but dismounted cavalry; go in now, with the brigade at hand, and go in hard. This Robinson did, as hard at least as his winded men could manage after crossing the gullied valley and wheezing up the incline, only to have the rebel line explode in their faces, a scant sixty yards away. In quality and volume — a sudden, heavy bank of flame-stabbed smoke, jetting up and out, and a rattling clatter much too loud for carbines — the fire left no doubt that the line was occupied, not by cavalry, as the attackers had been informed when they set out, but by infantry who met them with massed volleys and blasted them back down the slope, a good deal faster than they had climbed it on their way to the explosion.

Nor was that the worst of the affair. By now the second brigade, four regiments of Maryland troops whose enlistments were to expire before the month was out, had come up and begun its descent into the valley, coincident with the arrival of Anderson's corps artillery on the ridge ahead. Startled to find the first wave of attackers in retreat from momentary contact with the rebels, the second was caught and churned up fearfully by a deluge of projectiles. The Marylanders broke, scrambling rearward in a race with the comrades they had intended to support. Dismayed and angered, Robinson hurried forward to rally them in person, but went down with a bullet through one knee. His third brigade fared no better, being struck in the flank and scattered by a savage counter-attack, launched about as soon as it came up. This brought the casualty total to just under 1200 killed and wounded in less than an hour, while as many more were fugitives and stragglers, captured or otherwise unaccounted for. Robinson's knee wound cost him his leg, which was taken off that night. He was out of the war for keeps. And so, as another result of this brief engagement, was his division. It was disbanded next day, the remnants of its three cut-up brigades being distributed among the other divisions of the corps. Demoralized or not, these reinforcements were badly needed by all three, for they had suffered cruelly in the wake of Robinson's fiasco; Anderson's second division had arrived by then to strengthen the rebel line against the Federals, who were committed division by division, as fast as they came up, and division by division were repulsed. By the time Meade arrived, around midday, Warren had done his worst. He had to admit that he could not get over or around the Confederate intrenchments with what was left of his corps. Meade told him to hold what he had, then summoned Sedgwick from his reserve position, north of Alsop, to add the weight of his three divisions to the attack.

This took time — five hours, in all; Sedgwick's men were weary too — but the interim was livened, at any rate for the gossip-hungry clerks and staff, by a personality clash. Sheridan dropped by army headquarters, still fuming about last night's "interference," and Meade, losing his famous temper at last, retorted hotly that the cavalry had been doing less than had been expected of it ever since the campaign opened. That the charge was true did not make it any more acceptable to Sheridan, who replied, bristling, that he considered the remark a calculated insult. Meade recovered his balance for a moment. "I didn't mean

After noon on May 9, Union General John Sedgwick was summoned from a reserve position north of Alsop.

that," he said earnestly, placing one hand on the cavalryman's shoulder in a conciliatory gesture. Sheridan stepped back out of reach ("All the Hotspur in his nature was aroused," a staff observer later wrote) and continued his protest. If the cavalry had done less than had been hoped for, he declared, it was not his fault, but Meade's; Meade had countermanded his orders, interfered with his tactical dispositions, and worst of all had kept his troopers hobbled by assigning them such unprofitable and distractive tasks as guarding the slow-plodding trains and providing escorts for the brass. If results were what Meade wanted, he should let the cavalry function as it was meant to function — on its own, as a compact hard-hitting body. Give him a free rein, Sheridan said, and he would tackle Jeb Stuart on his own ground, deep in the Confederate rear, and whip him out of his boots. The argument continued, both men getting madder by the minute, until Meade at last decided there was only one way to resolve their differences. He went to Grant.

Three days ago, the general-in-chief's reaction to a similar confrontation had been decisive. "You ought to put him under arrest," he had said of the riled-up Griffin. Today though, having heard Meade out, he seemed more amused than angered: especially by the bandy-legged cavalryman's reported claim that he would whip Jeb Stuart out of his boots if Meade would only turn him loose. "Did Sheridan say that?" he asked. Meade nodded. "Well," Grant said, "he generally knows what he's talking about. Let him start right out and do it."

Meade, having thus been taught the difference between eastern and western insubordination, returned to his own headquarters and issued the order; Sheridan would take off next morning, with all three of his divisions, on a maneuver designed to provoke Stuart into hand-to-hand combat by threatening the capital in his rear. Meantime Sedgwick was coming up. By 5 o'clock he had his three divisions in line alongside what was left of Warren's four, and all seven went forward, more or less together, in a final attempt to turn the day's disjointed fighting into a Union victory by taking possession of Spotsylvania, a mile and a half beyond the rebel works. It failed, as the earlier attacks had failed, because Lee again managed to get enough of his veterans

★

— in this case, Ewell's lead division — up to the critical point in time to prevent a breakthrough. His losses had been light today, while Meade's had been comparatively heavy. "The ground was new to everyone, and the troops were tired," Meade's chief of staff explained.

For Grant, who smoked as he watched the sunset repulse, the day had been a grievous disappointment. Not only had he failed to pass Lee's front, but the resultant tactical situation in which he now found himself seemed to favor the defensive at least as much as had been the case in the one he abandoned, just last night, in the belief that it offered him little or no chance to achieve the Cannae he was seeking. Moreover, though he said that he left the Wilderness because he saw no profit in assaulting the works Lee's men had thrown up in the brush, the fortifications here were even more formidable, laid out on dominant ground between unfordable rivers, and getting stronger by the hour. Still smoking, he looked out across the shallow valley where so many of Warren's men had fallen — tousled rag-doll shapes becoming indistinguishable as the daylight faded into dusk — then turned, as imperturbable as ever, and rode back to his tent, there to make a study of the situation, based on such information as had been gathered.

Today's reconnaissance (for that was all it came to, in the end) had been costly, and next morning it grew more so, although nothing so patently wasteful as a repetition of yesterday's headlong approach to the problem was attempted. While Hancock and Burnside were on the march, summoned to come up on the right and left, Warren and Sedgwick limited their activities to improving their intrenchments and making a cautious investigation of the Confederate position. Restricted in scope by the absence of the cavalry, which had taken off soon after sunrise to challenge Stuart, this last was a gingerly business at best. Rebel marksmen, equipped with imported Whitworth rifles mounting telescopic sights, were quick to draw a bead on anything blue that moved, especially if it had a glint of brass about the shoulders. Moreover, in addition to this lack of respect for rank, they seemed to have none for the supposed reduction of accuracy by distance, with the result that there was a good deal of ducking and dodging on the Union side, even though the range was sometimes as great as half a mile. This not only interfered with work, it was also thought to be detrimental to discipline and morale. John Sedgwick looked at it that way, for one, and reproved his troops for flinching from a danger so remote. "What? Men dodging this way for single bullets?" he exclaimed when he saw one outfit react in such a manner to a far-off sniper. "What will you do when they open fire along the whole line? I am ashamed of you. They couldn't hit an elephant at this distance." The soldiers wanted to believe him, partly because they admired him so — "Uncle John," they called him with affection — but the flesh, being thus exposed, was weak; they continued to flinch at the crack of the sharpshooter's rifle, even though it was a good 800 yards away, and at the quick, unnerving whiplash of near misses, which seemed to part the hair of every man at once. "I'm ashamed of you, dodging that way," Sedgwick said again, laughing, and repeated: "They couldn't hit an elephant at this distance." Next time the glass-sighted Whitworth cracked, a couple of minutes later, Sedgwick's chief of staff was startled to see the fifty-year-old general stiffen, as if in profound surprise, and slowly turn his head to show blood spurting from a half-inch hole just under his left eye. He pitched forward, taking the unbraced colonel down with him, and though the doctors did what they could to help, they could not staunch or even slow the steady spurt of blood from the neat new hole beside his cheekbone. He smiled strangely, as if to acknowledge the dark humor of what had turned out to be his last remark, and did not speak again. Within a few minutes he was dead.

Sudden as it was, his death was a knee-buckling shock to the men of his corps, who had made him the best-loved general in the army. Besides, when corps commanders started toppling, alive one minute and dead the next, struck down as if by a bolt of blue-sky lightning, who was safe? All down the line, from brigadiers to privates, spirits were heavy with intimations of mortality. Sorrowfully, the staff carried his body back to army headquarters and laid it in a bower of evergreens beside the road, there to receive the salute of passing troops till nightfall, when he began the journey north to Cornwall Hollow, his home in the Connecticut Berkshires. Nor was the grieving limited to those who had served under him, or even under the same flag today; R. E. Lee, across the way, was saddened by this final news of his old friend. Meade wept, and Grant himself was stunned when he heard that Sedgwick had been hit. "Is he really dead?" he asked. Later, after characterizing the fallen general as one who "was never at fault when serious work was to be done," he told his staff that Sedgwick's loss was worse for him than the loss of a whole division. For the present, though, he found it hard to accept the fact that he was gone. "Is he really dead?" he asked again.

One fact was clear, in any case, and this was that a great many men of various ranks, now alive, were likely to be dead before long if they were ordered to overrun the intrenchments to their front. Formidable as these works had seemed at sundown, they were downright awesome this morning after an unmolested night of labor by the troops who manned them. Studded with guns at critical points throughout its convex three-mile length, Lee's Spotsylvania line was constructed, Meade's chief of staff declared, "in a manner unknown to European warfare, and, indeed, in a manner new to warfare in this country." Actually, it was not so much the novelty of the individual engineering techniques that made this log-and-dirt barrier so forbidding; it was the combination of them into a single construction of interlocking parts, the canny use of natural features of the terrain, and the speed with which the butternut veterans, familiar by now with the fury of Grant's assaults, had accomplished their intricate task.

★

*U*nion soldiers cluster around the fallen
General John Sedgwick only moments after he declared
rebels "couldn't hit an elephant at this distance."

Traverses zigzagged to provide cover against enfilade fire from artillery, and
head logs, chocked a few inches above the hard-packed spoil on the enemy side
of the trench, afforded riflemen a protected slit through which they could take
unruffled aim at whatever came their way. Where there were woods in front of
the line, the trees were slashed to deny concealment for two hundred yards or
more, and wherever the ground was open or insufficiently obstructed, timber
barricades called abatis were installed within easy rifle range, bristling with
sharpened sticks to entangle or slow the attackers while the defenders, more or
less at their leisure, picked them off. For Grant, the prospect was altogether
grim. To assault seemed suicidal, and yet to do nothing was militarily unsound,
since a stalemate under such circumstances might well allow Lee to detach
troops for operations against Butler or Sigel, back near Richmond or out in the

Shenandoah Valley. On the other hand, to maneuver him out of position again by swinging wide around one of his flanks would amount to nothing more than a postponement of the inevitable showdown, which in that case would occur in closer proximity to his capital and would probably result in his being reinforced by units from the garrison charged with its ultimate defense. Grant pondered these three alternatives, unwelcome as they were, until about midday, when Burnside, coming up on the left, provided information which suggested a fourth alternative, more acceptable than the others. While making his far-out eastern swing across Ni River, the ruff-whiskered general reported, he had encountered Confederate infantry, and though he had not had much trouble driving them off, it seemed to him that they might be the leading element of a detached force of considerable strength, engaged in a deep penetration of the Federal left rear for a strike at the army's Fredericksburg supply base.

Burnside could scarcely be classed as a skilled assessor of enemy intentions, but in the absence of Sheridan's cavalry, which might otherwise have been sent out to confirm or refute the validity of the report, Grant accepted the information at face value, partly on grounds that such a move would be altogether in character for Lee. By now, after the buffeting he had taken in the course of the

An abatis – a barricade of tree branches with sharpened points – protects a line of Confederate trenches on the battlefields of the Wilderness Campaign.

★

past five days, the old fox must be groping rather desperately in his bag of tricks for some such table-turning maneuver as the one he had devised, under similar circumstances, when he sent Jackson wide around Pope's flank for a strike at the supply base in his rear, compelling that hapless commander to abandon his position in short order. Grant's reaction was equally characteristic, and quite different. Instead of allowing concern for his base to deflect him from his purpose, he saw in this supposed development a chance to strike from an unexpected direction while his opponent's attention was distracted and his army was divided. Hancock, who had come up on the right, was instructed to detach one division, as a possible reinforcement for Burnside, and proceed westward with the other three for an upstream crossing of the Po. A fast march down the opposite bank — first south, to reach the road from Shady Grove, then eastward along it to the bridge one mile west of the Block House — would put him in position for a second crossing, well below the point where the rebel flank was anchored, and a sudden descent on Lee's left rear. At worst, this should bring the Confederates out of their intrenchments by obliging them to turn and meet the unexpected threat; while at best, assailed as they would be from two directions, north and south, it would result in their destruction. In any case that was the plan, devised in reaction to Burnside's report, and Grant considered it well worth a try, especially since the ablest of his surviving corps commanders was charged with its execution.

Hancock crossed upstream that afternoon, putting in three pontoon bridges, and encountered only sporadic opposition from butternut horsemen on the prowl. Even so, he had not reached the Shady Grove Road, leading eastward to the downstream point where he was to make the crossing that would land him in Lee's rear, before darkness obliged all three divisions to call a halt in the woods on the south bank. An early start next morning — Tuesday, May 10 — brought the head of the column within easy reach of Blockhouse Bridge by sunup. To Hancock's surprise, there on the opposite bank, fortifications had been thrown up overnight and were occupied in considerable strength, bristling with guns trained expectantly on the bridge and its approaches. Once more, with the help of his hard-working cavalry, Lee had forestalled a maneuver designed to discomfit or destroy him; Hancock could only regret that he had not waited until this morning to make his upstream crossing, in which case he would not have afforded the rebels a full night to work on their plans for his reception. Not much given to spilt-milk thinking, he devised an alternate crossing, half a mile downriver, and got one division in motion at once, intending to follow with the other two, when a courier arrived from Meade with instructions for a quick return by two of his divisions to their former position in line on the right of Warren. He himself was to come back with them, the message directed, to take charge of his and Warren's corps for an all-out frontal attack on the Confederate intrenchments at 5 o'clock that afternoon.

He scarcely knew what to make of this sudden change of plans. By now, one brigade of the advance division was across the river; he had only to follow with the other two divisions and Lee's flank would be turned; instead of which, apparently, Meade intended to revert to a direct assault, Fredericksburg style, on fortifications that were admittedly the most formidable ever constructed by an army in the field. Still, orders were orders, comprehensible or not. Recalling the crossed brigade, lest it be gobbled up in the bridgehead it was holding, he left his lead division behind, with instructions to continue what had now become no more than a demonstration, and set out at once with the other two to recross the Po by the three bridges they had installed with such high hopes the day before.

Back on the main front, to which Hancock was returning, Grant had ordered the change in plans as a result of Lee's failure to sustain Burnside's assessment that he had detached a major portion of his army for a strike at the Union supply base. In point of fact, what the IX Corps had encountered on its approach march, down across the Ni the day before, had not been infantry at all, but more of Stuart's ubiquitous cavalry, dismounted as skirmishers to delay the Federal concentration; Burnside had simply been mistaken, here as elsewhere in his career, and Grant decided that if Lee had not divided his army, it would be unwise for him to divide his own, particularly if this involved detaching Hancock, his most dependable lieutenant, who would be needed to help meet whatever crisis Lee had it in mind to precipitate, not in theory but in fact. Accordingly, he had had Meade summon Hancock back to his former position alongside Warren, who had also contributed to the decision by informing his superiors that, despite his failure yesterday, he believed he could score a breakthrough today if he was properly supported. It was true, the attack would be made against what seemed to be the most impregnable part of the rebel line, but when Warren declared that he had examined it carefully and believed it could be broken, Grant was altogether willing to give him the chance to prove his claim. Hancock would come up on his right, and Sedgwick's corps was already posted on his left; at 5 o'clock they would all go forward together, and if Warren's judgment proved sound, Lee's defenses would be pierced, his position overrun, and his army shattered. Richmond then would be Grant's for the taking, which in turn would mean that the war was approximately over, all but the incidental task of picking up the pieces.

It did not work out that way for a variety of reasons. Like Sheridan two days ago, Warren was anxious to accomplish something solid that would cancel his poor showing up to now, and this apparently made him oversanguine in his assessment of the chances for a breakthrough, as well as overeager to get started. Faulty judgment thus laid the groundwork for a failure which impatience served to enlarge. Around 3.30, with Sedgwick's corps alerted on his left and one of Hancock's divisions back in position on his right, he decided that to wait another hour and a half for jump-off time, as scheduled, would be to risk

*G*eneral Winfield Scott Hancock (center) and
II Corps staff officers pose for one of Mathew Brady's
photographers during the Wilderness Campaign.

losing the opportunity he believed he saw. Or perhaps he acted out of knowledge that Hancock, when he came up on the right, would take command by
virtue of his rank. In any case he appealed to Grant, through Meade, for
permission to attack at once. Always ready to encourage aggressiveness, Grant
was willing, and Warren — who had put on his dress uniform that morning,
evidently for the purpose of making a good appearance on what he hoped
would be his finest day since Gettysburg — went forward, around 4 o'clock;
into chaos. Exposed in the slashings and snagged by the abatis, his troops were
badly cut up, their ranks thrown into disorder by artillery and rifle fire from the
flanks and dead ahead. Some among the bravest pressed on to within point-
blank range of the rebel works, and a few even made it to the crest of the parapet.
But that was all; there was no penetration anywhere along the line. Warren kept
trying, only to have the process repeated. He was deeply discouraged at seeing
his hopes break in blood on the rim of the intrenchments, even though Grant
and Meade were not: not so deeply, at any rate, that it caused them to discontinue
the effort to score a breakthrough here today. When Hancock arrived soon after
5 o'clock with his other division, back at last from his overnight excursion on
the far side of the Po, he was ordered to resume the attack at 6.30, taking charge
of all the troops on the right, his own and Warren's.

Elsewhere along the concave Union line, north and northwest of Spotsylvania, results had been no better up to now. Posted astride the Fredericksburg Road to block the movement Lee failed to make, Burnside had scarcely been engaged; his only consequential loss today was the commander of his lead division, Brigadier General T. G. Stevenson, a young Bostonian of high promise, who was killed instantly, much as Sedgwick had been the day before, by a long-range sniper. Sedgwick's corps, headed now by Horatio Wright, who was also a Connecticut-born professional, had made no more of a dent in the enemy defenses than Warren's corps had done, but a close-up look at the rebel works had given one brigade commander a notion of how to go about making a good deal more than a dent.

This was Colonel Emory Upton, a twenty-four-year-old New Yorker who had graduated from West Point less than a month after Sumter and since then, aside from a brief, unhappy period as a drill instructor of volunteers, had

Speed and precision being the main elements, together with a clear distribution of duties, Upton took the dozen unit commanders forward to the line of departure . . .

served with distinction in all the army's battles, winning five promotions along the way. Strong on theory, as well as action, Upton returned from a personal examination of the Confederate fortifications to report to his division chief, Wright's successor Brigadier General David Russell, that he believed he knew a way to score a breakthrough in short order. His notion was that the troops should attack on a narrow front, four lines deep, without pausing to fire until a limited penetration had been achieved; whereupon the first line would fan out left and right to widen the breach and the second would plunge straight ahead to deepen it, supported by the third and fourth, which would form the reserve and be called upon, as needed, in any or all of the three directions. Russell liked the plan and took Upton to see the corps commander, who liked it too. In fact, Wright liked it so well that he not only gave the young colonel twelve regiments to use in the attack, but also arranged to have a full division standing by to exploit whatever success was gained. Speed and precision being the main elements, together with a clear distribution of duties, Upton took the dozen unit commanders forward to the line of departure, along the edge of a dense belt of pines 200 yards from the rebel works, and indicated to each of them just what was expected of him. The point selected for assault was about midway down the western face of a salient which Ewell's corps had occupied to deny the Federals

★

possession of some high ground where they might otherwise have posted batteries to enfilade this central portion of Lee's line, the two wings of which slanted
sharply back from the salient or "angle," as it was called. Rebel guns were thick
in there, thicker than anywhere else along the line, but it was Upton's plan to
get among them fast and overwhelm the crews before they had much chance to
use them. Having explained all this to the individual leaders, and shown them
their objectives on the map and on the ground, he told them to bring their regiments forward, one at a time to avoid attracting attention to the build-up, and
post them under cover for the assault, which was set for 6 o'clock, one hour
before sunset and two before dark.

At ten minutes past the appointed time, having waited for the pre-
arranged bombardment to die down, Upton gave the signal and the column
started forward with a cheer, three regiments in each of its four lines. Almost
at once the rebel guns took up the challenge, blasting away at the mass of
bluecoats running toward them across the field, but despite the delay involved
in breaking through the tangled abatis, set up about midway between the
woods and the intrenchments, men of all three leading regiments were
mounting the parapet within five minutes of the jump-off. These first arrivers
were shot or bayonetted or clubbed back — Upton later reported that at this
stage the defenders "absolutely refused to yield the ground" — but as others
came up, the weight of numbers began to tell. Presently there was
hand-to-hand fighting in the trenches, which broke off when the second wave
of attackers arrived and the badly outweighed Confederates turned and ran for
their secondary defenses, just under 200 yards in their rear. Many did not
make it, being captured or shot down. Meantime the first Federal line had
fanned out left and right, widening the gap, and the reserves were surging forward to support the second in its continued penetration. So far, everything had
worked precisely as Upton had planned; the rebel line was broken. Whether the
break would be extended, or even remain — Confederate reinforcements were
coming in fast by then from other parts of the salient — depended now on the
division Wright had given the assignment of exploiting just such a success as
had been gained.

This was not one of his own divisions, but the one that had been detached from Hancock when he crossed the Po the day before. Originally intended
for support of the IX Corps, it had been attached to Wright when the threat to
Burnside turned out to be nonexistent, and Wright had given its commander,
Gershom Mott, instructions to support Upton by advancing simultaneously on
the apex of the "angle," thus to divert the attention of the defenders away from
the main effort, midway down the western face of the salient; after which he was
to move fast to consolidate, and if possible enlarge, whatever gains had been
scored in that direction. As it turned out, he was only too successful, both for

his own sake and for Upton's, in carrying out the first half of this assignment. Forming his two brigades in full view of the objective, half a mile away, Mott did such a thorough job of attracting the attention of the rebels (particularly the gunners, who had crowded into that narrow space no fewer than 22 pieces of artillery with which to take him under fire across half a mile of open ground) that his division was knocked to pieces within minutes. Already badly shaken by their Wilderness experience, the troops milled about briefly under this pounding, some of them attempting ineffectively to return the fire with their outranged rifles, then scuttled backward in confusion, seeking cover and concealment. Staff officers, sent out to search for them that evening, found them deep in the rearward woods, huddled in groups about their regimental flags and boiling coffee to help them recover from the shock. Like Robinson's division, which had gone out of existence as a result of its misadventure two days ago, Mott's too would presently be abolished, the remnant of its two brigades being assigned three days afterward to another division in Hancock's corps.

But that was later. A more immediate consequence of the rout was that Upton's breakthrough went for nothing, not only because he was left without support, but also because the defenders now were free to concentrate all their attention and strength on healing the breach. This they were quick to do, obliging Upton to fight his way out of the rebel lines with much of the fervor and urgency he had displayed while fighting his way in. Darkness, gathering fast

Confederate prisoners captured during Colonel Emory Upton's May 10 charge rush to the rear past the Shelton house in this sketch by Alfred Waud.

after sundown, was a help in the disengagement; all twelve regiments made it back to their own lines, having suffered about one thousand casualties. That was also about the number they inflicted, mostly in the form of prisoners taken in the initial rush and escorted into the Federal lines before the counterattack obliged their captors to follow in their wake. Far on the right, Hancock's attack, deferred till sunset, was repulsed at about the same time, as decisively as Warren's had been earlier, and Burnside continued his pointless vigil on the left. Night came down as the fighting ended. Men sat around campfires and discussed the events of the day, which provoked much blame of Mott and praise for Upton. Across the way, notes faint in the distance and filtered through the trees, a Confederate band lent an eerie touch to the scene by playing "Nearer, My God, to Thee," but this was offset to some extent, or anyhow balanced, when a Union band responded with the "Dead March" from *Saul.*

One of Upton's warmest admirers was the general-in-chief, who rewarded him with a battlefield promotion — subject, of course, to Washington approval — "for gallant and meritorious services." Much encouraged by the young colonel's tactical contribution, which he saw as the key to Lee's undoing if the maneuver could be repeated on a larger scale and properly supported, Grant was in high spirits. A headquarters orderly saw him talking to Meade about the prospect that night with unaccustomed animation, puffing rapidly on a cigar. "A brigade today," he was saying; "we'll try a corps tomorrow."

Thinking it over he realized however that tomorrow would be too soon. One trouble with today's attack was that it had been launched with not enough daylight left for its full exploitation; dawn would be a much better time in that regard, and the preceding darkness would help to conceal the massing of large bodies of troops within charging distance of the rebel works. So Grant, having ruled out tomorrow, decided that the assault would be delivered at first light on the following day, May 12 — which would also give him plenty of time for briefing all commanders, high and low, and an unhurried movement of units, large and small, into their designated jump-off areas. Given the method, the tactical execution was fairly obvious. Hancock would be shifted from the far right to the center, where he would be in charge of the main effort, and he would make it with his whole corps, against the very point that Mott had failed to hit today, the apex of the "angle," the military theory being that the tip of a salient was hard to defend because fire from the lines slanting back from that forward point could not converge on a force advancing from dead ahead. It was true, this theory had not applied too well on that same ground today; Mott had been wrecked before he got within reach of the objective. But Hancock's assault would be delivered Upton-style, without pauses for alignment or for firing, and if it worked as well for him as it had worked for Upton, his men would be up to the enemy works, and maybe over them, before the defenders had time to offer much resistance. Moreover this attack, unlike the one today, would be heavily supported. Burnside, off on the left, would move up close tomorrow night and launch a simultaneous assault next morning against the salient's eastern face, while Wright and Warren kept up the pressure on the right and the far right. Further details could be worked out next day, when the formal order was drawn up. In any case, after Upton's demonstration late today, a Tuesday, Grant had little doubt that Lee's defenses would be breached on Thursday and that careful planning would see to it that the breach was enlarged to victory proportions. He went to bed in a better frame of mind than he had done on any of the other five nights since May 4, when his army completed its crossing of the Rapidan unopposed.

That his mood was still the same on Wednesday, hopeful and determined, was demonstrated shortly after breakfast by his response to a request from a distinguished visitor, U. S. Representative Elihu B. Washburne of Illinois, that he give him some word of encouragement to take back to Washington with him. Grant's congressional guardian angel from the outset of the war, Washburne had spent the past week at headquarters, where, incongruous in somber civilian broadcloth amid the panoply of the staff, he had been something of a puzzle to the troops; they could not figure who or what he was, until a wit explained that the general, with his usual concern for the eventualities, had brought his private undertaker along on the campaign. Now that he was returning to his duties at

*In this May 11 Edwin Forbes sketch, members of a
Federal II Corps battery lounge against the log revetments
of their earthwork along the Brock Road.*

the capital, the congressman told Grant as they stood outside the latter's tent to say goodbye, it might be a good idea to relieve the anxiety of the President and the Secretary of War by sending them some word on the progress of the fighting here in Virginia. "I know they would be greatly gratified," Washburne said, "if I could carry a message from you giving what encouragement you can as to the situation." Grant looked doubtful. He was aware that anything of the kind would be released to the public, and he did not want to be hurt, as others before him had been hurt, by the boomerang effect of overoptimistic statements. Pleased though he was with his progress so far, he replied, he knew that the road ahead was a long one and he was therefore "anxious not to say anything just now that might hold out false hopes to the people." He hesitated, then added: "However, I will write a letter to Halleck, as I generally communicate through him, giving the general situation, and you can take it with you." He stepped inside the tent, sat down at his field desk, and after heading a sheet of paper, "Near Spottsylvania C. H., May 11, 1864 — 8.30 a.m.," scribbled a couple of hundred words, puffing away at his cigar as he wrote. "We have now ended our sixth day of very hard fighting," he informed Halleck. "The result up to this

★

time is much in our favor. But our losses have been heavy, as well as those of the enemy. . . . I am now sending back to Belle Plain all my wagons for a fresh supply of provisions and ammunition, and purpose to fight it out on this line if it takes all summer. . . . I am satisfied the enemy are very shaky, and are only kept up to the mark by the greatest exertions on the part of their officers and by keeping them intrenched in every position they take."

When he finished he had a clerk make a fair copy, which he then signed and folded and gave to Washburne, along with a farewell handshake, before returning to work on his plans for tomorrow's dawn assault. Staff officers read the retained draft of the letter, one afterwards recalled, without finding in it anything unusual or "epigrammatic" until a few days later, when the New York papers reached camp with excerpts from it splashed across their front pages in large headlines — particularly a phrase or sentence which someone, either the copyist here or another at the far end, polished up a bit: "I propose to fight it out on this line if it takes all summer." That caught the attention of the editors, and through them the public, with a force unequaled by anything Grant had said or written since the Unconditional Surrender note at Donelson, more than two years ago. "I propose to move immediately upon your works" had passed into history as a watchword signifying Federal determination to press for total victory over the forces in rebellion, and so too, now, did "I propose to fight it out on this line if it takes all summer."

Grant's assessment of the Confederates as "very shaky" indicated that he had not really believed it would take "all summer" to settle the issue at hand that Wednesday morning, north of Spotsylvania. By midafternoon — coincident with a sudden change in the weather, brought on by a light drizzle of rain that dropped the temperature from the unseasonable high it had been holding for the past few days — the field order for tomorrow's attack was being distributed to the commanders of all four corps. Already in close proximity to the enemy along their respective portions of the line, Warren and Wright would remain more or less where they were, and Burnside had only a limited adjustment to make. It was otherwise with Hancock, who had to shift three of his divisions into position with the fourth, Mott's, which by now, although considerably diminished and dejected, had been reassembled just in rear of the area where it had begun its ill-fated advance the day before. The division he had left beyond the Po when he returned with the other two, in accordance with orders from Meade, had also recrossed the river after a clash with a rebel force Lee sent over from his right, and in this rear-guard action the division had had to leave behind a gun that, in the haste of the withdrawal, got wedged so tightly between two trees that it could not be freed. Hancock took this hard, the more so because it was the only piece of artillery the II Corps had ever lost in battle, and he was determined to get full revenge tomorrow.

★

Just now, though, he had his hands full getting his troops into position for the attack at first light, which the almanac said would come at 4 a.m. The march began at dusk, along a narrow road soon churned to mud by a pelting rain that seemed to be getting harder by the hour. It was midnight before the head of the column reached the jump-off area and the four divisions, three of them wet and cold from their rainy march, started forming in the dripping woods. This too was a difficult business, for more reasons than the unpleasantness of the weather or the loss of sleep and lack of food. Here on reconnaissance earlier that day, unable to see far or clearly through the steely curtain of rain, Hancock had tried to get Mott's disheartened men to drive the enemy pickets back so he could get a look at the objective; but little or nothing came of the attempt — they had too vivid a memory of what those 22 guns up there had done to them the day before — with the result that his examination of the apex of the "angle," along with most of the intervening ground across which he would charge, had practically been limited to what he could learn from the map. And so it was tonight, in the rain and darkness. The best Hancock could do was give his division commanders a compass bearing, derived from the map by drawing a line connecting a house in their rear with a house in the approximate center of the rebel salient, and tell them to move in that direction when they received his order to advance.

Four o'clock came, but not daylight; the almanac had not taken the rain or fog into account. Finally at 4.30, though there still was scarcely a glimmer of light from what the compass showed to be the east, word came for the lead division to go forward, followed closely by the other three.

★ ★ ★ **F**earing **the worst as they stumbled** forward through fog so dense that it held back the dawn, Hancock and his soldiers were in better luck than they had any way of knowing. For one thing, those 22 guns assigned to defend the apex of the salient up ahead, which they expected to start roaring at any moment, tearing their close-packed ranks with shot and shell within seconds of hearing a picket give the alarm, were by no means the threat they had been two days ago, when they all but demolished one of these four divisions attempting this same thing on this same ground. They were in fact no threat at all. They were not there. They had been withdrawn the night before, as the result of an overdue error by Lee, whose intelligence machinery, after a week of smooth if not uncanny functioning, had finally slipped a cog.

Reports of activity beyond the Union lines had been coming in from various sources all the previous afternoon. A lookout perched in the belfry of a Spotsylvania church, which commanded a view of the roads in rear of the enemy left, informed headquarters of what seemed to be a large-scale withdrawal in that direction, and this was confirmed between 4 and 5 o'clock by two messages

★

from Lee's cavalryman son, whose division — left behind by Stuart when he took out after Sheridan, two days ago, with three of his six brigades — was probing for information in that direction. Heavy trains were in motion for Fredericksburg, young Lee declared, and Federal wounded were being taken across the Rappahannock in large numbers to Belle Plain, eight miles beyond on the Potomac. "There is evidently a general move going on," he notified his father. Here as in the Wilderness, the southern commander was alert to the danger of having his opponent steal a march on him, and here as there he was prepared to react on the basis of information less than conclusive or even substantial. Such activity in Grant's left rear could mean that, having found the Spotsylvania confrontation unprofitable and restrictive, he had one of two strategic shifts in mind: 1) a limited retreat to Fredericksburg, where he would consolidate his forces and better cover his supply line for a subsequent advance by land or water, or 2) another swing around the Confederate right, to interpose his army between Lee and Richmond. From Lee's point of view, though a similar endeavor had failed four days ago, the latter was the more dangerous maneuver, one that he simply could not afford to have succeed. In this case, however, he believed from the evidence that what Grant was about to attempt was a withdrawal to the Rappahannock line, and he wanted to prevent this — or, more strictly speaking, take advantage of it — almost as much as he did the other. In conversation with two of his generals about an hour before sundown he told why.

It began as a discussion of Grant's worth as a tactician. Lee was visiting Harry Heth's headquarters, on the far right near the courthouse, as was A. P. Hill, up and about but still not well enough to return to duty, when a staff officer happened to remark that, in slaughtering his troops by assaulting earthworks, the Union commander was little better than a butcher. Lee did not agree. "I think General Grant has

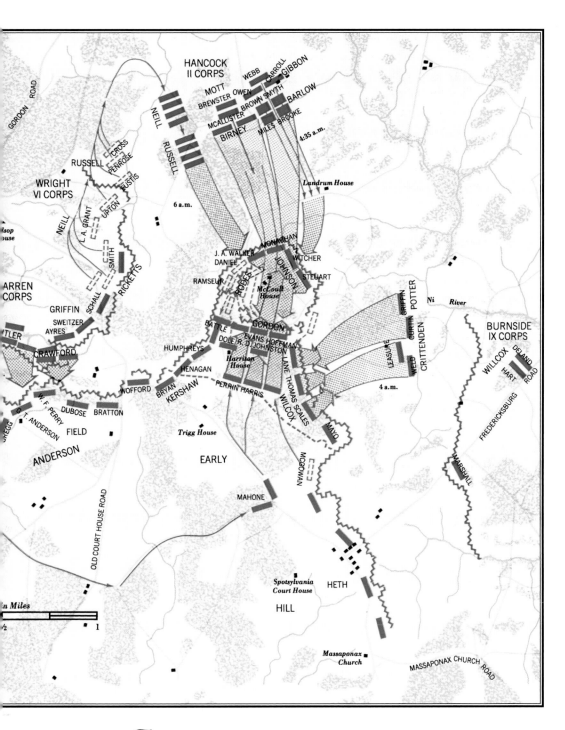

GORDON ROAD

HANCOCK
II CORPS

WEBB   CARROLL
        GIBBON

MOTT
BREWSTER OWEN
          SMYTH   BARLOW
MCALLISTER BROWN
NEILL   BROOKE
      BIRNEY   MILES
RUSSELL   4:35 a.m.

RUSSELL   Landrum House

NEILL   CROSS
         PENROSE
RUSSELL   EUSTIS

WRIGHT
VI CORPS   6 a.m.
        L. A. GRANT UPTON
Alsop
House   MONAGHAN
                J. A. WALKER WITCHER
         SMITH   DANIEL
ARREN   JOHNSON
CORPS   SCHALL RAMSEUR STEUART
        RICKETTS   McCoull
  GRIFFIN   RODES House
   SWEITZER
   AYRES   GORDON   Ni River
TLER   BATTLE EVANS HOFFMAN   GRIFFIN POTTER
  CRAWFORD   HUMPHREYS DOLE R. D. JOHNSTON   CURTIN CRITTENDEN
                      Harrison   LEASURE WELD BURNSIDE
        HENAGAN   House   IX CORPS
  W. F. PERRY BRYAN PERRIN HARRIS   4 a.m.   WILLCOX DELAND
  G. T. ANDERSON KERSHAW   HART ROAD
GREGG DUBOSE BRATTON WOFFORD   LANE THOMAS WILCOX
       FIELD   Trigg House   SCALES
  ANDERSON   MAYO   FREDERICKSBURG
                                                MCGOWAN
        OLD COURT HOUSE ROAD   EARLY
                                                    MARSHALL
                      MAHONE

                                            HETH
                    Spotsylvania
                    Court House
                         HILL

                                      Massaponax
                                      Church   MASSAPONAX CHURCH ROAD

n Miles
/2   1

This map shows the fighting on May 12. Union troops overran
the Mule Shoe but were repulsed. The battle raged into
the night, and by daybreak next morning Lee had withdrawn.

★

managed his affairs remarkably well up to the present time," he said quietly. Then he turned to Heth and told him what he had come for. "My opinion is the enemy are preparing to retreat tonight to Fredericksburg. I wish you to have everything in readiness to pull out at a moment's notice, but do not disturb your artillery till you commence moving. We must attack those people if they retreat."

Hill spoke up, pale but impetuous as always. "General Lee, let them continue to attack our breastworks. We can stand that very well."

The talk was then of casualties, and though no one knew the actual number of the fallen on either side (Grant in fact had lost about 7000 men by now in front of Spotsylvania, while Lee was losing barely one third that many) all expressed their satisfaction with the present position, which they were convinced they could maintain longer than the Federals could afford to keep assaulting it. Lee rose to go; "We must attack those people if they retreat," he had declared, and in parting he explained what he meant by that. "This army cannot stand a siege," he said. "We must end this business on the battlefield, not in a fortified place."

From there he rode in the rain to the center, where Ewell had disposed his three divisions to defend the salient, one along its eastern face and the apex, another along its western face, where Upton had scored an abortive break-through yesterday, and the third in reserve, posted rearward under instructions to move quickly in support of any stricken point along the inverted U of the intrenched perimeter. Dubbed the "Mule Shoe" by its defenders in description of its shape, the position was a little under a mile in depth and about two thirds as wide, heavily wooded for the most part and crisscrossed by a few narrow, winding roads. Because of this last, which would make removal of the guns a difficult business in the dark and the deepening mud, Lee told Ewell to get the batteries that were posted in the forward portion of the salient withdrawn before nightfall, in order to avoid delaying pursuit of the Federals when word arrived that their retreat was under way. It was close to sunset now, and while Ewell got to work on this Lee rode to First Corps headquarters on the left. After giving Anderson the instructions he had earlier given Heth — to be ready to pull out at a moment's notice, but to leave his artillery in position until then — the gray commander returned to his tent to get what sleep he could between then and 3.30, his usual rising time at this critical stage of the campaign.

Within the salient, as night wore on and the rain came down harder, a feeling of uneasiness, which began with the departure of the guns, pervaded the bivouacs and trenches. At first it was vague — "a nameless something in the air," one soldier was to call it, looking back — but after midnight it grew less so, particularly for the men who held the "toe" of the shoe-shaped line and were closest to the enemy position. A sort of rumble, slow but steady, came from the saturated darkness out in front; some likened it to the muffled thunder of a wa-terfall, others to the grinding of a powerful machine. Veterans who heard it, over and under the pelting of the rain, identified it as the sound of troops in motion by the thousands. Either a retreat was under way, as Lee had said, or else a heavy attack was in the making. If it was the latter, there was difficulty in telling whether the enemy was moving to the left or right, for a strike at Anderson or Early, or massing for another assault on the Mule Shoe. One of Edward Johnson's brigade commanders, Brigadier General George H. Steuart, a Maryland-born West Pointer, went out to his picket line for a closer investigation. He had not listened long before he decided that the Federals not only were preparing an attack, but were aiming it at him. His next thought was of the gun pits standing empty along his portion of the works, and he went at once to Johnson to urge the prompt return of his artillery, parked since sundown back near Spotsylvania. Old Allegheny passed the request to Ewell, who approved it. All 22 of the withdrawn guns would be back in position by 2 o'clock, he said.

When the appointed time had come, but not the guns, Steuart's anxiety mounted. After waiting another hour he went again to Johnson, who had a staff officer make the round of the brigades with orders for the troops to turn out and check the condition of their rifles, while another rode back to inform Ewell that the artillery had not arrived as promised. All this time, that muffled grinding sound continued in the outer darkness. Shortly before 4.30, just as the fog began to lift a bit, Johnson was relieved to learn that the missing guns were returning up the road from the base of the salient. Before they came in sight, however, the sound out front in the paling darkness rose in volume and intensity, drawing nearer, until it became the unmistakable tramp of a marching host. From a distance of about 300 yards a mighty cheer went up — the deep-chested roar of charging Federals, as distinguished from the high-throated scream that was known as the rebel yell — and heavy masses of blue infantry, close-packed and a-bristle with bayonets glinting steely in the dawn, broke through the fog directly in front of the apex of the salient. Alerted, the Confederates rose and gave the attackers point-blank volleys. In some cases the fire was effective, while in others it was not, depending on whether unit commanders had acted on the warning to have their men draw the dampened charges from their rifles and reload. Not that it mattered tactically; for whether their losses were high or low, the various

*M*aryland-born Confederate General George H. Steuart was captured during the fighting on May 12.

Confederate General Edward Johnson, called "Old Clubby" for the cane he carried courtesy of a leg wound, was captured during the fighting at the Mule Shoe salient.

elements of the dense blue mass surged up and over the parapet, into the trenches. Johnson, who was sometimes called "Old Clubby" because of the stout hickory stick he used as a cane to favor the leg he had been shot in, two years back, limped about amid the confusion and implored his troops to keep fighting, despite the odds; the guns would soon be up to settle the issue, he told them, and for a moment it seemed to be true. The lead battery unlimbered, there in the toe of the Mule Shoe, and managed to get off one round each from two of the pieces. But that was all. "Stop firing that gun!" the cannoneers heard someone shout as they prepared to reload, and looked around to find scores of rifles leveled at them by hard-eyed Federals who had broken the gray line. They raised their hands. Others were less fortunate, taking fire from all directions before they knew the place had been overrun. "Where shall I point the gun?" a rattled corporal asked a badly wounded lieutenant. "At the Yankees," he replied with his last breath. But the two rounds already gotten off were all that were fired before all but two of the 22 guns were surrendered, most of them still in limber on the road.

Lee was breakfasting by lantern light when the rapid-fire clatter erupted in the Mule Shoe to inform him that the enemy, far from retreating, was launching an assault upon his center, which he had stripped of guns the night before. From the volume of sound he knew the attack was a heavy one, and presently, when he mounted Traveller to ride in that direction, he saw at first hand that, so far at least, it had also been successful. Fugitives fled past him, streaming rearward, with and without their weapons. "Hold on!" he cried, removing his hat so they would know him. "Your comrades need your services. Stop, men!" Some stopped and some kept running past him with a wild look in their eyes. "Shame on you men; shame on you!" he called after them in his deep voice. "Go back to your regiments." As he drew near the base of the salient he met an officer from Edward Johnson's staff riding to bring him word of what had happened up ahead. Pouring in through a quick break just east of the apex, which was held by Stonewall Jackson's old Manassas brigade, the Federals had fanned out rapidly, left and right, to come upon the adjoining brigades from the flank and rear. Johnson himself had been taken, after being surrounded and very nearly shot because he would not stop hobbling about, brandishing his hickory club and calling for his troops to rally, even though a whole company of blue-coats had their rifles trained on him. Steuart too was a prisoner, along with a number of his soldiers, and the Stonewall Brigade had surrendered practically en masse when the enemy came up in its rear and blocked the possibility of escape. In all, no less than half of Johnson's 5000-man division had been shot or cap-tured in the first half hour of fighting, along with twenty guns and well over half of the regimental flags.

That was the worst of it. On the credit side, Lee was presently to learn, Rodes's division, by "refusing" its flank adjoining the break at the apex, was holding fast to the western face of the salient, and Wilcox had managed to do the same on the right, where Early's line joined Ewell's, even though an attack of nearly equal strength had been made against that point by Burnside at about the same time Hancock struck. This meant that, up to now at any rate, the breakthrough was laterally contained. Whether it could also be contained in depth was another matter, and it was to this that Lee gave his immediate atten-tion. "Ride with me to General Gordon," he told the orphaned staff man, and continued to spur Traveller toward the open end of the Mule Shoe, where Gordon's division had been posted with instructions to support Rodes or Johnson in such a crisis as the one at hand.

Gordon had already begun to meet the situation by sending one of his three brigades forward on a wide front, the men deployed as skirmishers to blunt the Federal penetration, and was preparing to counterattack with the other two, his own Georgians and Pegram's Virginians, when Lee rode up. "What do you want me to do, General?" Gordon asked. Lee wanted him to do just what he was doing, and said so, knowing only too well that unless the Union drive was stopped his army would be cut in half. Gordon saluted and returned to the work at hand. However, as he was about to give the signal to go forward he looked back and saw that Lee, faced with a crisis as grave as the one six days ago in the Wilderness, was responding in the same fashion here at Spotsylvania. Still with his hat off, he had ridden to a position near the center of the line, between the two brigades, with the obvious intention of taking part in the charge. Horrified — for he knew how great the danger was, even here near the base of the salient, having just had his coat twitched by a stray bullet out of the woods he was about to enter — the young brigadier wheeled his horse and rode back to confront his gray-haired chief. "General Lee, this is no place for you," he told him. "Go back, General; we will drive them back." Soldiers from both brigades began to gather about the two horsemen for a better view, and Gordon spoke louder, wanting them to reinforce his plea. "These men are Virginians and Georgians. They have never failed you. They never will. Will you, boys?" The answer was prompt and vociferous. "No! No!" "General Lee to the rear; Lee to the rear!" "We'll drive them back for you, General!" Lee kept looking straight ahead, apparently determined not to be put off, until a tall Virginia sergeant took the matter into his own hands by grabbing Traveller's rein, jerking his head around, and leading him rearward through the cheering ranks.

Behind him Lee heard Gordon's voice ring out above the roar of battle, which grew louder as the breakthrough deepened: "Forward! Guide right!" And while the Virginians and Georgians crashed into the woods to come to grips with the attackers, as they had promised they would do, the southern commander resumed his higher duties. Of these, the most immediate was to find some means of strengthening the counterattack now being launched, and in this connection his first thought was of the fugitives, the troops blown loose from their units when the forward part of the salient went. "Collect together the men of Johnson's division and report to General Gordon," he told the orphaned staffer. That would help, though probably not enough. He thought then of Mahone's division, detached from Early two days ago to meet the threat from across the Po at Blockhouse Bridge, and sent word for Mahone to leave one brigade in the newly dug intrenchments there, protecting his flank, and move at once with the other three to reinforce Gordon's effort to restore the integrity of his broken center.

In point of fact Gordon was already doing remarkably well on his own, first by stemming, then by reversing the flow of the blue flood down the salient. His success in this unequal contest — in effect, a matching of three brigades against four divisions — was due in part to the fury of his assault, inspired by Lee, and in part to the assistance given by the hard-core remnant of Johnson's division, as well as by the troops from the adjoining divisions of Rodes and Wilcox, whose interior flanks hooked onto the wings of his line as he advanced. All this helped; but perhaps the greatest help came from the Federals themselves, who by then were in no condition, tactically or otherwise, to offer sustained resistance to what Gordon threw at them. Boiling over the works and onto unfamiliar ground, a maze of trenches and traverses, thickly wooded in spots and cluttered with prisoners and debris, they scarcely knew which way to turn in order to make the most of the breakthrough they had scored with such comparative ease and speed. The impetus at this point came mainly from the rear, as more and more of Hancock's men continued to pour into the salient; eventually there were close to 20,000 of them in an area less than half a mile square, with such resultant jumbling of their ranks that what had been meant to be a smoothly functioning military formation quickly degenerated into a close-packed mob, some of whose members were so tightly wedged against their fellows that, like muscle-bound athletes, they could not lift their arms to use their weapons. It was at this discordant stage that Gordon struck, and the effect of his fire on the men in that hampered mass of blue was appalling. A bullet could scarcely miss its mark, or if it did it struck another quite as vital. Turning to breast the pressure from the rear, where there was little knowledge of what was going on up front, they broke as best they could, a stumbling herd, and fled back up the salient to gain the protection of the intrenchments they had crossed on their way in. Gordon's troops came after them, screaming and firing as they ran.

Down the eastern face of the salient, the critical point being near its base, where Ewell's line joined Early's, Burnside had attacked at about the same

They scarcely knew which way to turn in order to make the most of the breakthrough they had scored with such comparative ease and speed.

time Hancock did; but there was less confusion here, on both sides, for the simple reason that there had been no penetration. Recoiling, the three blue divisions — made up of greener, less determined men than the veterans under Meade — found what cover they could, within range of the rebel works, and contented themselves with firing at whatever showed above the parapet. This gave Wilcox so little trouble that he was free to assist in Gordon's counterattack, thus helping to keep Hancock off his flank. Across the way, down the western face of the salient, Rodes was able to do the same, for the even simpler reason that he had not been hit at all; not yet. But then at 6 o'clock, with Hancock's attackers tamped firmly back into the toe of the Mule Shoe, Wright struck. He came up hard, with everything he had, against that portion of Rodes's front where Upton had scored the original breakthrough, two days back. Rodes managed to prevent a repetition of that archetypical success, though only by the hardest. Much of the fighting was hand-to-hand, across the works, but Wright's attack, like Hancock's, was muscle-bound, hampered by its bulk; he too had close to 20,000 men and he was mindful of Grant's concern that he bring the weight of every one of them to bear. Rodes kept his badly outnumbered division in position, but he knew that the line might go with a rush at any moment under all that pressure. Accordingly, he sent word to Lee that if he was to prevent a second breakthrough — potentially even more dangerous than the first, since it would put the attackers in rear of practically every Confederate in the salient — he must have reinforcements, and have them quick.

They were already on the way from Blockhouse Bridge. Sent for earlier to strengthen Gordon's counterattack, the three brigades from Mahone's division could be used instead to shore up Rodes; provided of course that they came up in time. Impatient at their nonarrival, Lee rode westward in rear of Anderson's position — which had not been attacked, so far, but was under fire from Warren's long-range artillery — to meet them and save time by redirecting their march to the hard-pressed west face of the salient, where the Federals were hammering at the works. Presently he came upon the lead brigade, Carnot Posey's Mississippians, now under Brigadier General Nathaniel Harris, a thirty-year-old former Vicksburg lawyer. Lee rode alongside Harris, giving instructions, and the Union gunners, spotting the column in brisk motion across the way, lengthened their ranges to bring it under fire. They concentrated mainly on the horsemen at its head, with the result that Lee had to give all his attention to Traveller, who began to rear wildly amid a flurry of plunging shot and bursting shell. Lee kept his seat, doing what he could to calm the animal, but Traveller kept rearing. It was well he did; for as he went back on his hind legs, boxing the air with his forehoofs, a solid shot, which otherwise would have killed or maimed both horse and rider, passed directly under his belly. Horrified, the Mississippians began to yell: "Go back, General! Go back! For God's sake, go back!" They tried to get between him and the exploding shells, urging him to hurry out of range, but Lee was in no more of a mind to retire from this fourth Lee-to-the-rear tableau than he had been to quit the other three. His blood was up, now as before; anxiety was on him. At last he said, "If you will promise me to drive those people from our works, I will go back." The soldiers cheered and, while Lee watched admiringly, took up the march at a faster rate, joining Rodes in time to prevent a breakthrough which one of his brigadiers had just warned him was only minutes away.

Now, however, this second phase of the contest, which ended with the approximate restoration of Lee's line, merged into the third, a struggle even fiercer than the two that had gone before. Tamped back into the toe of the Mule Shoe, Hancock's troops found cover by recrossing the log parapet and taking shelter behind it. There they stayed and there they fought, sometimes at arm's length, much as Wright's men were doing on their right, down the western face of the salient, where the region of Upton's abortive penetration acquired a new name: The Bloody Angle. The term had been used before, in other battles elsewhere in the war, but there was no doubt forever after, at least on the part of those who fought there, that here was where the appellation best applied. It soon became apparent to both sides that what they were involved in now was not only

*In this Alfred Waud sketch, Union soldiers near
the Bloody Angle tempt fire from a foe just
opposite their trench with hats held aloft on ramrods.*

fiercer than what had gone before, today, but was in fact more horrendous than what had gone before, ever. This was grimmer than the Wilderness — a way of saying that it was worse than anything at all — not so much in bloodshed, although blood was shed in plenty, as in concentrated terror. These were the red hours of the conflict, hours no man who survived them would forget, even in his sleep, forever after. Fighting thus at arm's length across that parapet, they were caught up in a waking nightmare, although they were mercifully spared the knowledge, at the outset, that it was to last for another sixteen unrelenting hours. "All day long it was one continuous assault," a Pennsylvanian would recall. But in truth it was as much a defense as it was an attack, on either side, and the two were simultaneous. Neither victory nor defeat was any longer a factor in the struggle. Men simply fought to keep on fighting, and not so much on instinct as on pure adrenalin. Slaughter became an end in itself, unrelated to issues or objectives, as if it had nothing whatever to do with the war. Troops were killed by thrusts and stabs through chinks in the log barricade, while others were harpooned by bayonetted rifles flung javelin-style across it. Sometimes in this extremity even the instinct for self-preservation went by the board. From point to point, some wrought-up soldier would leap up on the parapet and fire down into the opposite mass of blue or gray, then continue this with loaded rifles passed up by comrades until he was shot down and another wrought-up soldier took his place. Rain fell, slacked, fell again in sheets, drenching the fighters and turning the floor of their slaughter pen to slime. Down in the trenches, dead and wounded men were trampled out of sight in the blood-splotched mud by those who staggered up to take their posts along the works, until they too were dropped or forced to retire because their weapons became so powder-fouled from rapid firing that they could not be loaded to fire again. High though the casualties were along this portion of the line, they would have been much higher if there had been time or room for taking aim. As it was, the largely unaimed fire — particularly heavy from the Federal side, where men were stacked up twenty deep in places — passed over the heads of the Confederates to destroy a

Heavy rains turn the battlefield into a quagmire as Union troops advance against a rebel breastwork in the seemingly endless fighting on May 12.

whole grove of trees within the salient; some, including an oak nearly two feet in diameter, were actually felled by the chipping bullets, which, to the amazement of a Vermont brigadier, continued their work until the fallen trunks and limbs "were cut to pieces and whipped into basket-stuff." One of Wright's officers, fighting in the Bloody Angle, tried afterwards to sum up what he had lived through. "I never expect to be believed when I tell of what I saw of the horrors of Spotsylvania," he wrote, "because I should be loath to believe it myself were the cases reversed."

Warren's infantry moved out at last, shortly after 9 o'clock, in a full-scale assault on the Confederate left, but this was broken up so effectively by Anderson's artillery and massed small-arms fire that not a Federal reached the works along this portion of the line. Severely hurt, the attackers recoiled and did not venture out again, permitting Lee to detach a brigade from each of the two First Corps divisions as reinforcements for Ewell in the Mule Shoe. They were sorely needed. It was noon by then and men were falling there from nervous exhaustion as well as from wounds. Veterans who had survived the worst this war afforded, up to now, went through the motions of combat after the manner of blank-faced automatons, as if what they were involved in had driven them beyond madness into imbecility; they fought by the numbers, unrecognizant of comrades in the ultimate loneliness of a horror as profoundly isolating in its effect as bone pain, nausea, or prolonged orgasm, their vacant eyes unlighted by anger or even dulled by fear. There were exceptions. One man, for example, stopped fighting to plunder an abandoned knapsack, and finding clean clothes in it, stripped off his butternut rags to exchange them for the laundered finery, underwear and all, then returned cheerfully to the grisly work at hand, apparently refreshed. But for the most part they had that look, well known to experienced officers of the line, of troops whose numbness under pressure might give way at any moment to utter panic, an abrupt collapse of all resistance. Unit commanders began to send word to superiors that the men were near their limits of endurance, but the answer was always the same: Hold on longer, a little longer, until a new line of intrenchments, under construction across the base of the salient by Martin Smith's engineers, could be completed to provide shelter for the troops when they withdrew. So they kept fighting, albeit mechanically, up in the blood-drenched toe of the Mule Shoe and down its western shank, and Hancock and Wright kept battering, although they too had most of the same problems with regard to keeping their larger masses of men involved in the meat-grinder action along those two portions of the line.

Sunset, twilight, and the following darkness brought no slackening of the struggle; 9 o'clock came, then 10, and then 11; "Not yet" was still the answer to urgent requests for permission to retire to the line being drawn across the gorge of the salient, half a mile in rear of the apex which had been

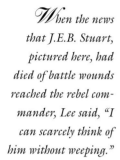

When the news that J.E.B. Stuart, pictured here, had died of battle wounds reached the rebel commander, Lee said, "I can scarcely think of him without weeping."

under bloody contention for the past eighteen hours. Finally, at midnight, word arrived and was passed along the zigzag curve of trenches — defined against the moonless blackness by the wink and glare of muzzle flashes, fitful stabs of pinkish yellow stitching their pattern back and forth across the parapet — for a piecemeal disengagement to begin. Unit by unit, so stealthily that they were not detected, the weary graybacks stumbled rearward through the bullet-tattered woods to where the new line had been dug. It was close to dawn before the last of them completed their somnambulistic withdrawal and took up their position in the works near the Brock Road. Daybreak showed the abandoned salient held only by corpses, the sodden trenches yawning empty save for these and other shattered remnants of the all-day battle. Still hugging the outward face of the log barricade, the Federals did not cross it even now that the defenders had departed, and the Confederates were glad that this was so. Exhausted, out of contact at last, blue and gray alike slept on their arms in the mud where they lay, oblivious to the pelting rain. Lee had preserved the integrity of his position, but at a cruel cost, having had nearly 3000 of his hard-core veterans captured and a somewhat larger number killed or wounded. Grant had lost as many, if not more; 6820 was the subsequent Federal count for this one day, a figure almost as great as the total for the three preceding days, when the Confederates lost fewer than one third as many. The gray army, fighting for the most part behind intrenchments, had managed to maintain its one-for-two ratio of casualties suffered and inflicted since the start of the campaign. But that was by no means the whole story of comparable attrition, which, as it applied to the men of highest rank on the two rosters, was just the other way around. Eight days of combat had cost the Army of Northern Virginia better than one third of its corps, division, and brigade commanders — 20 out of 57, killed or captured or severely wounded — while its adversary was losing barely half as many, 10 out of 69. And presently word arrived that still another Confederate general was to be added to the doleful list, one whose loss might prove the hardest to bear of them all, since his absence in the past had left the army and its famed commander groping blind.

Soon after the blue assault was launched, on the morning of May 12, Lee received a telegram informing him of the mishap, which had occurred within ten miles of Richmond the afternoon before. "Gentlemen, we have very bad news," he announced to a group around him; "General Stuart has been mortally wounded. A most valuable and able officer — " He paused, as if in search of further words for a formal statement, but then gave up and merely added in a shaken voice: "He never brought me a piece of false information." His sorrow was commensurate with his personal affection for, and his military debt to, the stricken horseman. Still, throughout the long day's fight at Spotsylvania, he kept hoping that somehow Jeb would pull through this crisis, as he had escaped so many other dangers over the past three years. Late that night, however, shortly before the withdrawal to the line still under construction across the base of the embattled salient, a second message came; Stuart was gone. Lee put his hands over his face to conceal his emotion. Presently he retired to his tent to master his grief, and when one of the dead cavalryman's staff officers arrived to tell him of Jeb's last minutes, back in Richmond, he remarked: "I can scarcely think of him without weeping."

★   ★   ★

Epilogue

$\star$ $\star$ $\star$ **In the spring of 1864,** Ulysses S. Grant, recently appointed general-in-chief of all the Union armies, was being celebrated in the nation's capital. Uncomfortable with all the attention from the public and the press, he was even more put out with the mess Nathaniel Banks was making of his Transmississippi campaign. Attempting to expand and consolidate the Federal hold on Louisiana and Texas along the Red River, Banks sought glory at the expense of his relationship with William Tecumseh Sherman and with Grant, neither of whom much cared for the expedition. When Richard Taylor soundly drubbed Banks, Grant grumbled that the Federal forces had followed a familiar pattern and "acted independently and without concert, like a balky team, no two ever pulling together." It was a pattern that Grant, heading down to the Rappahannock to take charge of and reorganize the Army of the Potomac still then in winter quarters, intended to change.

The Confederates continued to rack up spring successes on top of the Red River victory. Bedford Forrest, who even now still considered Federal-occupied northern Mississippi and western Tennessee his personal recruiting grounds, launched a successful raid through the region to Paducah, Kentucky, that culminated in the taking of Fort Pillow. Immediately the northern press attacked the declassé, former slave-trader for his "massacre" of the Black troops defending the fort. In North Carolina, too, the South celebrated the exploits of the ironclad *Albemarle* in retaking Plymouth and threatening New Bern. Back in Richmond, Jeff Davis, besieged by domestic political disputes including such outrages as a plan from Georgia's Governor Joseph E. Brown for something like a separate peace, was hardly in a frame of mind to welcome reports of such minor victories, especially as he worried about the Union's spring offenses in Virginia and Georgia. Then came the devastating accidental death of his young son Joe. Grim, but determined as ever, Davis tried to prod Joseph E. Johnston into action against Sherman at Chattanooga and ordered Longstreet to rejoin Lee in Virginia.

Meanwhile Grant had reorganized his army from top to bottom, shifting troops from headquarters and supply functions, even from heavy artillery fortifications, to join the fighting ranks of the foot soldiers. He was ready now to implement his grand strategy of four coordinated, simultaneous blows against the Confederate armies in the field: Benjamin Butler would lead an army up the James River; Franz Sigel would work his way along the Shenandoah Valley; Sherman would strike out from Chattanooga for Atlanta; and George Meade, directly under Grant, would attack Lee and fight him, wherever he went. Lee, for his part, planned to make Grant pay dearly for every engagement until he destroyed the North's will to wage war. If he could stand Grant to a bloody draw, chances were Abraham Lincoln would lose the upcoming election, and perhaps the United States would sue for peace.

During the first two days of the Wilderness Campaign, Grant certainly paid dearly, losing some 18,000 men. But instead of retreating, he ordered his men south, and they cheered him for it. Lee guessed correctly that Grant was headed for Spotsylvania Court House and was waiting when the Federals arrived on May 11. At dawn next day, Grant sent 20,000 men against the Confederate center and captured the breastworks along a curved salient called the Mule Shoe. Lee counterattacked and reclaimed the log works, but the battle raged on, surging back and forth all day. The two armies lost nearly 12,000 men, and Lee fell back as fighting continued around Spotsylvania for several days. To the northern press, the Union commander vowed to fight along this line all summer should it prove necessary. And fight he would, if not exactly along that line, at other spots on the way to Richmond, for forty days altogether, until the slaughter at Cold Harbor would give even Ulysses S. Grant pause.

By then Ben Butler would find himself bottled up by P. G. T. Beauregard between Richmond and Petersburg and Franz Sigel would lose his job for skedaddling back down the valley. Only Sherman would live up to Grant's expectations, starting from Chattanooga on May 6 to roll inexorably south and chase rebel forces under Joe Johnston out of one position after another, right up to the outskirts of heavily fortified Atlanta. There a frustrated Jeff Davis would remove that ever-ready-to-retreat commander on the eve of Federal attack and replace him with an inexperienced John Bell Hood, much to Sherman's surprise and satisfaction.

★   ★   ★

Picture Credits

The sources for the illustrations are listed below. Credits from left to right are separated by semicolons, from top to bottom by dashes.

Dust jacket: Front: Massachusetts Commandery of the Military Order of the Loyal Legion of the United States and the U.S. Army Military History Institute (MASS-MOLLUS/USAMHI), copied by A. Pierce Bounds; **rear,** Library of Congress, Neg. No. B8184-10006; **flap,** photo by Larry Shirkey. **8-10:** Courtesy Civil War Library and Museum, Philadelphia, Pa., copied by Blake A. Magner. **14:** The White House Collection, courtesy the White House Historical Association. **17:** National Museum of American History. **21:** Special Collections (Orlando Poe Collection), United States Military Academy Library, West Point, N.Y., copied by Henry Groskinsky. **24:** Special Collections, United States Military Academy Library, West Point, N.Y. **27:** National Portrait Gallery, Smithsonian Institution, Washington, D.C., Meserve Collection No. 1369. **28:** Courtesy Chris Nelson. **30:** State Historical Society of Wisconsin. **33:** Courtesy of The Cincinnati Historical Society Library. **34:** Manuscript Department, Tulane University Library. **38:** United States Army Military History Institute, Carlisle Barracks, Pa., copied by A. Pierce Bounds. **42-44:** Painting by James Madison Alden, courtesy Museum of Fine Arts, Boston, reproduced with permission, © Museum of Fine Arts, Boston, all rights reserved. **49:** Collection of Michael Kramer, photographed by Larry Sherer, assisted by Andrew Patilla. **50:** Courtesy Atlanta History Center. **53:** Courtesy Frank and Marie-Thérèse Wood Print Collections, Alexandria, Va. **55:** Drawing by C. E. H. Bonwill, The Print and Picture Collection, The Free Library of Philadelphia. **59:** Library of Congress. **62, 66:** Courtesy Frank and Marie-Thérèse Wood Print Collections, Alexandria, Va. **70, 75:** Maps by Walter W. Roberts. **78:** Courtesy Frank and Marie-Thérèse Wood Print Collections, Alexandria, Va. **83:** Library of Congress. **85:** Massachusetts Commandery of the Military Order of the Loyal Legion of the United States and the U.S. Army Military History Institute (MASS-MOLLUS/USAMHI), copied by A. Pierce Bounds. **86:** Zenda, Inc. **89:** From *The Photographic History of the Civil War,* vol. 10, Review of Reviews Co.,

New York, 1912. **90:** Zenda, Inc. **93:** National Archives Neg. No. 111-B-2780. **97:** Massachusetts Commandery of the Military Order of the Loyal Legion of the United States and the U.S. Army Military History Institute (MASS-MOLLUS/USAMHI), copied by A. Pierce Bounds. **98:** From *The Photographic History of the Civil War,* vol. 10, Review of Reviews Co., New York, 1912. **101:** State Historical Society of Missouri, Columbia. **104:** From *The Photographic History of the Civil War,* vol. 10, Review of Reviews Co., New York, 1912. **108:** Museum of the Confederacy, Richmond, Va., copied by Katherine Wetzel. **112:** Massachusetts Commandery of the Military Order of the Loyal Legion of the United States and the U.S. Army Military History Institute (MASS-MOLLUS/USAMHI), copied by A. Pierce Bounds. **115:** Courtesy Frank and Marie-Thérèse Wood Print Collections, Alexandria, Va. **117:** Courtesy Paul de Haan. **123:** Michael Waskul Collection, courtesy L. M. Strayer. **125:** Library of Congress, No. B8172-6574. **128-130:** The Western Reserve Historical Society, Cleveland, Ohio. **134:** North Carolina Department of Cultural Resources, Division of Archives and History, Raleigh. **139:** U. S. Department of the Interior, National Park Service, Adams National Historical Park, Quincy, Mass. **140:** Courtesy Meserve-Kunhardt Collection, Mt. Kisco, N.Y. **143:** Courtesy Frank and Marie-Thérèse Wood Print Collections, Alexandria, Va. **144:** Courtesy The Lincoln Museum, Fort Wayne, Ind. (#497). **147:** Library of Congress. **150:** Special Collections (Orlando Poe Collection), United States Military Academy Library, West Point, N.Y., copied by Henry Groskinsky. **153:** Courtesy Frank and Marie-Thérèse Wood Print Collections, Alexandria, Va. **155:** Painting by Paul Louvrier, West Point Museum Collection, United States Military Academy, photographed by Henry Groskinsky. **159:** From *History of the Confederate States Navy* by Thomas J. Scharf, published by The Fairfax Press. **160:** Courtesy Frank Wood. **162:** Map by Walter W. Roberts. **165:** Library of Congress. **168:** Painting by E. F. Andrews, Kentucky Museum, Western Kentucky University, Bowling Green, Ky., photographed by Bill LaFevor. **170:** Library of Congress. **174-176:** Library of Congress, Neg. No. B8184-10602. **179:** Map by Peter McGinn.

★

180: Drawing by Edwin Forbes, Library of Congress. 183: Massachusetts Commandery of the Military Order of the Loyal Legion of the United States and the U.S. Army Military History Institute (MASS-MOLLUS/USAMHI), copied by A. Pierce Bounds. 184: Library of Congress. 186: Drawing by Edwin Forbes, Library of Congress. 188: National Archives, Neg. No. 111-B-5046. 191: Zenda, Inc. 192: Massachusetts Commandery of the Military Order of the Loyal Legion of the United States and the U.S. Army Military History Institute (MASS-MOLLUS/USAMHI), copied by A. Pierce Bounds. 200: Library of Congress, Forbes #127. 204-206: Painting by Julian Scott, courtesy Robert A. McNeil, photographed by Sharon Deveaux. 208: Library of Congress. 211: Massachusetts Commandery of the Military Order of the Loyal Legion of the United States and the U.S. Army Military History Institute (MASS-MOLLUS/USAMHI), copied by A. Pierce Bounds. 213: Library of Congress, Forbes #218. 216: Map Division, Library of Congress, photographed by Larry Sherer. 219: The Valentine Museum, Richmond, Va. 220: William A. Turner Collection. 223: Massachusetts Commandery of the Military Order of the Loyal Legion of the United States and the U.S. Army Military History Institute (MASS-MOLLUS/USAMHI), copied by A. Pierce Bounds. 225: Library of Congress. 226: The Valentine Museum, Richmond, Va. 229: Library of Congress, Waud #656. 230: U. S. Army Military History Institute (USAMHI), photographed by A. Pierce Bounds. 232: Cook Collection, The Valentine Museum, Richmond, Va. 235: James C. Frasca, photographed by Andy Cifranic. 237: From *The Story of a Cannoneer under Stonewall Jackson,* by Edward A. Moore, The Neale Publishing Company, 1907, copied by Philip Brandt George. 238: Texas State Library & Archives Commission (#1995/160-M-74). 241: Courtesy Historical Times, Inc. 242: Library of Congress, Waud #157. 245: Museum of the Confederacy, Richmond, Va. 248: Confederate Museum, Charleston, S.C., photographed by Harold H. Norvell. 248: Confederate Relic Room, Columbia, S.C., photographed by Larry Sherer, assisted by Andrew Patilla. 250: From: *From Manassas to Appomattox: Memoirs of the Civil War in America,* by James Longstreet, J. B. Lippincott Co., Philadelphia, 1896. 252: Massachusetts Commandery of the Military Order of the Loyal Legion of the United States and the U.S. Army Military History Institute (MASS-MOLLUS/USAMHI), copied by A. Pierce Bounds. 253: Albion Historical Society Collection at USAMHI, copied by A. Pierce Bounds. 254: Library of Congress, Waud #535. 258: Library of Congress, Waud #695. 262: Drawing by Edwin Forbes, Library of Congress. 264-266: Library of Congress, Neg. No. LC-B8184-5037. 269: The Valentine Museum, Richmond, Va. 270: Map Division, Library of Congress, photographed by Larry Sherer. 275: Library of Congress, Forbes #217. 277, 280: Massachusetts Commandery of the Military Order of the Loyal Legion of the United States and the U.S. Army Military History Institute (MASS-MOLLUS/USAMHI), copied by A. Pierce Bounds. 283: "Death of General Segwick" by Julian Scott, Drake House Museum, Historical Society of Plainfield, photographed by Henry Groskinsky. 284: Massachusetts Commandery of the Military Order of the Loyal Legion of the United States and the U.S. Army Military History Institute (MASS-MOLLUS/USAMHI), copied by A. Pierce Bounds. 287: The Cincinnati Historical Society. 290: Library of Congress, Waud #752. 293: Library of Congress, Forbes #212. 296: Map by Walter W. Roberts. 299: Erick Davis Collection, copied by Jeremy Ross. 300: Museum of the Confederacy, Richmond, Va. 305: Library of Congress, Waud #741. 306: From *Battles and Leaders of the Civil War,* vol. 4, edited by Robert Underwood Johnson and Clarence Cough Buel, The Century Co., New York, 1887. 308: Cook Collection, The Valentine Museum, Richmond, Va.

Index

Numerals in italics indicate an illustration of the subject mentioned.

107, 108
Cincinnati: 25, 37, 41
City Belle: 113
City Point: 35, 178, 215
Clark, John S.: 66
Clark's Mountain: 189, 212, 275
Cloutierville: 87
Columbus, Mississippi: 147
Columbus, Ohio: 151
Conestoga: 55
Conscription, 173, 180; bounties, 180
Contraband goods, seizure of: 48-49, 61-62
Cooke, James W.: 158, *159,* 160
Copperheads: 142
Corbin's Bridge: 277
Corinth: 46
Corps d'Afrique: 61
Cotton: 48-49, 61
Couchatta Chute: 85
Covington: 113
Crawford, Samuel W.: 225-226
Crawfordville: 132
Cricket: 89, 92
Crook, George: 34
Culpeper: 40, 41, 206
Culpeper Mine Ford: 268

D

Dalton: 30, 127, 163
David's Ferry: 113
Davis, Jefferson: 127, 167; Confederate efforts
    and, 195, 197-198; core of the Confederacy, 142;
    criticism of, 131-135; death of son, 196-197;
    exchange of letters with Vance, 131-132, 135;
    impossibility of peace negotiations, 135-137;
    military offensive, 135, 137-138, 163; securing
    foreign recognition, 135, 138-141
Davis, Jefferson, Jr.: 196
Davis, Joseph Evan: 196, 197
Davis, Varina Howell: 196, 197
Decatur, Alabama: 156
Demopolis: 30
Donaldsonville: 124
Donelson: 46
Dunn's Bayou: 113
Dwight, William: 77, 124

E

Early, Jubal A.: 218, 241, 251, 269, 276
Eastport: 56, 89, 92, 118
Edwards Ferry: 157
Elizabeth City: 158

Eldorado Landing: 103
Elkin's Ferry: 99, 100
Elliott, George: 158
Ely's Ford: 189, 201, 202, 207, 208, 260, 267
Emma: 113
Emory, William H.: 77, 88, 119
England: 138-141
Eugenie, Empress: 139
Ewell, Richard S.: 267, 270, 274, 275; Spotsylvania
    battle, 281, 298, 307; in the Wilderness, 198, 203,
    214, 217, 218, 219, 220, 221, 222, 228, 230, 231,
    234, 239, 241, 246, 251, 253

F

Fagan, James: 98, 99, 103, 104, *105,* 106
Farragut, David G.: 30
Field, Charles W.: 233, 238, 242, 249, 250, 269, 274
Finegan, Joseph: 145, 172
Flat Creek: 241
Florida: 145
Forrest, Nathan Bedford: 145-152, 155, 156-157, 172
Fort De Russy: 51-52, *53,* 57
Fort Henry: 90
Fort Hindman: 92, 115, 116
Fort Monroe: 35, 178, 179, 192
Fort Pillow: 150-156
Fort Sherman: *30-31*
Fort Smith: 47, 96
France: 28, 45, 47, 138, 139
Franklin, William B.: 65, 66-67, 69, 71, 73, 77, 80,
    81, 119, 124
Fredericksburg: 41, 210, 217, 246, 268
Frémont, John C.: 38

G

Galveston: 47
Germanna Ford: 189, 201, 202, 207, 209, 210, 224,
    227, 231, 257, 260, 267
Germanna Plank Road: 209, 218, 222, 224, 231,
    252, 256
Getty, George W.: 227
Gettysburg: 20, 141
Gibbon, John: 227
Gilmore, Quincy A.: 35
Gordon, John B.: 267, 268, 270; Spotsylvania
    battle, 301-302, 302; in the Wilderness, 219, 225,
    226, 241, 251, 252, 253, 257
Gordonsville: 169, 187, 214
Grand Design plan: 11-41, 170, 177, 187; authorities
    in Richmond and, 166, 172; Transmississippi
    operations, 26-27
Grand Ecore: 54, 56, *62-63,* 65, 69, 74, 75, 78, 80,

Pemberton, John C.: 23
Pendleton, William N.: 268
Petersburg: 35, 168, 178
Phelps, S. Ledyard: 89
Pickett, George E.: 217, 242, 243
Pine Bluff: 96, 98
Piney Branch Church: 261
Pittsburg: 118
Pleasant Hill: 63, 65, 66, 73-77, *78-79,* 145
Plymouth: 157, 158-162
Po River: 270, 273, 276, 285, 287, 302
Poague, William: 236, *237,* 239, 240
Poison Spring: 101-102, 145
Polignac, Camille Armand Jules Marie: 69-70, 76, 81, 87
Polk, Leonidas: 30, 31, 127, 156, 163, 187
Pollard, Edward A.: 134-135
Pope, John: 23, 32, 36, 41, 199
Port Hudson: 45, 61
Porter, David Dixon: 49, 55-56, 81, 84, 85, 89, 90-*93,* 94, 110, 115, 116-117, 118, 119, 145
Posey, Carnot: 304
Potomac River: 20, 296
Prairie d'Ane: 100, 145
Presidential election of 1864: 142, 144, 172, 193-194
Price, Sterling: 59, 79, 96, 97-98, 99-100, *101,* 106, 107, 108, 145
Princeton: 106
Prisoners-of-war, exchanging: 184

R
Rapidan River: 32, 167, 168, 169, 189, 200, 201, 202, 203, 207, 209, 210, 213, 215, 246, 256
Rapidan Station: 187
Rappahannock River: 168, 172
Rappahannock Station: 170, 209
Rawlins, John A.: 17, 23, 256-257
Red River: *86,* 145; 45-127
Red River campaign: 45-127; casualties of, 12, 126; "gorilla" operations, 87; naval operations: 49, 51, 55-56, 110-118; results of, 125-127
Richard's Shop: 214, 216, 233
Richmond: 26, 28, 32, 33, 34, 35, 84, 142, 146, 168, 169, 171, 172-173, 178, 210, 261, 268, 273, 276, 283; communication between Transmississippi and, 145; rail connections with Petersburg, 215
Richmond *Examiner:* 134
Richmond, Federicksburg & Potomac Railroad: 268
Ricketts, James B.: 230, 252
Rio Grande: 47
Roanoke Island: 160

Roanoke River: 157
Robinson, John C.: 278-279
Rodes, Robert E.: 218, 219, 301, 303-304
Rosecrans, William S.: 29, 172
Rosser, Thomas L.: 272, 274
Russell, David A.: 288
Russell, Lord John: 140
Russia: 138

S
Sabine Crossroads: 67-71, 78, 81, 100; casualties, 72
Sabine Pass: 47
Sabine River: 46, 59
Saint Johns River: 145
St Louis: 126
St Louis *Republican:* 52, 125
Saint Paul's Church (Richmond): 141
Saline River: 94, 103, 172
Salomon, Frederich S.: 100, 105
San Antonio: 48
Sandusky Bay: 252
Savannah: 142
Schofield, John M.: 30
Scott, Winfield: 27
Seddon, James A.: 165, 166
Sedgwick, John: 274; death of, 281-282, *283;* Spotsylvania battle, 279, *280;* in the Wilderness, 209, 210, 223, 230, 231, 234, 241, 252, 253, 256, 257, 261, 262, 263
Selma: 145
Seward, William H.: 16, 140
Seymour, Truman: *252*
Shady Grove: 272, 277, 285
Shady Grove Church: 210, 211, 216, 268, 270, 274
Shaler, Alexander: 252, *253*
Shelby, J. O.: 98, 103
Shenandoah Valley: 32, 33, 40, 168, 178, 215, 284
Sheridan, Phil H.: *190-*191, 207, 243, 261, 276; Spotsylvania battle, 277-278, 279-280, 286
Sherman, John: 37
Sherman, William T.: *27,* 36, 37, 49, 50, 83, 127, 145-146, 156, 157, 172, 187; Grant's plan and, 22, 24, 25, 26, 28, 29, 30, 31
Shreveport: 28, 29, 46, 47, 48, 49, 53, 56, 58, 59, 63, 79, 82, 84, 96
Sigel, Franz: 32-33, 34, 41, 177-178, 192, 215
Signal: 113
Simsport: 51, 52, 119
Slidell, John: 139
Smith, Andrew J.: 51, 53, 54, 57, 64, 65, 72, 73, 76, 77, 83, 85, 87, 118-119, 121, 124
Smith, Edmund Kirby: 50, 57, 58-60, 67, 71, 78, 81,

SHELBY FOOTE, THE CIVIL WAR,
A NARRATIVE
VOLUME 10 RED RIVER TO SPOTSYLVANIA

Library of Congress Cataloging-in-Publication Data
Foote, Shelby.
    [Civil War, a narrative]
    Shelby Foote, the Civil War, a narrative / by Shelby
Foote and the editors of Time-Life Books. — 40th
Anniversary ed.
        p. cm.
    Originally published: The Civil War, a narrative.
New York : Random House, 1958-1974, in 3 v.
    Includes bibliographical references and indexes.
    Contents: v. 10. Red River to Spotsylvania
    ISBN 0-7835-0109-9
    1. United States—History—Civil War, 1861-1865.
I. Time-Life Books. II. Title.
E468.F7 1999   99-13486
973.7—dc21   CIP

10 9 8 7 6 5 4 3 2 1

OTHER TIME-LIFE HISTORY PUBLICATIONS

Our American Century	*The American Indians*
World War II	*Lost Civilizations*
What Life Was Like	*Time Frame*
The American Story	*The Civil War*
Voices of the Civil War	*Cultural Atlas*

For information on and a full description of any of
the Time-Life Books series listed above, please call
1-800-621-7026 or write:
Reader Information
Time-Life Customer Service
P.O. Box C-32068
Richmond, Virginia 23261-2068

Time-Life Books is a
division of Time Life Inc.

TIME LIFE INC.
PRESIDENT and CEO: Jim Nelson

TIME-LIFE BOOKS
PUBLISHER/MANAGING EDITOR: Neil Kagan
SENIOR VICE PRESIDENT, MARKETING:
Joseph A. Kuna
VICE PRESIDENT, NEW PRODUCT
DEVELOPMENT: Amy Golden

EDITOR: Philip Brandt George
Art Director: Ellen L. Pattisall
Editorial Assistant: Patricia D. Whiteford

Correspondent: Christina Lieberman (New York)

ZENDA INC.

Editor: Charles Phillips
Managing Editor: Candace Floyd
Administration: Patricia Hogan
Design and Production:
Gore Studio, Inc.: Bruce Gore (cover)
The Graphics People: Susan Ellen Hogan,
Mary Brillman, Roger Neiss

Separations by the Time-Life Imaging Department

NEW PRODUCT DEVELOPMENT: Director,
Elizabeth D. Ward; Project Manager, Karen Inge-
bretsen; Director of Marketing, Mary Ann Donaghy;
Marketing Manager, Paul Fontaine; Associate Marketing Manager, Erin Gaskins

MARKETING: Director, Peter Tardif; Marketing
Manager, Nancy Gallo; Associate Marketing
Manager, Kristen N. O'Shea

Executive Vice President, Operations: Ralph Cuomo
Senior Vice President and CFO: Claudia Goldberg
Senior Vice President, Law & Business Affairs:
Randolph H. Elkins

Vice President, Financial Planning & Analysis:
Christopher Hearing
Vice President, Book Production: Patricia Pascale
Vice President, Imaging: Marjann Caldwell
Director, Publishing Technology: Betsi McGrath
Director, Editorial Administration: Barbara Levitt
Director, Photography and Research:
John Conrad Weiser
Director, Quality Assurance: James King
Manager, Technical Services: Anne Topp
Senior Production Manager: Ken Sabol
Manager, Copyedit/Page Makeup: Debby Tait
Chief Librarian: Louise D. Forstall